Not Just *Any* Dress

Studies in the Postmodern Theory of Education

Joe L. Kincheloe and Shirley R. Steinberg
General Editors

Vol. 220

PETER LANG
New York • Washington, D.C./Baltimore • Bern
Frankfurt am Main • Berlin • Brussels • Vienna • Oxford

Not Just Any Dress

NARRATIVES OF MEMORY, BODY, AND IDENTITY

EDITED BY
Sandra Weber & Claudia Mitchell

PETER LANG
New York • Washington, D.C./Baltimore • Bern
Frankfurt am Main • Berlin • Brussels • Vienna • Oxford

Library of Congress Cataloging-in-Publication Data

Not just any dress: narratives of memory, body, and identity /
edited by Sandra Weber, Claudia Mitchell.
p. cm. — (Counterpoints; vol. 220)
Includes bibliographical references and index.
1. Women's clothing. 2. Clothing and dress—Psychological aspects.
3. Clothing and dress—Symbolic aspects. 4. Body, Human—Social aspects.
I. Weber, Sandra. II. Mitchell, Claudia.
III. Series: Counterpoints (New York, N.Y.); v. 220.
GT1720. N67   391'.2—dc22   2003027181
ISBN 0-8204-6118-0
ISSN 1058-1634

Bibliographic information published by **Die Deutsche Bibliothek**.
Die Deutsche Bibliothek lists this publication in the "Deutsche
Nationalbibliografie"; detailed bibliographic data is available
on the Internet at http://dnb.ddb.de/.

Cover photo by Shannon Walsh

Cover design by Lisa Barfield

The paper in this book meets the guidelines for permanence and durability
of the Committee on Production Guidelines for Book Longevity
of the Council of Library Resources.

© 2004 Peter Lang Publishing, Inc., New York
275 Seventh Avenue, 28th Floor, New York, NY 10001
www.peterlangusa.com

All rights reserved.
Reprint or reproduction, even partially, in all forms such as microfilm,
xerography, microfiche, microcard, and offset strictly prohibited.

Printed in the United States of America

To the memory of Carol Shields, Jo Spence and the "one and the many" feminist writers who have come before us and for whom issues of dress, body, and identity have always been so central to acts of memory and imagination

Contents

List of Figures xi

Acknowledgments xiii

PART I: OUR DRESSES/OUR SELVES

1 "Dress Stories" 3
   Sandra Weber & Claudia Mitchell

2 That Saturday night all her clothes fell apart and broke into song 11
   Lorri Neilson Glenn

PART II: GROWING UP WITH DRESSES

3 Collecting Loss: Photographs, Dresses, "Paperies" 15
   Carol Mavor

4 Communion Dress Violations 39
   Kathleen O'Reilly Scanlon

5 "I'll Never Find a Dress": Shopping for the Prom 45
   Catherine Derry

6 No Red Shoes 57
   Sandra Weber

PART III: DRESS AND SCHOOLING

7 Boxed-in by My School Uniform 61
Sandra Weber

8 Tunique Desires 67
Lyse Lemieux

9 In Front of the Closet: (Ad)dressing the Academic 73
Candis Steenbergen

10 Was It Something I Wore? 83
Claudia Mitchell

11 My Green Robe: Scholae Personae 89
Madeleine R. Grumet

12 Curse You Descartes! My Academic Gown 99
Sandra Weber

13 Basic Black: A Wardrobe Primer for Seasoned Academic Women 105
Lorri Neilson Glenn

PART IV: DRESS RITUALS AND MOTHERS

14 A Credit to Her Mother 111
Annette Kuhn

15 Fashioning Pregnancy: The Maternity Dress in Clothing Catalogues .. 127
Jennifer Musial

16 The Christmas Doll 137
Ardra L. Cole

17 Constraining Mother: Corsetry, Control, and Comfort 145
Gary Knowles

18 (Wo)man Time and M(other) Sins 157
Celeste Snowber

PART V: OF DRESSES AND WEDDINGS

19 Bridesmaid dress: Thick Description 163
  Claudia Mitchell

20 Try This One On for Size: Poetic Notes from
  Wedding Dress Research 165
  Kathryn Church

21 Nailing It: My Wedding Dress 171
  Jo Visser

PART VI: DRESSING IDENTITY

22 Made in China 183
  Xiao Lan Curdt-Christiansen

23 Revealing Veiling and Unveiling 191
  Roksana Bahramitash

24 Scarf Signatures 207
  Joan Reider

25 Love Affair with My Isishweshwe 211
  Liz Ralfe

26 Fashion Statement 219
  Charlotte Hussey

PART VII: BODIES, DRESS, AND MORTALITY

27 At the Ugly Ducklings Anonymous Meeting 223
  Lorri Neilson Glenn

28 Writing Bare-breasted 225
  Celeste Snowber

29 Not Just Any Little Black Dress 229
  Ilana Abramovitch

x • Not Just Any Dress: Narratives of Memory, Body, and Identity

30 Dressing Death: Elsie Never Wore a Prom Dress 239
Claudia Mitchell

31 Fashion for the Soul 247
Kathy Sands

PART VIII: INTERPRETIVE DRESS

32 Theorizing Dress Stories 251
Sandra Weber & Claudia Mitchell

References 273

Contributors 283

Name Index 289

Subject Index 293

List of Figures

3.1. Author's family album picture. Grandmother in a dress with an enormous cotton bow, Father and Uncle at the 1935 Chicago World's Fair. 18
3.2. Hawarden, Clementina Viscountess Hawarden, ca. 1861–1862. All of Hawarden's photographs are untitled and undated. The Board of Trustees of the Victoria and Albert Museum. 22
3.3. Hawarden, Clementina Viscountess Hawarden, ca. 1862. 23
3.4. Hawarden, Clementina Viscountess Hawarden, ca. 1861–1862. 25
3.5. elin o'Hara slavick, "BROTHER YOU HELD ME OVER THE WATERS," dress from *A Wall of Incoherent Dresses*, 1991. Courtesy of the artist. 27
3.6. Sally Mann, *The Easter Dress*, 1986. Copyright Sally Mann. Courtesy Houk Friedman, New York. 31
4.1. Photo of author as a child in her Communion dress. 40
5.1. Photo of author and date at the prom, 1988. 52
8.1. "2 Tuniques," 1987. Neoprene rubber. 8' × 10'. Lyse Lemieux. Courtesy of the artist. 67
8.2. "La peau de Mme Ives (mère) 2," 2003. Latex rubber gauze, 22.5" × 47". Lyse Lemieux. Courtesy of the artist. 69
12.1. Photo of the author. University graduation, 1969. 100
14.1. Photo of author as infant. 111
14.2. Photo of author as a child. 116
14.3. Photo of author as a child. 122
15.1. "Front Cover." JC Penney Maternity Collection Catalogue. Spring/Summer 2001. 129

15.2.	Pumpkin Maternity Catalogue. Fall 2000.	134
16.1.	Photo of the author age 4, Christmas doll photograph courtesy of the Cole family album.	137
20.1.	Close up of bow on bridal gown.	165
20.2.	Bridal gown with sash.	166
20.3.	Close-up of bead work on bridal gown.	167
21.1.	"Crucifiction," Jo Visser. Courtesy of the artist.	171
22.1.	The author's adaptation of traditional Chinese dress.	183
23.1.	Photo of the author as a young woman.	191
23.2.	Photo of the author.	191
24.1.	Photo of author, 1966.	207
25.1.	Photo of Isishweshwe, 2003.	211
25.2.	Photo of Isishweshwe, 2003.	214
25.3.	Photo of Isishweshwe, 2003.	215
26.1.	Photo of author, 1995.	219
29.1.	Black dress with flowers. Courtesy of the author.	229
32.1.	Prom Dress #1: I am a woman now. Art installation by Sandra Weber and Sophie Cloutier. Photograph by Stephanie Anne Weber Biron	259

Acknowledgments

It was a cold January day in Montreal. Three of us, Sandra Weber, Claudia Mitchell and Kathleen O'Reilly Scanlon were stepping carefully down the ice-covered slope of McTavish Street towards Thomson House to celebrate Kathleen's successful defence of her doctoral dissertation. She had spoken about the significance of her memory of her communion dress, a topic which sparked a great deal of discussion during the defence about the meanings of particular dresses. Even as we walked down the hill, the discussion continued, with one of us—we are no longer sure who—declaring "after all it was not just any dress." The birth of the Not Just Any Dress (NJAD) project!

Where to start in acknowledging the inspiration, enthusiasm, dedication . . . and sheer hard work of so many people?

We begin by thanking the talented contributors to this book for their collaboration, their eloquence, and their generosity. Without them, this project would have foundered.

We also wish to acknowledge with thanks the financial support of the Social Sciences and Humanities Research Council of Canada for its ongoing support to the Image and Identity Research Collective and our work on memory, photography and narrative in relation to body and identity.

We particularly want to thank the following publishers for giving us permission to reprint chapters or sections of chapters: Duke University Press (*Collecting Loss*, Carol Mavor), Verso (*A Credit to Her Mother*, Annette Kuhn), Indiana University Press (Scholae Personae: Masks for Meaning, Madeleine Grumet), Backalong Books ("Elsie Never Had a Prom Dress," Claudia Mitchell).

A further foundation on which this book rests is our documentary video work related to "dressing for the prom"—a project that draws on the passion for detail of so many women who we wish to thank: Honore Kerwin-Borrelli, Faith Butler, Sarah Mitchell, Catherine Derry, Barbara Pyontka, Dorian Mitchell, Jo Visser, Stephanie Weber Biron, Karen Clandining, Lara Nasser, Ricardo Arthur, and the graduating students from Lachine High, 2000, as well as the talented film-makers, Monica Mak and Sophie Cloutier with whom we collaborated closely to produce *Dress Fitting* and *Canadian Pie*.

To our many graduate students who over the last several years have participated in classes and seminars at McGill University, Concordia University, the University of British Columbia in Canada and the University of Natal and the University of the Witwatersrand in South Africa, we offer our thanks for their useful comments, intelligent ideas, feedback, and in some cases, narrative contributions to the book.

We very much appreciate the encouragement and the enthusiastic support for our dress-body project that we have received from so many people who have attended our presentations at various conferences: Canadian Association of the Study of Women in Education, the Herstmonceux "Castle Conference" on Self-Study of Teaching Practices, the Popular Culture Association, the American Educational Research Association, the "Making Appearances" Conference in Brisbane, and the International Federation of Teachers of English Conference.

And, on behalf of all of the contributors to this book, we would especially like to thank our Research Assistants who provided their invaluable assistance, tracked down permission rights, and just generally kept the whole "NJAD" project running. We acknowledge with deep gratitude the highly capable assistance of Anna-Marie Sellon and Shannon Walsh in the early stages, Catherine Derry forever, and Candis Steenbergen whose impressive editorial skills and willingness to work around the clock played a crucial role in the completion of the final manuscript.

Finally, a book like this would never get started or finished if it weren't for the ongoing support of our much loved partners, Michel Boyer and Ann Smith, and the inspiration we derive from women everywhere of style, persistence, character, strength, and panache, among whom we count our daughters, our mothers, and our grandmothers.

PART I
Our Dresses/Our Selves

CHAPTER 1

Sandra Weber
Claudia Mitchell

"Dress Stories"

Oh my, what a beautiful dress!
I have nothing to wear! Really!
Will you look at that dress she is almost wearing!
This dress makes me look fat!
Is this dressy enough to wear to the party? How dressed up do I have to be?
I'm looking for an outfit that will make people at work take me seriously.
Not that dress! I won't wear it! I don't care what the dress code is.
Do you think this colour suits me?
What a frumpy dress! Ages her ten years, I swear.
That's funny, you don't look like a teacher.
(REMARKS OVERHEARD OR UTTERED IN
THE COURSE OF OUR LIVES THUS FAR)

Dresses! We love them, we hate them, we gawk at them, we covet them, we long for them, we disdain them, we buy them, we make them, we wash them, we iron them, we wear them, we refuse to wear them, we work in them, we dance in them, we stain them, we tear them, we mend them, we remodel them, we ridicule them, we take them for granted, we grow out of them, we curse at them, we give them away, we forget them, we remember them with shame or longing, we store them away lovingly, we toss them crumpled on the floor, we hang on to them for ages even when they no longer fit, we hand them down, and sometimes, we even burn them. If dresses could talk, what stories might they tell?

Ask women to talk or write about dresses, and without much prompting, they will regale you with detailed snippets from their lives, anecdotes that start out ostensibly about clothes, but end up being about so much more—events, family, community, relationships, body-image, feelings, aspirations, attitudes, beliefs and thoughts about all sorts of things.[1] In the telling or writing of these autobiographical stories, an item of clothing becomes a springboard, an axis of rotation, or a structural grounding for a detailed account of life events. Sometimes it is the photograph of the item of clothing that both sparks and shapes the memory, and other times it may be the material object itself still hanging in a closet or stored in a trunk in someone's attic or basement that is the prompt. The item of clothing may serve as a symbol to represent a significant theme or issue in the author's life that emerges as the story unfolds. While these dress tales are usually very personal in nature, they also point unfailingly to matters of social and cultural import. We have labeled these special sorts of narratives *"dress stories."*[2]

These "dress stories," whether or not they are "true" in their details, whether or not they really happened (or happened the way they are remembered), bear the traces of our past experience and provide insight into how we perceive and make sense of our lives. Dress stories reveal much more than we may realize about who and how we are in the world and what sort of culture we are living in. Indeed, we have become convinced that one of the best ways to interview women (and perhaps men too) about almost anything is to ask them about their clothes! If you ask some one, for example, to tell you what it means to have an "identity" or what it means to be "embodied," or how they view the world, or what their conception of culture is, all you get in response may be blank stares. However, if you ask someone to tell you about what they are wearing or wish they were wearing or are glad they are not wearing, you will get a surprising amount of useful information on identity, body, and culture.

It is when talking about mundane, concrete, material objects from our everyday lives that we often uncover the multiple and culturally constructed meanings that a whole range of events and experiences can have for us.[3] Although we may not be immediately aware of it, talking about clothes forces us to speak, directly or indirectly, about our bodies, about details of material culture, about context, about commerce and commodification, about social expectations and personal aspirations, about media influence, family relationships, work, play, values, social structures, and more. "One of the great voids of dress history" writes Lou Taylor, "has been its failure to examine emotional responses to clothing and appearance."[4] In this book, we make a start.

Dress Stories as Research Method

Clothing, as objects of material culture, can act both as entry points for personal (and private) autobiography in relation to questions of identity, as well as entry points for understanding the social components of identity as read through individual and collective responses to a particular clothing artefact—what might be described as *"the wearer's view."* Convinced of the potential dress offers as a method of inquiry into identity processes and embodiment,[5] we began writing stories about particular items of clothing, and invited a small number of writers, including scholars and poets who are connected with our interdisciplinary research group, *The Image and Identity Research Collective (IIRC)*,[6] to do the same, resulting in this edited volume of carefully crafted autobiographical and literary pieces. Academics and poets, it turns out, have a lot to say about their clothes (if someone asks), and are skilful in using dress to write thoughtfully and artfully about things that matter. Shining the spotlight on an item of clothing simultaneously illuminates a range of phenomena lurking just underneath or beside the garment itself, starting with the body.[7]

This book thus draws together a number of dress stories—narrative essays, short stories, and poems in which dress becomes the organizing feature for looking at body and identity in women's lives within a birth-to-death framework in North American and Western society. In some cases, respondents to our invitation to write for this book have chosen items that reflect a particular rite of passage of social and institutional significance; others have chosen garments that take on some sort of individual symbolism (as in "the dress I was wearing when . . ."). What is apparent in both sets of accounts is that *dress might be read as both phenomenon and method.*

The idea of the personal read against the social, with all the inherent tensions and contradictions that produces, seems to us to be very useful and appropriate in relation to the textual evidence of clothing. East-West "border crossing" elements in some of the dress stories serve not only to contextualize dress as culturally laden, personally mediated signs and symbols, but also underline the impossibility of arriving at a singular interpretation of any dress. This collection warns against simplistic notions of identity. The interaction of individual and social processes is further explored as many of the authors pursue the idea of "not just any dress" in relation to a particular rite of passage in which a dress has traditionally been used as a social marker or symbol, laden, before it is ever bought or made, with heavy layers of historical and cultural meaning.

Some of the contributors to this collection use poetry or photography to represent their autobiographical inquiry, reminding us that dresses are first and foremost visual objects. Working with material culture, the authors draw variously on critical memory work (much of it photography-based), autobiographic narrative inquiry, popular culture, feminist theory, and poetic inquiry to tell their insightful stories. The power of these narratives and poems is predicated on the simple fact that we all have bodies and usually wear clothes, both in private and in public. Moving back and forth from private spaces to public ones, each chapter tells a compelling tale that revolves around at least one garment and features an unexpected twist of plot or language that interrogates the common assumptions usually associated with the buying or making or wearing of the dress. Thus for example, a communion dress becomes an affront to the clergy, a wedding dress, a declaration of defiance, a corset, a symbol of a mother's sternness, and a bathrobe, a teacher's garment. Bought or made, then worn, forgotten, remembered, reconstructed and reinterpreted, each dress offers new glimpses into how we construct meaning in our daily lives.

The narrative research methodology underlying this collection capitalizes on the ways that any woman's autobiography is in some respects every woman's biography, and on how no two experiences or images are exactly alike yet can have much to say to each other, even when they seem to be portraying contradictory world views or realities. Beyond the semiotic, tactile, and visual aspects of the clothes themselves, the essays, stories, and poetry delve into what dresses can reveal about fundamental aspects of personal and social experience, aspects which helped us group the pieces into sections and derive their themes: childhood; schooling; professional identity; presentation of self; dress as ritual; dress and identity; dress and culture; conformity and difference; dress and sexuality; dress and our mothers; body size and body-image; gender socialization; popular culture, power relations, aging and mortality.

Dresses, Dressing, and Women

Women's dress experiences are the focus here (even in the chapter by a male author), although men's bodies, identities, and values echo through many of the pieces. Although men do wear dresses in certain cultural contexts, the dresses and garments featured here are those that have been associated closely, for better or for worse, with women. The focus of most pieces is not on dress as an abstract concept or as an historical artefact or even as a concrete object to be analyzed, but rather on *dresses-in-use, dresses embodied, dresses worn*. In short, it is the act of dressing and the experience and construction of meaning around and through dresses that is front and center.

The stories do not set out to exemplify or typify or speak for every woman. They are personal and often difficult to write, exposing, as they often must, some of the author's background, biases, vulnerabilities, silences, feelings, and beliefs. Dress stories, as we conceive them, are not the same thing as the Story (history) of Dress.[8] And yet, through their *unique particulars,* they *cumulatively* point to certain aspects of dress, body, and identity that could have ramifications for almost any one, thereby making a real contribution to the fields of Dress Studies,

Cultural Studies, Women's Studies, and Education where experiential accounts of wearing clothes are scarce indeed. As Tseelon points out, although there is a plethora of semiotic and sociological analyses and historical accounts of dress and an abundance of philosophizing of the body, approaches to the clothed body that are grounded in people's own accounts of their experience are too few in number.[9] Through the use of various forms of "dress stories"—critical memoir, photography, poetry, autobiographical narratives—this book helps to address this imbalance.

Dress Story Genres

Some of the keenest insights into the meaning of clothing are to be found both in literature, in the novels and short stories by such writers as Jane Austen, Margaret Atwood, Alice Walker, and Alice Munro, and in the photography and textile installations around the theme of dresses that are being staged with increasing frequency in museums, galleries, as can be seen, for example, in the work of Annette Messager, Suzanne Lacey, and Jana Sterbak. The ability of novelists and artists to evoke both the visible and tangible as well as the invisible, ethereal power of dress convinced us to feature photographs and literary genres. When carefully constructed and de-constructed, literary narratives about dresses can become effective forms of critique, social commentary, and even theory. This becomes evident in reading the wide range of genres represented in the collection, ranging from the photography-based memory-work of Kuhn and Mavor; the literary prose of Grumet, Knowles, and Mitchell; the reflective stories of Cole, Derry, Ralfe, Reider, Steenbergen, and Visser; the essay by Musial; the critical reminiscences of Bahramitash, Curdt-Christiansen, and Weber; to the poetry of Church, Hussey, Lemieux, Neilson Glenn, Mitchell, Sands, Snowber, and Weber. As this collection demonstrates, dresses turn out to be amazingly strong, supple, and adaptable to different genres, acting always to evoke the intimate relationship between the personal and social elements of our everyday experience, and, as we see, for example, in O'Reilly Scanlon's and Abramovitch's compelling short stories, of our not so everyday experiences as well. And throughout, we see dress mediating identity and the body as only clothes can.

Like all stories, poems, and literary texts, dress stories invite a variety of readings between and through and beyond the lines, multiple interpretations through one's own embodied experience, knowledge, biases, background, beliefs, and creative imagination. For those readers interested in pursuing dress-body studies beyond this volume, in addition to detailed endnotes, we have gathered all the chapters' references into one convenient reference list at the end of the book.

Notes

1. In an article entitled "The narrative anecdote" published in the *Journal of Education for Teaching* (1993) *19* (1), 71–82, Weber draws on van Manen's work to contend that the humble and too often overlooked anecdote should be accorded more respect and attention as a rich data source that holds underestimated epistemological value.
2. Although the term "dress stories" is our own, we see some affinity between our work and they way that Banim, Green, & Guy explored aspects of women's identity through their day-to-day use of clothes and the meanings the women they interviewed attached to their clothing. M. Banim & A. Guy (2001). Dis/continued selves: Why do women keep clothes they no longer wear? In A. Guy, E. Green, & M. Banim (Eds.) *Through the Wardrobe: Women's Relationships with Their Clothes* (Oxford & New York: Berg, 2001). We also note the significance of work on other topics that use short, personal autobiographic narrative to evoke larger social issues, such as Wendy Chapkis' powerful collection *Beauty Secrets: Women and the Politics of Appearance* (Boston: South End Press, 1986).
3. This careful attention to the capacity of details to evoke the meaning of experience is at the heart (albeit in different ways) of both anthropologist Clifford Geertz's notion of "thick description" and Max van Manen's most useful approach to hermeneutic phenomenology as articulated in his book, *Researching Lived Experience: Human Science for an Action Sensitive Pedagogy* (London, Ontario: The Althouse Press, 1990). In a different way, it is also at the heart of the work of Roland Barthes as well as the many scholars who work with material culture.
4. L. Taylor, *The Study of Dress History* (Manchester and New York: Manchester University Press, 2002) 102.
5. See in particular, chapter 4, "Clothes make the Teacher? Adornment and Identity" in Weber & Mitchell's *That's Funny, You Don't Look Like a Teacher! Interrogating Images and Identity in Popular Culture* (Falmer Press, 1999) and also chapter 4, "Undressing and Redressing the Teacher's Body" in Mitchell & Weber's *Reinventing Ourselves as Teachers: Beyond Nostalgia* (Falmer Press, 1999).
6. IIRC is a project initiated by Sandra Weber (Department of Education and the Simone de Beauvoir Institute, Concordia University) and Claudia Mitchell (Faculty of Education, McGill University). The collaborators of the *Image and Identity Research Collective* share an interest in developing interdisciplinary, image-based research methodologies and artistic forms of representation for the Humanities and Social Sciences. In our individual and collective projects, we variously use video, film, photography, performance, and fictional practice to research questions relating to gender, age, body, popular culture, and/or identity. Many of our projects involve critical self-study and collective inquiry. Members of the collective use the website (www.iirc.mcgill.ca) to post their work and to "house" bibliographies and other resources that are useful for image-based research. In collaboration with IIRC, Mitchell and Weber have also established Taffeta Productions, directing and producing several video documentaries related to the body and identity: *Dress Fitting* and *Canadian Pie* (both related to dressing for the prom), and *Fire + Hope* (on youth, gender and HIV/AIDS in South Africa).
7. The growing attention paid by scholars such as Joanne Entwistle (2001) to the notion of the dressed body (what we like to call "dress-body") and to the way clothing acts as a mode of embodiment is particularly important to reading between the lines of "dress stories."
8. Although most of the dress stories we present here document a more personal rather than a social history of particular garments, we enthusiastically acknowledge the importance of work that is carefully documented and grounded in history by scholars such Christopher

Breward, Diane Crane, Amy De la Haye, Joanne Eicher, Anne Hollander, Valerie Steele, and Elizabeth Wilson (see references at the end of the book).

9. E. Tseelon, *The Masque of Femininity: The Presentation of Women in Everyday Life*. (London: Sage, 1995) 4, and Tseelon, "Ontological, Epistemological and, Methodological Clarifications in Fashion Research: from Critique to Empirical Suggestions," in A. Guy, E. Green, & M. Banim (Eds.) *Through the Wardrobe: Women's Relationships with Their Clothes* (Oxford & New York: Berg, 2001).

CHAPTER 2

Lorri Neilson Glenn

That Saturday night all her clothes fell apart and broke into song.

A white sports coat and a pink carnation, blue suede
shoes and a ramalama ding dong
itsy-bitzy teeny-weeny yellow polka dot bikini
we wear short shorts, do
wappa do
       (Find your
high heel sneakers, ride my
pink Cadillac in your polka dot vest and
man oh man—)
mamma may have, and
papa may have, but god bless your
boots of Spanish leather, and the big
panama with
a purple hat band.
Obla di,
Obla
Da. You're the
devil with a
blue dress, blue
dress, blue dress, devil with a blue dress
and green-
sleeves, and a coat of many
colours, coo-coo
ca-choo.

Baby's in black, but I'm forever in
blue jeans, wanting nights in
white satin, and a ten-
gallon hat, obla di obla da,
      what to
do, who to be, the mask or the
mirror, or the lady in red. A string of
pearls, scarlet ribbons, scarlet
ribbons for her
hair,
hung down in
ringlets, she was a
nice girl, a proper girl, but—

(He cuts down
trees, he wears high heels, suspenders and a
bra)

Goin' to town with my best dress on,
Goin' to town with my best dress on.

Do-lang, do lang, do lang.
Do-lang, do lang, and
along comes a lady in lacey sleeves. She had a
dark and a rovin' eye, and I didn't know what
she was headin' for, but it was too
late. If you

want to destroy my sweater, hold this thread as
I walk away, hold

this thread as I—
Shuwap, shubee-doo
wap,
obla di obla da,
you can leave your hat on.

(you can leave your hat on).

PART II
Growing Up with Dresses

CHAPTER 3 *Carol Mavor*

Collecting Loss: Photographs, Dresses, "Paperies"

> *All women . . . are clothing fetishists.*
> SIGMUND FREUD[1]

> *What they [clothing and photographs] have in common is that they are simultaneously presence and absence. They are both an object and a souvenir of a subject, exactly as a cadaver is both an object and souvenir of a subject.*
> CHRISTIAN BOLTANSKI[2]

I fetishize two things in my life: clothing, especially old clothing, clothing with a past, and photographs. And it was not until recently that I understood that my desires for each were woven closely together. My story is stitched with fetishistic embroidery: "Collecting Loss" threads, pokes, pulls, ties and knots the letters of a beautiful, if melancholic, F-E-T-I-S-H that is decidedly female and feminized. I adamantly pick up dangling silken threads and tiny pearls and bright-and-somber-colored glass beads by pulling the fetish into view as unquestionably attached (with umbilical threads) to mothers, grandmothers, daughters, girls.

According to Freud's work on fetishism, the fetish is solely the prerogative of men; women are often hysterics, but they are almost never fetishists. As Apter points out, "despite his admission at the Vienna Psychoanalytic Society in 1909 that 'all women . . . are clothing fetishists,'" Freud typically supplies a male agent to the perversion by associating it with male homosexuality and coprophilic pleasure.[3] In response to Freud, Apter gives fetish objects to (retrieves them for) women in special boxes and bureaus and albums and other private places enshrouded with veils, fabrics, and furs, whose sole purpose is to preserve the relics of departed loved ones. The stories of loss range from spoiled love to death to merely growing up. Inside these feminine spaces we find letters, pressed flowers, locks of hair, nail clippings, pieces of clothing. The fetish objects, from the trivial to the exquisite, are most often passed down and gathered by the women of the family, "by hook or crook" (a translation of à-bric-à-brac) in a continual process of "acquisition and exchange"—which can be met with heated emotions (ranging from intense love to harbored jealousy to violence) between sisters, between mothers and daughters.[4] Apter points out that this "bric-a-brac–cluttered world" has been largely overlooked, even when it reaches a space of "manic collectomania," because it has been naturalized as part of feminine culture. Apter's examples of female fetishes, taken from literature and art, are often visual, sometimes olfactory, but the majority of them relate to a sense of touch.

My "bric-a-brac–cluttered world" is also haptic. My fingers are beckoned by a baby dress of white cotton eyelet, an abandoned pink baby blanket woven with satin ribbons, a once white wedding veil yellowed crisp, Grandfather's old camel mohair coat eaten by moths, a tiny but heavy glass-beaded bag (royal blue, deep rose, white and gold) cinched with a silk cord, tiny shoes of soft worn mildewed leather pressed flat by storage and polished powder blue. These are the things that clutter and fill the recesses of my home, my memories, my body.

Crucial to this world are my photographs: some are made of soft matte paper printed with sepia tones, others are made of glossy paper printed in stark black and white, others are losing themselves in the faded tones of early color photography, still others feature the surreal spaces of the Polaroid camera. My family's bureaus, albums, and boxes (and those of many other middle-class families) have been filling up with photographs ever since the invention of the *carte de visite* and the never-ending succession of photographic inventions: mass-produced hand cameras (the Brownie, the Kodak, the Lilliput, the Tom Thumb, the Frena); drug store developing; Sears value packs; school portraits; disposable cameras; digital processing. Using such products of the photographic enterprise, my own grandmother spent the last years of her life preparing elaborate scrapbooks/photograph albums on each of her two sons to be left to us after her death.

An Album

My father's album (which he sent directly to me after my grandmother's death) begins and ends with photographs not of him, but of my mother when they were first married; the year was 1953. This blunt, one might even say shocking, beginning is an ending. It is the ending of something that I am only beginning to understand now: a final severing of that (umbilical) something between a mother and her son—that something that began with my father's tumbles inside his mother, his elbow poking between her ribs, in the months before his birth in 1926. Though my father remained devoted to my grandmother, marriage changes things between a son and a mother. As I turn the black pages weighted with pictures and other memorabilia (cards for birthdays, graduations, birth, bereavement, an occasional newspaper clipping), I feel as if I am watching one of the old Super-8 family movies that we never had—only in reverse. (When I was a child I loved watching other people's home movies this way.) Stopping and starting, the timing is all off; parts are left out. My heart feels heavy with the weight of the black-and-white photographs. I discover that the album finally ends (begins?) with pictures of my baby-father at seven months: white wicker pram, floppy cotton brimmed cap, lips tucked in, as contemplative as he is today.

In between the first page with the pictures of my mother as a young bride, her lips darkened with red lipstick (when I came along, her lips would be frosted pink), and the last page with pictures of my father as baby, there are many more pictures and things: a small lock of hair inside a tiny, tiny envelope inscribed in my grandmother's writing (small, tight, cursive) with the words "My curl," meaning my father's curl (I cannot bear to look inside); military pictures of my father in sailor caps and active-duty clothes and dress uniforms with harsh brass buttons; photographs of the three of them (my grandmother in a white dress with an enormous cotton bow of an unknown color, like the wings of a giant butterfly, like angel wings on the wrong side of her body, she appears ready to alight, her smile is the sign of a joy so pure that it fills her with helium lightness—my laughing father in short pants—his brother in long pants) taken in succession as they happily stride toward the camera at the 1935 Chicago World's Fair—my grandfather out of the frame, as he almost always is (figure 3.1).

By arranging his life backwards, my grandmother has reconstructed my father's life as if it ends, like some forbidding myth, with their beginning. As James Clifford has told us, "Living does not easily organize itself into a continuous narrative."[5] It is only after we have lived through cycles of our lives, in recollection, in photographs, that a narrative comes through. Afterward, we tell narratives that may be partly true, but they are also narratives that must be fictionalized in order for us to make sense of our lives . . . in order to survive. "We are condemned to tell stories," but we cannot, in our heart of hearts, believe that they are altogether true.[6]

I learned from my grandmother that it is the mother's duty to create palpable narratives of our lives. It is the mother's duty to love things. My grandmother passed on to me this love of things (which is both wonderful and burdensome). Yet, not all things can be passed on; not all pictures make it into the album. Though I begged for and got my grandfather's old chair, he is virtually absent in the album. In one photograph I find him, but he is barely visible in the front seat of the Packard. In another picture, I find him striding into the back door of the cabin, but he turns his face away from the camera; the car grimaces and returns the

18 • Growing Up with Dresses

Figure 3.1. Author's family album picture. Grandmother in a dress with an enormous cotton bow, Father and Uncle at the 1935 Chicago World's Fair.

camera's gaze for him. In a family picture with unidentified aunts, my grandfather stands so far apart from my father's hand, which reaches out, futilely trying to pull him in, that it is as if he were not in the picture at all. There is a silent gap between my grandfather and father. Like a parenthetical phrase skipped, the space between them is calling to be read. Despite the silences that many of my grandmother's objects give way to, I collect the things that she has given to me: the chair, the albums, the huge Parisian turn-of-the-century glass vase whose surface imitates carved turtle shell, the odd dark little oil painting of a monk playing the trombone (painstakingly painted with a fine brush and plenty of linseed oil), the silver spoons collected from all over the world, the white fluted wedding teacups, so thin that you can see through them, as if they were made of paper or skin.

A Keeper: Henriette Barthes

In *Camera Lucida* (the book that Roland Barthes wrote after his mother's death, the last book that he would publish before his death), the referent's "umbilical" connection to the actual photograph is a maternal metaphor informed by his relationship to his mother. Just as Barthes' search for perfect lovers in *A Lover's Discourse* (and his posthumous *Incidents*) often turns on memories of, experiences with, the mother, even D.W. Winnicott's maternalized psychoanalytic theories, Barthes' search for the most meaningful, most moving, most touching, most poignant, most wounding photograph turns out to be a search for the perfect photograph of her, turns out to be *the* perfect photograph: the famed Winter Garden Photograph. Threading together incidents, anecdotes and semiotic squibbles on the meaning of photography, *Camera Lucida*'s well-strung speech suspends Barthes and his stories like old-fashioned pearls on a metaphorical string of umbilicus forever clasped around his mother's tender neck. Umbilicus becomes real/reel, a "carnal medium":

> The photograph is literally an emanation of the referent. From a real body, which was there, proceed radiations which ultimately touch me, who am here; the duration of the transmission is insignificant; the photograph of the missing being, as Sontag says, will touch me like the delayed rays of a star. A sort of *umbilical cord* links the body of the photographed thing to my gaze: light, though impalpable, is here a carnal medium, a skin I share.[7]

and

> The air is the luminous shadow which accompanies the body; and if the photograph fails to show this air, then the body moves without a shadow, and once the shadow is severed as in the myth of the Woman without a Shadow, there remains no more than a sterile body. It is by this tenuous *umbilical* cord that the photographer gives life; if he cannot, either by lack of talent or bad luck, supply the transparent soul its bright shadow, the subject dies forever.[8]

A photograph is but a shadow of what once was there, but now is gone. Not unlike the mother "whom we all have to live without sooner or later."[9] She comes and she goes.

Camera Lucida developed quickly (April 15–June 3, 1979), like a photograph. In fact, it developed extra quickly, like a Polaroid picture, like purple spring crocus, like a last breath before death. Barthes died in 1980, the year that *Camera Lucida* was published. Critically injured when "knocked down by a laundry truck while crossing the street in front of the Collège de France," he lingered; he could not recover.[10] "Though he recovered sufficiently to receive visitors, he died four weeks later."[11] It has been suggested that he died of a broken heart, of broken heart strings. Barthes himself predicted his death by lethal sorrow, as he writes in *Camera Lucida*: "Once she was dead I no longer had any reason to attune myself to the progress of the superior Life Force (the race, the species) — From now on I could no more than await my total, undialectical death."[12] In the last letter that he wrote to Richard Howard, four months before the accident, the broken Barthes, bereft of desire, wrote: "Don't think me indifferent or ungrateful—it's just that since

Maman's death there has been a scission in my life, in my psyche, and I have less courage to undertake things. Don't hold it against me. *Ne m'en veuillez pas.*"¹³

Without her, Barthes fears that he will desire nothing, that he will no longer speak his mother tongue *(la langue maternelle)*. He finds himself to be alone. As Barthes remarks in *S/Z,* long before his loss of Maman: "When it is alone, the voice does no labor, transforms nothing: it [merely] *expresses;* but as soon as the hand intervenes to gather and intertwine the inert threads, there is labor, there is transformation."¹⁴ For Barthes, the labor that comes from the body, the hand that intervenes, produces "*text, fabric, braid:* the same thing." But without *Maman,* labor might no longer be possible: the braid [the umbilicus] is under the dark shadow of the scissors. To be reduced to a "unity of meaning" is "to *cut the braid.*"¹⁵

Like many mothers, Henriette Barthes, Roland Barthes' mother, was also a "keeper" of bric-a-brac. Shortly after her death, Barthes, finding himself lost, went through boxes of photographs, relics of their lives spent together and apart. Barthes claims that at that moment, he was not looking for her, that he had no hope of finding her. He, after all, had already cut himself off from her, had faced his/her absolute loss. "I had acknowledged that fatality, one of the most agonizing features of mourning, which decreed that however often I might consult such images, I could never recall her features (summon them up as a totality)."¹⁶ Yet his desire belies him; he continues his looking. Sorting through the pictures, he finds her caught not so much by the camera, but rather by the objects in the pictures that define her. The objects that he writes about, some of which are clothing, are rich in fetishistic lure:

> With regard to many of these photographs, it was History which separated me from them. Is History not simply that time when we were not born? I could read my nonexistence in the clothes my mother had worn before I can remember her. There is a kind of stupefaction in seeing a familiar being dressed *differently*. Here, around 1913, is my mother dressed up—hat with a feather, gloves, delicate linen at wrists and throat, her "chic" belied by the sweetness and simplicity of her expression. This is the only time I have seen her like this, caught in a History (of tastes, fashions, fabrics): my attention is distracted from her by accessories which have perished: for clothing is perishable, it makes a second grave for the loved being. In order to "find" my mother, fugitively alas, and without ever being able to hold on to this resurrection for long, I must, much later, discover in several photographs the objects she kept on her dressing table, an ivory powder box (I loved the sound of its lid), a cut-crystal flagon, or else a low chair, which is now near my own bed, or again the raffia panels she arranged above the divan, the large bag she loved (whose comfortable shapes belied the bourgeois notion of the "handbag").¹⁷

The photographs, objects themselves, record objects within them (dress, dressing table, ivory powder box): things that stand in for her, not wholly, but partially. It is no wonder that he never "recognized her except in fragments."[18] These mother-objects are tied to her and to Barthes, who never really cut the cord, even, perhaps, especially, after death.

Because photographs so poignantly speak of death and loss, they wound us, prick us, reach us like "the delayed rays of a star."[19] Every photograph is a record of a moment forever lost—snapped up by the camera and mythically presented as evermore. The family album is always torn by the sorrows of loss: lost childhoods, lost friends, lost relatives, lost memories, lost objects, lost newness. Pressed into the album, not without joy, the images depress the beholder; they speak in melancholic tones. "With the Photograph, we enter into flat Death."[20]

And like childhood and new woolen winter coats and linen blouses and mothers and silk dresses and felt hats and distant cousins and grandmothers, photographs deteriorate, spoil, die, benumb, weaken. "Not only does it [the photograph] commonly have the fate of paper (perishable), but even if it is attached to more lasting supports, it is still mortal: like a living organism, it is born on the level of the sprouting silver grains, it flourishes a moment then ages . . . Attacked by light, by humidity, it fades, weakens, vanishes."[21]

The photograph dies like a body. And like a body, we simply cannot throw it out. (We bury the dullest, even the ugliest, photographs in drawers and boxes.) To tear or to cut the photograph is a hysterical action. (My friend Patricia snatched some albums away from her father. I was shocked to see that he had cut her mother out of every one of the pictures, even the wedding photographs. What absolute violence!) Such undue alterations—as in my friend's missing mother, or the ripped picture found at the bottom of a box, or those blank spaces in my father's album where paper corners mark a picture's escape—captivate me for the ways they suggest untold, unimaged, lost, and often purposely forgotten stories.

Yet most of us are anxious to preserve our images of ourselves and our loved ones (as whole and as undamaged), like "flies in amber," as Peter Wollen has written.[22] So, we often ask ourselves, what are we to do with these traces of bodies that fill bureaus, boxes, shelves, attics, basements, closets? It is as if our pictures contained thin ghosts of the actual person photographed (of our aunt, our cousin, our mother, our childhood friend, our self). We are haunted by our family photographs. If thrown away, Barthes writes, "What is it that will be done away with, along with this photograph which yellows, fades, and will someday be thrown out, if not by me—too superstitious for that—at least when I die? Not only 'life' (this was alive, this posed live in front of the lens), but also, sometimes—how to put it?—love."[23]

Likewise, clothing is perishable, and because it takes on the body (it takes form, smells, dirt) it makes "a second grave for the loved being," even before death, but especially after death.

22 • Growing Up with Dresses

A Keeper (of Dresses): Clementina, Viscountess Hawarden

In the photographs taken by Clementina, Viscountess Hawarden (1822–1865), beautiful old dresses and other objects of fancy dress inform the poignantly torn edges of the photographs (figure 3.2). Hawarden's oeuvre focuses almost entirely on her lovely adolescent daughters (especially her favored model who was also named

Figure 3.2. Hawarden, Clementina Viscountess Hawarden, ca. 1861–1862. All of Hawarden's photographs are untitled and undated. The Board of Trustees of the Victoria and Albert Museum.

Figure 3.3. Hawarden, Clementina Viscountess Hawarden, ca. 1862.

Clementina), whom she pictured in tantalizing selections from her closets of fancy dress alongside exquisite objects (a curvaceous vase, a large looking-glass, an Indian traveling cabinet). Like many Victorian mothers of her class, Hawarden collected photographs of her growing girls and either she or another family member or servant or friend pasted them into albums. But unlike the standard images found in Victorian family albums, these photographs were taken by the mother herself and seem to overflow with folds of sexuality and an invitation to touch: a daughter pulling up her dress and underskirts to reveal an ankle criss-crossed with ribbons; a daughter in her corset and petticoat before a mirror; two daughters in pounds of petticoats and silk, one nestling her head on the breast of the other; a sister dramatically, yet subtly, pulling on a tender lock of her sister's hair (figure 3.3). ("She clipped a precious golden lock/ She dropped a tear more rare than pearl," Christina Rossetti.[24])

Even the edges of the photographs give way to touching. After being cut and torn from the family albums (for reasons still unclear), they were donated to London's Victoria and Albert Museum by Hawarden's granddaughter, still another Clementina (Clementina Tottenham), who had inherited 775 photographs from her mother. (The pictures arrived in 1939.) No longer in the heart of the home (the family album), but in the Museum's humidity-controlled, acid-free environment, their scarred borders, their ripped and cut edges, remain poignant signs, permanent scars, of their short but dramatic flight from Hawarden's home (5 Princes Gardens, South Kensington) to one of Britain's premier cultural institutions) right around the corner. Their palpable edges, always overlooked (even misleadingly "repaired" in the first published book of Hawarden's pictures), mark a transformation from the often dismissed maternal collection to the official paternal space of the museum.[25] Hawarden's cut, ripped and torn pictures perform images as full of historical incompleteness: like bits of shard gathered; like jigsaw puzzle pieces scattered; like mixed-up cups and saucers; like a board game in a box, with colored plastic cars and houses, little silver markers, a pair of dice, cardboard cards to draw from, but no directions . . . and no one remembers how to play. I am drawn to their loss as a pictured memory, a becoming beauty, with all the folds and wrinkles of an old flouncy dress, of a Proustian *Search* for the scallop-shaped "madeleine cake," "so richly sensual under its severe, religious folds."[26] In the technical jargon of sewing, wrinkles are called "memory."[27]

I am particularly taken by a particularly joyful Hawarden photograph of her daughter and namesake Clementina teaching two of her siblings to take "the first steps of a dance"[28] (figure 3.4). Daughter Clementina is pictured as developing as beautifully as the new buildings of South Kensington behind her. Clementina full of confidence, full of love, full to the brim with her mother's indulgences, skips outward, pulls up her skirt. This photograph is unusual among the hundreds of others in that Clementina is not in "fancy dress" but in an 1830s ordinary vintage dress, which very well may be an old dress of her mother's.[29] Clementina is about fifteen.

For me, wearing the clothes of a loved one or a friend, in which her smells come forth, in which her body has worn the cloth smooth or through, is akin to carrying a photographic image with me. Her body caresses me. I like to wear lockets with photographic images tucked inside. The locket (say, with a picture of Oliver or Ambrose or Augustine inside) or Amy's old dress, or my father's royal purple letter sweater from high school, or someone else's great aunt's abandoned hat—all carry specters of my loved ones: I sense them skin to skin.

I guess that is why we have to keep so much in our dressers (which function as miniature museums of our archived selves): "the function of any drawer is to ease, to acclimate the death of objects by causing them to pass through a sort of pious site, a dusty chapel, where, in the guise of keeping them alive, we allow them a decent interval of dim agony."[30] Like a photograph, the drawer of saved objects functions as a space between life and death. For not only do our photographs, our objects, signify death, they also (in the spirit of the fetish) keep death away. Collecting these objects in the nooks and crannies of our homes keeps them and our memories and ourselves alive. Objects keep death away by helping us to remember. Milan Kundera writes on memory's close link to death: "Forgetting . . . is the great private problem of man;

Figure 3.4. Hawarden, Clementina Viscountess Hawarden, ca. 1861–1862.

death as the loss of self. But what of this self? It is the sum of everything we remember. Thus, what terrifies us about death is not the loss of future but the loss of past. Forgetting is a form of death ever present within life."[31] I am so afraid of forgetting.

Sartorial Memories

Elin o'Hara slavick's mother never wanted to forget the childhoods of her five daughters. She feared the loss of the past. And she must have, I imagine, feared a loss of herself. In addition to the family photographs and the Super-8 home movies, slavick's mother saved most of their dresses. The dresses were worn by slavick and her sisters to Mass, to school, to birthday parties, and to family gatherings. As a result, the girls were often photographed in these dresses.

Not so long ago, slavick told her mother that she wanted to use the worn and mended dresses in an artwork; she wanted to embroider her own text onto them (figure 3.5). slavick's mother, a female fetishist in her own right, agreed to send the material of her maternal collectomania to her youngest daughter, the one who used to get mad and kick people's shins. (I still am surprised that the mother agreed to give them up.) The dresses, like my father's family album, came to slavick in the mail. Like my father's family album, they contained the histories of a family. Like my father's album, they prompted memories.

Trained as a photographer, slavick has reconstructed her childhood, not with photographs, but in response to photography. (As Susan Sontag writes in *On Photography*, "Now all art aspires to the condition of photography."[32]) slavick sees the dresses as photographs of how she remembers her body:

> The work is informed ... primarily by my own small memory of being a girl. An investigation of my childhood produces a synthesis of distorted memory, my real history, and my adult desire to interpret and remember. Poetic and confessional texts are sewn in the dresses that my mother saved since my childhood. Each dress becomes a surrogate of my body, a photograph of the memory of my body. The absence of actual photographic imagery of that body implies the loss of multiple bodies; the hiding body, the invisible body and the dead child body which we all possess within our adult selves.[33]

But unlike the photographs that are found in the usual family album, slavick's dresses take on images that are almost never found in family pictures. "slavick's childhood dresses no longer can pretend innocence. They are transformed through adult texts and become surreal evidence in the absence of the original snapshots that they might have been."[34] The dresses function like the missing pictures in an album, or the tears alongside Hawarden's photographs. They manage to picture the unsaid. For example, on the creamy soft bodice of a beautiful cotton dress, with a full green skirt whose hem holds the extra weight of a full four inches from being turned up for one of the girls so that it could dance just above her knees, slavick has stitched:

> MOTHER, YOU PUT COLD VINEGAR
> CLOTHS ON MY SUNBURNT
> BODY.
> THE CLOTHS WERE STEAMING
> WITH YOUR BREATH
> AND I KEPT BREATHING.
> I FELL ASLEEP AND DREAMED.
> I LOVED YOU.

Figure 3.5. elin o'Hara slavick, "BROTHER YOU HELD ME OVER THE WATERS," dress from *A Wall of Incoherent Dresses*, 1991. Courtesy of the artist.

It is a family picture: a child's sunburnt body, maternal care, child sleep, a child's profound love for her mother. But it is not an image that many of us could find in our family album. Pain, nakedness, the unposed, the unconscious, the smells of the home, the breath of the mother, the unmasked, a grown child's sleep, the everyday, a sensual confession—such steam and chill are rarely there.

Like most of us, Reynolds Price can find only "innocent" and "posed" pictures in his family's collection. As he writes in the afterword to Sally Mann's *Immediate Family:*

> [My parents] exposed yards of film, not only in their frank satisfaction in a child but also in pursuit of visible proof that I was glad to be their product, a moon to their sun—and I generally was—but they likewise early enlisted my cooperation in a long concealment or denial that my becoming moon had hid a dark face, which was where I lived for far more hours—and now for nearly six decades—than any of them would have wanted to hear, not to mention confirm in permanent image. Like most veterans of family photographs then, my face and body—so far as they manage to outlast me—will survive as a highly edited version of the whole person I managed to be behind an ever-ready grin.[35]

Price would "give a lot to have a stack of black-and-white pictures of moments" that captured such things as the "furious look" in his "father's gray eyes on a warm Sunday evening" when he told his wife that "she'd stolen his share" of Price and his brother.[36] But there are no such pictures for Price, for most of us. Family albums are closely edited; they "tend to include [only] those images on which family members can agree, which tell a shared story."[37]

Most families agree on the same shared stories: Happy Holiday, Happy Vacation, Happy Graduation, Happy Birthday, Happy First Bicycle, Happy New Home, Happy New Baby, Happy Wedding. Though as family members we can read other stories between the lines, there are solid similarities among family pictures (the pose, the occasion, the smiles, sometimes the clothes), a general covering-over that "perpetuate[s] dominant familial myths and ideologies." It is in this way that all family pictures are masked: they assume the mask of the familial. "Photography," writes Barthes, "cannot signify (aim at a generality) except by assuming a mask."[38]

Yet, in a play of contradiction, childhood photographs often seem like an extraordinary touch of the real: evidence of the unmasked self. Looking through my father's family album, I see all of the essential traces of him: his quiet way, his tight-lipped smile, something moral and self-assured, his surprising love for wearing silly hats that stands in direct contrast to his hatred of costume, the pure pleasure he feels in being with the right people, his always very thick hair, a comfortableness with his own body, his love of dogs, his devotion to his mother. Some will say that I am reading what I want to see into these photographs. Nevertheless, I see the essential image of my father that is "utopically," as Barthes argues in *Camera Lucida*, *"the impossible science of the unique being."*[39]

Our childhood photographs are an extraordinary touch of the real because they are able to capture an essence of a unique being that we carry within ourselves from birth to death indexically. Like footprints in the sand or fingerprints in wax, photographs leave a trace of the referent. All photographs are traces of a skin that once was. Balzac understood this; this is why he feared losing thin ghosts of himself, like layers of skin, with each photograph "taken."[40] Barthes is in touch with Balzac when he writes: "The photograph is literally an emanation of the referent. From a real body, which was there, proceed radiations which ultimately touch me, who am here."[41] Maybe this is why, when I see an old childhood photograph of my father, my grandmother, myself, I have an urge to touch it, to really feel it. And, even though I (really) feel nothing but smoothness, in my body, in my heart, I feel a weighty ache, a pang of loss. I believe, like Balzac, like Barthes, that the child before me is touching me. He weighs me down, she weighs me down, with grains of light that emanate from a small body that wears such childhood things as short trousers, cotton dresses, white cotton shirts (without collars), striped sweaters (with pointy collars), socks that bag and crinkle at the ankle.

Like slavick, many of us feel the loss of the body/bodies of our own childhood. Indeed, many of us feel that our childhood selves are dead. We mourn the loss. We try to bring the child back. We save toys and clothes and other mementos from our childhood days: souvenirs that try to replace the loss. Childhood and death, as Lynn Gumpert has remarked, are closely linked:

> Although these themes at first appear at odds with one another, they share some fundamental similarities. We never know death directly; as Wittgenstein has succinctly observed, "Death is not lived through." Thus we must broach the subject from a distance, from observation. And while childhood is most definitely lived through, when analyzed or discussed, it is again almost invariably from a distance, from the vantage of adults who must rely on fragmented recollections and observations.[42]

Bringing the dresses out of the closet was a way for slavick to touch the child that had died, that she had left behind—not only the death of her own child body, but also that of the little brother who drowned. On a small silken slip that once rubbed against small silken girls, slavick stitched the following:

I ATE FOOD IN THE BASEMENT,
I SUCKED LILACS.
I KICKED MY SISTER'S SHINS.
I PICKED DANDELIONS AND SOLD THEM
FOR A QUARTER.

> I WANTED UGLY THINGS AND COULDN'T SWIM.
> A BROTHER HAD DROWNED.
> SICK EVERY SWIMMING DAY, HAND UNDER
> MY DRY THIGHS,
> BROTHER, YOU HELD ME OVER THE WATERS.

Reading slavick's dress pulls me into the closet of the family album of my mind's eye. Childhood images flash before me. Though I had no brother who drowned, I had a little cousin who died. I hid behind my bed. And even though he did not drown and even though I could swim, I hid in the bushes on swimming day. I did not sell dandelions, but I sold things that I made, really dumb things, door to door. Ugly things were really beautiful to me too, like my favorite toys made of bright colored plastic on various themes of grotesque cuteness. But like most of us, while I have some photographs of my creepy collection of dolls and stuffed animals, I have no pictures of devastating emotions, and maybe it is just as well.

But Sally Mann has taken pictures of such things. Pictures such as that of Emmett sporting a shockingly bloody nose and mouth, Emmett with a back speckled by frightening chicken pox, Jessie with an eye painfully swollen and saddened by what I hope is only a bug bite, mar the perfection of childhood that we all try to invent, not only for ourselves but for our own children, for history itself. With each smiling photograph of the combed and primped child that we dutifully place in the album, the frame, the note to Grandma, we image childhood as undamaged and undamaging: far away from death. We preserve our children in an emulsion of Neverland, an imaginary place of tiny first teeth that never pop out. Yet Jessie bites (we see her teeth marks on her mother's arm in Mann's 1985 photograph *S*) and slavick kicked her sister's shins.

Jenny's mom, Barbara, showed me where my boys were to sleep for the night. The two beds were covered with beautiful aging quilts made of hundreds of tiny squares, the very size of old photographs, like those taken and printed and pasted in my father's album. Caressing one of the old quilts, Barbara explained to me that each square was from an old dress worn by her and her sisters. Each square, patterned with tiny flowers, dots, and funny abstractions, lightly colorful in their muted washed-out colors, were dresses taken, like photographs: they represented years at home, with mother, father, and siblings. Infused with the "texture of perfume," each square, as if bites of (Proustian) madeleine cake, brought back memories.[43] Some good. Some bad. Some banal. They too, like my father's album, carried the weight of the past. Each seam was a memory, a seed sown. I thought of slavick's dresses and I thought of the things that I hoarded in my closets.

Remembering that rainy night in Virginia and the quilts made of lost dresses, I recall a photograph taken not by but of Sally Mann. Perched on a swing, wearing the Easter dress that had been made for her by her mother and grandmother, she is only six years old. You can see the lovely little dress showing its bright face again in Mann's *The Easter Dress* (figure 3.6). Like the dresses in the slavick family, passed down from mother to daughter, Mann has continued the process of acquisition and exchange by passing the Easter dress down to her daughter Jessie. In Mann's photograph, Jessie holds out the bright white pleated cotton skirt, sprinkled with flowers, into a wide smile for the camera. A little sister in a white baby dress hunts in the weeds—for what? I am charmed. But I am also haunted, not only by Jessie's brother, who pulls himself along the wire fence (his face strangely hooded, his legs in shorts), but especially by the torn nightdress that hangs on the clothesline. The nightdress—caught in the gentle breath of the Blue Ridge mountains, caught between the movement of an elderly man's dancing steps and the blur of a winged creature—is ripped at the back and at the hem. This dress is a horrible dress. Hanging and blowing like shed skin, it is a souvenir of loss, amongst shadows of change.

Figure 3.6. Sally Mann, *The Easter Dress*, 1986. Copyright Sally Mann. Courtesy Houk Friedman, New York.

I am reminded of my children's little baby sweaters and the grief that I felt (and still feel) when I discovered that they had been ravished by moths. I try to convince myself that the loss tears at my body, not theirs. I try to console myself with Barthes' words on the pleasure of "abrasions," the pleasure found in "the site of loss, the seam, the cut, the deflation."[44] But one hole gives way to another tear. I become acutely aware of my futile attempts to fill the holes with family albums of becoming pictures.

(Ad)dressing Writing

But what comes closer to satisfying my pangs of loss is not saving photographs, but rather writing: writing like I was constructing the perfect dress. I learned to (ad)dress my writing as sewing through the author-tale(r)-seamstress-mender Marcel Proust.[45] Proust writes as if making a dress.

Stitching writing into sewing is a metaphor elegantly developed by Proust in his lengthy *A la recherché du temps perdu (In Search of Lost Time)*. I have usurped the stitches that he has dropped through the hands of the book's Narrator's beloved and talented servant Françoise. The Narrator, as mirrored "character" of Proust himself, is trying to find the voice and structure required for the novel that he so desperately wants to write. Eventually the reader comes to understand Françoise's sewing as the ultimate model for completing the perfect novel. Yet, the Narrator (Proust) is not able to see the value of Françoise's "art" until late in the book.

At the beginning of the first volume *(Swann's Way)*, it is the image of the cathedral that serves as principle model for the Narrator's ambitions of what his own novel will be. Proust's cluttered church of Saint-Hilaire in his beloved Combray, with its "sturdy architecture, handsome stained-glass windows, secret crypt and distinguished bell tower," is offered to the reader as the "first representation of form and structure in the book."[46] But as it turns out in the final volume of the novel *(Time Regained)*—like a garment pulled right side out to show off the beauty that had been held hostage by the wrong side of the fabric, bared seams, unsightly threads and frayed edges—it is the exquisite sewing done by Françoise that becomes the most exquisite metaphor for the Narrator's true ambition. In the following passage, the Narrator discusses mending his notes and rewrites for the novel (his "paperies"):

> And—for at every moment the metaphor uppermost in my mind changed as I began to represent myself [as a writer] more clearly and in a more material shape the task upon which I was about to embark—I thought that . . . under the eyes of Françoise, who like all unpretentious people who live at close quarters with us, would have a certain insight into the nature of my labours . . . I should work beside her and in a

way almost as she worked herself . . . and, pinning here and there an extra page, I should construct my book, I dare not say ambitiously like a cathedral, but quite simply like a dress. Whenever I had not all my " paperies" near me as Françoise called them, and just the one that I need was missing, Françoise would understand how this upset me, she would always say that she could not sew if she had not the right size of thread and the proper buttons. And then through sharing my life had she not acquired a sort of comprehension of literary work. . . ?[47]

The Narrator's memory of his first meeting with Françoise, the one who would critically provide his approach to writing, indeed his "comprehension of literary work" (ultimately to cut it up and restructure it as if one were sewing the perfect dress, mirroring how this talented woman picked the best pieces of meat and enriched it with the perfect juices when she was slowly and carefully making her exquisite boeuf à la mode), took place at the home of his Aunt Léonie during a New Year's visit to Combray. It is a memory of "spun sugar" (sucre filé): an image of madeleine (sweet memory) and sewing (spinning one's novel) in one.

> No sooner had we arrived in my aunt's dark hall than we saw in the gloom, beneath the frills of snowy bonnet as stiff and fragile as if it had been made of spun sugar, the concentric ripples of a smile of anticipatory gratitude. It was Françoise, motionless and erect, framed in the small doorway of the corridor like the statue of a saint in its niche.[48]

In particular, Françoise has a special talent for transforming old clothes (clothing with a past) into something new, which though different, is reminiscent of slavick's own sartorial memory dresses. Fairly early in the long novel *(Within a Budding Grove)* we learn, for example, how Françoise transformed the Narrator's great-aunt's old cloak and hat into a delightful, perfect, charming costume. By removing the bird from the hat and adding a "velvet band, the loop of ribbon that would have delighted one in a portrait by Chardin or Whistler," Françoise proved her "simple but unerring taste."[49] By turning the cloak, which had been "decorated with a hideous pattern and jet beads" inside out to expose an "'inside' of plain . . . faded cherry-coloured cloth," Françoise metamorphosized the once shabby coat into a lovely one: "the discreet nap of her fur collar, brought to mind one of those miniatures of Anne of Britanny painted in the Books of Hours by on old master, in which everything is so exactly in the right place."[50] Like Chardin, Whistler or an old master who paints Books of Hours, Françoise (whom the Narrator refers to elsewhere as "the Michelangelo of our kitchen,"[51]) is a great artist-writer-seamstress in her own right. Proust, one might argue, like Françoise, writes with the old and makes it new.

Proust's early process of writing that appears as fragments of life in his *Carnet* de notes (1908–1918) or his copious letters written in pursuit of, say, a question about "a certain dress worn in the 1890s, or a famous witticism uttered during the Belle Epoque,"[52] as well as the handwritten drafts of the *Search* and the rewriting that took place once the manuscript had been typeset all produce exquisite swatches, whose materiality mirrors that of weaving and sewing. Shocking to anyone involved in publishing, once Proust's manuscript was set in type, he would proceed to "use typesetters the way other people use typists, or word processors."[53] Crowding "the margins with more and more new passages, all designed to enrich his design and to establish links [threads] among the various characters and scenes," even pasting new additions in strips that would fold out.[54] The end effect is beauty at play in the textures of form as content, and the textures of content as form. Just as the characters of the *Search*—the Narrator, Odette, Albertine, Swann, Françoise, Bergotte, the mother, the father, the grandmother and many, many more—exist in a labyrinth of layers of gardens, villages, homes, paths, conversations, deaths, marriages, parties, walks, theater visits and more and more, the manuscripts themselves were made in material layers: exquisite paper pastiches of "paperies." As Françoise used to say, "'Ah! if only, instead of this girl who makes him waste all of his time, Monsieur had got himself a nicely brought up young secretary who could have sorted all Monsieur's paperies for him!'"[55]

These "paperies" metaphorically play out Proust's realized desire to weave and connect all the details of life lived into his unfathomable literature (which itself was like an umbilical tie, a return to the maternal through his life and work). Walter Benjamin has described this Proustian fabric that leaves not a piece of string, yarn or thread unattended as a structure, a web that is "fiction, autobiography, and commentary in one, to the syntax of endless sentences (the Nile of language, which here overflows and fructifies the regions of truth), everything transcends the norm."[56] Benjamin runs the shuttle through the bright and somber yarns of the "warp" of the *Search* to emphasize that "the Latin word *textum* means 'web.' No one's text is more tightly woven than Marcel Proust's; to him nothing was tight or durable enough."[57] As Benjamin knows, Proust is at the mercy of the invisible weaver, who refuses to abandon the threads that have been unraveled through the course of a day come evening, in favor of collecting and rearranging these tender and loosened offshoots, to bring on new meaning. As Benjamin writes: "For the important thing for the remembering author is not what he experienced, but the weaving of his memory, the Penelope work of recollection. Or should one call it, rather, a Penelope work of forgetting."[58] Just as the *Search* is as much about forgetting as it is remembering, the Narrator both generates and covers up time, like a writer, like Proust, like Barthes. It is through Benjamin's description of the tightly-woven Proustian text that I now understand why I have been of late, cradling myself in the memory of these lines spoken by the Narrator in reference to Françoise and the pleasure she derived in consoling herself with "the knowledge that she would one day be buried in her own fine sheets, marked with her name, not darned at all (or so exquisitely darned that it merely enhanced one's idea of the skill and patience of the seamstress), a shroud from the constant image of which in her mind's eye she drew a satisfactory sense, if not actually of wealth and prosperity, at any rate of self esteem." Françoise's perfect sheets, "not darned at all (or so exquisitely darned that it merely enhanced one's idea of the skill and patience of the seamstress)," are the perfect white sheets that are now bound in the book that buried Proust, like a baby swaddled, like a corpse wrapped. The paperies of the *Search* are nearly hidden, now just traces of a collage that once was, that enhance one's idea of the skill and the patience of the writer: of Proust as an exquisite seamstress who works with impalpable threads.

My writing as dress is made of words that grew from the magic of cloth, from the invisibly-thimbled tips of my typing fingers. I pull the dress over my body and find that I am grazed by the wrinkles (memories) of my grandmother's photo album that she made for my father: my father's curl, the photograph of my grandmother in a white dress with an enormous cotton bow of an unknown color, like the wings of a giant butterfly, like angel wings on the wrong side of her body. As I button up the front placard, I take hold of Barthes' mother-objects: the Winter Garden Photograph, "a cut crystal flagon . . . a low chair . . . raffia panels . . . the large bag that she loved." As I try to straighten and fluff the stiff, mesh petticoats under the skirt, I become lost in the folds of Hawarden's photographs of girls in great dresses: two daughters in pounds of petticoats and silk, one nestling her head on the breast of the other. As I tie the wide satin ribbon at my waist, I remember my child self, my old Easter dress, the photograph of Jessie Mann in her mother's Easter dress. As I look into the invisible mirror, I see nothing but I smell the delicious musty smell of slavick's dresses (that her sisters wore too) of "sucked lilacs" and "dry thighs," of acidic "cold vinegar" and Mother's "breath." As I quickly mend the fallen hem that catches on my heel, I take in the detail of Françoise's reparative sewing on the old cloak which had been "decorated with a hideous pattern and jet beads" but now has been turned inside out to expose a beautiful "'inside' of plain . . . faded cherry-coloured cloth." My dress, is *not just any dress*. It trembles with collecting loss.

Notes

This essay grows out of two related versions of an essay that first appeared in *Cultural Studies* II, no. 1 (1997) and as a chapter in my book *Becoming: The Photographs of Clementina, Viscountess Hawarden* (Duke: Durham and London, 1999).

1. Sigmund Freud, Minutes from the Vienna Psychoanalytic Society, 1909, published as "Freud and Fetishism: Previously Unpublished Minutes of the Vienna Psychoanalytic Society," ed. and trans. Louis Rose, *Psychoanalytic Quarterly* 57 (1988): 159, cited by Emily Apter. "Splitting Hairs," in *Feminizing the Fetish* (Ithaca, NY: Cornell University Press, 1991).

2. Christian Boltanski, cited by Lynn Gumpert, *Christian Boltanski* (Paris: Flammarion, 1994) 110.
3. Apter, "Splitting Hairs," 102.
4. Susan Stewart writes in *On Longing: Narratives of the Miniature, the Gigantic, the Souvenir, the Collection* (Durham, NC: Duke University Press): "The term *à-bric-à-brac*, which we might translate as 'by hook or crook,' implies the process of acquisition and exchange, which is the (false) labor of the collector," 159.
5. James Clifford, "On Ethnographic Allegory," *Writing and Culture: The Poetics and Politics of Ethnography*, ed. J. Clifford and G. Marcus (Berkeley: University of California Press, 1986) 106.
6. Ibid., 121. Here, because Clifford is writing about ethnographic allegories/stories, I am twisting his intended meaning a bit. Clifford's exact words are, "If we are condemned to tell stories we cannot control, may we not, at least tell stories we believe to be true."
7. Roland Barthes, *Camera Lucida: Reflections on Photography*, trans. Richard Howard (New York: Farrar, Straus & Giroux, 1981) 80–81. Originally published in French as *La Chambre Claire* (Paris: Editions du Seuil, 1980).
8. Ibid., 110.
9. Ibid., 75.
10. Culler, *Roland Barthes* (New York: Oxford University Press, 1983), 21.
11. Ibid., 21–22.
12. Barthes, *Camera Lucida*, 72.
13. Richard Howard, "Remembering Roland Barthes," in Steven Ungar and Betty R. McGraw, eds., *Signs in Culture: Roland Barthes Today* (Iowa City: University of Iowa Press, 1989), 35.
14. Barthes, *S/Z*, trans. Richard Miller (New York: Blackwell, Oxford: Oxford University Press, 1990), 160. Originally published in French as *S/Z* (Paris: Seuil, 1970).
15. Barthes, *S/Z*, 160.
16. Barthes, *Camera Lucida*, 63.
17. Ibid., 64–65.
18. Ibid., 65.
19. Ibid., 81.
20. Ibid., 92.
21. Ibid., 94.
22. Peter Wollen, "Fire and Ice," *Photographies* 4 (1984), quoted in Christian Metz, "Photography and Fetish," *October* 34 (fall 1985): 84.
23. Barthes, *Camera Lucida*, 94.
24. Christina Rossetti, "Goblin Market," in *The Complete Poems of Christina Rossetti*, vol. I, edited by R. W. Crump (Baton Rouge: Louisiana State University Press, 1979), 14.
25. All edges of Hawarden's photographs are magically intact in Graham Ovenden, *Clementina, Lady Hawarden* (London: Academy Editions; New York: St. Martin's 1984).
26. Marcel Proust, *Swann's Way*, Vol. I, *In Search of Lost Time*, translated by C.K. Scott Moncrieff and Terence Kilmartin, revised by D. J. Enright (New York: Random House, 1992), 63.). Hereafter, citations to this edition appear with the volume number of the (American), Modern Library, Random House edition with the page number in parentheses in the body of the text. There are six volumes to this edition, volume V contains both *The Captive* and *The Fugitive*. The British edition has different pagination.
27. Peter Stallybrass, "Worn Worlds: Clothes, Mourning, and the Life of Things," *Yale Review*, 81: 2, 36.
28. Virginia Dodier, catalogue raisonné (London: Victoria and Albert Museum, 1988), photograph D616.
29. Ibid.

30. Roland Barthes, *Roland Barthes by Roland Barthes,* trans. Richard Howard (New York: Farrar, Straus & Giroux, 1981), 61.
31. Milan Kundera in "After Word: A Talk with the Author by Philip Roth," in *The Book of Laughter and Forgetting,* trans. Michael Henry Heim (New York: Viking Penguin, 1981), 234-235," in *Christian Boltanski: Lessons of Darkness,* exhibition catalogue (Museum of Contemporary Art, Los Angeles, and New Museum of Contemporary Art, New York), 64.
32. Susan Sontag, *On Photography* (New York: Farrar, Straus & Giroux, 1973), 149.
33. Elin o'Hara slavick, artist's statement, in *Embodiment,* catalogue prepared in conjunction with the *Embodiment* exhibition, organized by Angela Kelly, Randolph Street Gallery, Chicago, 22 November-28 December 1991, 13.
34. Angela Kelly, introduction to ibid., 6.
35. Reynolds Price, "For the Family," in *Immediate Family,* by Sally Mann (New York: Aperture, 1992), unpaginated.
36. Ibid.
37. Marianne Hirsch, "Masking the Subject: Practicing Theory," in *The Point of Theory,* ed. by Mieke Bal and Inge E. Boer (New York: Continuum, 1994), 122.
38. Barthes, *Camera Lucida,* 34.
39. Ibid., 71.
40. Nadar, "My Life as Photographer," trans. Thomas Repensek, *October* 5 (Summer 1978), addresses this in his discussion of Balzac and the Daguerreotype: "According to Balzac's theory, all physical bodies are made up entirely of ghostlike images, an infinite number of leaflike skins laid one on top of the other. Since Balzac believed man was incapable of making something material from an apparition, from something impalpable—that is creating something from nothing—he concluded that every time someone had his photograph taken, one of the spectral layers was removed from the body and transferred to the photograph. Repeated exposures entailed the unavoidable loss of subsequent ghostly layer, that is, the very essence of life" (9).
41. Barthes, *Camera Lucida,* 80-81.
42. Gumpert, "The Life and Death of Christian Boltanski," 51.
43. Barthes uses this phrase to describe the voice of Proust in "Odors," in *Roland Barthes by Roland Barthes,* 135.
44. Barthes, *The Pleasure of the Text,* 8.
45. Proust, not coincidentally, was driven by photographicness and its ability to hold time and traces of the body. He treasured photographs of family and friends that, in turn, inspired the characters of the *Search.* Furthermore, Proust used the qualities of "photographicness" as both metaphor and objects of inquiry in the *Search.* See Mieke Bal's deftly argued *The Mottled Screen: Reading Proust Visually,* Trans. Anna-Louis Milne (Stanford, California: Stanford University Press, 1997), from the unpublished manuscript *Images proustiennes, ou comment livre visuellement,* which elaborates upon not only the novel's use of actual photographs and magic lanterns, but also upon Proust's photographic writerly effects of the zoom, the contact sheet, clarity and indistinction, the cutting out of details, over and under exposing images.
46. Roger Shattuck, "Lost and found: the structure of Proust's novel," in *The Cambridge Companion to Proust,* ed. Richard Bales (Cambridge, England: Cambridge University Press, 2001), 79.
47. Proust (VI, 509).
48. (I, 71).
49. (II, 309).
50. (II, 308-309).
51. II, 39.

52. Edmund White, *Marcel Proust* (New York and London: Viking Penguin, 1999), 133.
53. Ibid., 110.
54. Ibid.
55. (V, 319).
56. Walter Benjamin, "The Image of Proust," in *Illuminations: Essays and* Reflections, Ed. and with an Introduction by Hannah Arendt, Trans. Harry Zohn (New York: Schocken Books, 1968), 201.
57. Ibid., 202.
58. Ibid.

CHAPTER 4   *Kathleen O'Reilly Scanlon*

Communion Dress Violations

If you were raised Catholic in the late fifties and early sixties then the whole deal about the communion dress, or the new suit if you were a boy—most often your first suit—would be familiar to you. Nowadays I don't know how big a deal is made of one's First Holy Communion, but there are religion teachers who argue that the fanfare surrounding the ceremony needs to be underplayed, so that the kids don't lose sight of what's really important—that is, receiving the sacrament of holy communion for the first time.

But for me at the age of six, it was the fanfare—the stuff out of the ordinary—that has insured my remembering anything about the day at all. I remember being careful, as we had been instructed by the nuns and priests who had prepared us, not to bite down or actually chew the host, but instead to just let it be until it dissolved on its own. I recall the light feel and taste of nothingness—melting, thin cardboard merging and becoming one with my tongue. I also remember saying all the way up to the railing the most awful thing that I could imagine ("My mother's dead—my mother's dead"), ensuring that I would be somber, worried that I would give in to my usual impulse to laugh during the most solemn occasions. I also worried that I would sneeze or that the priest would drop the host, but mostly I worried that I wasn't worthy or pure enough. I remember the priests telling us about a woman who had been so evil and so full of sin that as soon as the host touched her lips she combusted, shriveling up into a blackened, smoking heap at the communion rail. Right there in the church, in front of everyone. When I returned to the pew, I buried my head in my hands, a more preventive gesture than a pious one: if I couldn't control my laughter, it would at least be hidden. As it turned out, I didn't laugh and even the boys, who

Figure 4.1. Photo of author as a child in her Communion dress.

routinely fooled around in class making farting sounds as they rubbed their armpits with their fists, were behaved that day.

There is a picture of me taken before we went to the church. I am standing in the front garden of my house, smiling, my hands clasped in front of me, dressed in a white, filmy dress and veil. No heavy silks or dull velvets—my mother's favorites—this time, I got something like everyone else. My mother was Jewish, but my father was Catholic and that is how I was raised. I attended Catholic schools and Mass each Sunday. My mother stayed out of any decisions having to do with religious things because she was afraid that she would do something wrong. That's why she allowed me to choose what I wanted—a white nylon dress, similar to the party dresses that my friends had and that I coveted. How I loved that dress, with its prim collar that folded down "just so," and the three shiny pearl buttons at the neck. The housekeeper called them *faux* pearls, making them sound very exotic.

Years later, my mother referred to the dress as a pretty but inexpensive one. "Why pay a lot for something you wear only once?" she reasoned.

But as it turned out, I did wear the dress more than once. Another incident involving my communion dress surfaced two years later when I was in Grade 3. One day, for no particular reason that I can recall now, I wore my Annie Oakley costume to school, a birthday gift from my father who was living in Toronto and home only on weekends. The outfit consisted of a white blouse and an attached red vest that was hemmed with leather fringe. The front of the matching skirt, also red with leather fringe, displayed a picture of a smiling and toothy Annie Oakley with two yellow braids. A cowgirl hat was perched jauntily on her head.

My friends admired the outfit in the school grounds, and as I walked into the school after the bell, I was unaware that my teacher would be annoyed or even take much notice. But when Sister stared at me throughout the whole of the morning prayers, her lips unmoving and closed tight throughout the entire *Our Father,* three *Hail Marys,* and the *Glory Be,* I felt her anger. Embarrassed and afraid, my face was hot and flushed as I sat down. Within seconds Sister was in front of my desk. The anger and old age etched on her face stared at me and then, in a voice loud enough for the classes next door to hear, she roared: "Get home and change!"

When Sister yelled it was usually at a misbehaving boy or if the class was noisy and not paying attention. Yelling caused different reactions—half the kids would go silent and the other half would stifle nervous giggling. I usually was in the latter group. But this time, the yelling was directed at me alone. I left my seat, and the humiliation rushed me out the door. On the way home, I picked leaves from the trees and brushed their velvet touch against my skin, comforting myself against the razor sharp anger and embarrassment of having been banished from class in disgrace. Reaching home, I rushed past the housekeeper who was tending my baby sister and went straight to my room. As I went through my closet for something to wear, I saw behind the winter coats and clothes I no longer wore, a small piece of familiar cloth still white and filmy—my communion dress beckoning—a reminder of more pleasant times. I tried the dress on and smoothed out the skirt. I looked in the mirror. Two years of growth had taken its toll; the dress was inches shorter now, but being a thin child I fit into it easily. The sun, shining in from the window, warmed me and made my image glint and sparkle. Surely Sister would approve of this. The communion dress would make up for the other outfit and warrant her saying when I returned, "Well now, that's a lot better."

I took one last look and left the second time for school that morning. As was the practice then, I knocked on the classroom door before entering, bowed my head slightly in Sister's direction and went to my seat. But before I made my way to the end of the row where I sat, Sister began yelling in the loudest voice ever heard in our Grade 3 class. "Get to the cloakroom!" I looked around and saw my classmates' faces—a combination of terror and sympathy—on mine. This time no snickering or muffled laughter interrupted the deafening silence. It was clear to me, and probably the others too, that we were witnessing something terrible. I knew only too well that that I—*I alone*—had caused this reaction. But I had no idea why. How could a nun—any nun—not approve of a communion dress? It was part of their persona; it went along with their reverence for all things holy: rosaries, holy pictures, holy water, and communion dresses. Or so I thought.

The cloakroom, where we stored our book bags and hung our coats in the winter, was separated from the rest of classroom by a dividing wall open at both ends. This was where Sister would send the rowdy boys and where the worst of them would get the strap. I stood in the cloakroom and waited, staring at the sweaters and book bags hanging on hooks, longing to find comfort in something familiar to offset the terror that was rapidly enveloping me. Thunderous silence, making everything still, was broken finally by the sounds of a desk drawer opening and shuffling feet, approaching. I knew what Sister had taken from the desk even before she announced to the class the words that made my face flush with shame. "Class, I want you to know that this is the first time that I have ever *had* to strap a girl. And I hope I never will have to again."

My humiliation, along with the burning sensation that echoed the snapping sound of the leather against my flesh, made my eyes water. I stared ahead knowing that the film of liquid that had formed veils on my eyes was waiting for its cue to spill down if I blinked. I received six straps on each hand (two more than anyone else that year), and I held out my palms for more. "That will do," Sister said, as she left the cloakroom with the strap bulging in the pocket of her habit. At recess time, my classmates wanted to see my still-reddened palms. The boys after some initial curiosity went off, but the girls, a comforting presence, stayed with me. Had it hurt? Wasn't I brave for not crying! I didn't feel brave, nor did I want their sympathy.

As I walked home from school that day, I saw my mother leaving the sanatorium where she worked. She took one look at me and shook her head, weary even before her workday was half over and said, "For God's sake, Kath, what on earth are you wearing?" I went up to my room, changed and left the dress—a crumpled heap of misery on the floor.

That evening at dinner, the familiar sounds of home comforted me. The CBC radio newsreader's voice was occasionally drowned out by the sounds of the wind rattling the windowpanes as we ate. My mother wasn't listening to the news; between bites and balancing my sister on her lap, she was talking about her day—about the woman at work whose brother had died at a canning factory, my father's arrival home next week, my sister's tantrums. I picked at my food.

"You're quiet tonight, Kath. Cat got your tongue?"

"No. Only thinking."

Once the dinner dishes had been cleared away, I went up to my room and stuffed the dress that had caused so much trouble into a brown paper bag. I took the lighter that was tucked into a pack of Black Cat cigarettes from my mother's handbag and with the winds howling I went into the backyard behind the fort that I had built in happier times.

Setting the bag on fire was harder than I thought. Sparks shooting up into the sky floated downwards like failed fireworks. After singing my eyelashes and several failed attempts, the bag finally started to burn. Slowly at first and then taking on a life of its own, it began to roll along the grass—a burning ball, gathering speed. Remembering the woman the priest had warned us about, I ran alongside—laughing—exhilarated by the sight of my communion dress, now a burning, melting mass of nylon, soaring like flying spiders into the approaching storm.

CHAPTER 5 *Catherine Derry*

"I'll Never Find a Dress": Shopping for the Prom

It's pink and strapless, a tulle floor-length gown with a sheer pink shoulder wrap, very fluffy and girly. My first prom dress lives on a headless mannequin in the office where I work (figure 5.1). It's there because my dress and I were part of documentary called *Dressfitting* and my office doubles as the research office space of its director.[1]

This dress has become quite a conversation piece—strangers walk into my office uninvited to admire it, my dress, and to tell me about their own prom dress or—in the case of one closet cross dresser—the dress he wished he had. When someone compliments my dress, I smile faintly and say "thank you," but I'm really thinking, "It may be beautiful, but it's not what I wanted." People who know me well, often say they can't picture me actually *wearing* that pale pastel dress, it's just not me. And they're right; the dress of my prom dreams would have been *black*. How did I end up with the fluffy pink dress?

My story begins in 1988, when I was a very turbulent teen. I had left home against my parents' wishes and was living in a dive downtown with my boyfriend. I had almost dropped out of school because of personal upheaval; my teachers were giving me a hard time about my living situation, my parents and I were constantly arguing about it, and I was trying to learn how to live on my own for the first time. I wasn't even sure if I was going to graduate. My family had promised me that if I actually did graduate, they would take care of all of the related expenses: my mom would pay for the dress for the ceremony and my aunt would take care of the prom dress. And so, when the good news came in mid-June, the three of us went shopping.

My father and my date were distinctly absent from the prom shopping expedition, something for which they were likely grateful! While the prom is considered an adolescent rite of passage; the night when boys and girls officially leave childhood behind, it has also been constructed as a uniquely feminine site where girls replicate expected heterosexual feminine norms.[2] The hype of popular culture suggests that the most important aspect of this occasion is the prom dress and the "feminine" activity of shopping for it. Most of the women interviewed in *Dressfitting* noted that they shopped for their dresses with their mothers. Who more appropriate to help find the dress that represents the epitome of adult feminine heterosexuality than a girl's mother?

When thinking of what I might want to wear to the prom, I had envisioned something black, satin and strapless. A sexy, sophisticated, little bit avant-garde dress (perhaps from *Le Chateau*). For me, the kind of dress I would wear was very important—a way of expressing my "alternative" identity. While clothing conveys social messages about the wearer to society, most girls seek to express their individuality and personality through their prom dresses.[3] Teen magazines insinuate further that the prom dress is the ultimate expression of self.[4]

This expression was particularly important to me as I had spent most of my school years being bullied and excluded. I wanted a dress that looked different than the others. One that would say, "I don't care about fitting in, I am above all that, I am more hip than the rest of you." I wanted my dress to reflect my punk rock affiliation, and black had to be the color. I wanted to say "fuck your conformist ideas of what a woman should look like, I'm doing it my way and still looking hot."[5] I wanted my dress to say, "I don't need to belong—I belong somewhere else." Yet, it was equally important was that my dress be be strapless, to show off my breasts; because even though I wanted to show that I didn't care about fitting in, I also wanted to say, "Look what a beauty you are missing."[6]

My expectations of the prom, like other teen girls, were highly influenced by pop culture: mostly movies and media images. My prom fantasies were especially fueled by Molly Ringwald (the alternative princess in *Pretty in Pink*), and Olivia Newton-John (the good-girl-turned-bad in *Grease*). These two fictitious characters represented the kind of teen I strove to be. I wanted to be hip like Molly and bad and sexy like Olivia. The best way to embody that spirit, I thought, would be in a black satin strapless dress.

Unfortunately, I faced three roadblocks along the path to the dress of my dreams: my mom's rules of "good taste," our timing, and my body. Even though my aunt was paying for the dress, my mom had a few rules. It couldn't be black (I spent the last few years wearing nothing but black and it drove my parents nuts, I don't know how many times they asked me if "I was on my way to a funeral"). The other rule was that it had to be tasteful, according to what I felt were my mom's overly conservative standards. No sexy over-the-top dress for me, which is was exactly what I wanted with every fiber of my being. My mom envisioned me more as a demure, innocent, pastel, and girl-next-door kind of girl, like Doris Day in an old 1940s movie. But I wanted to look like Madonna going to the prom.[7] I quickly realized that I wouldn't be wearing the showstopper I wanted, but the one thing I wouldn't concede was that it had to be strapless.

So, with my mom and I both compromising our visions and my aunt in tow, we set out to find the semi-perfect prom dress. Most girls in my school had started shopping for their dress in January, so by the time we had made it to the dress shops most of the dresses had been picked over. Then there was the problem of size. While my body wasn't overly large (I think I was about a size 13/14) my bosom was ample. I had never shopped for a fancy dress before, and I didn't know that my size would be a hindrance. All of the dresses we found at the malls seemed made for tiny girls only. The few beautiful and sophisticated dresses I did see were made in sizes 3–7. Ugly flowered tents were made in my size. I tried on a few strapless dresses, but my boobs either fell out or were squished down in an unflattering fashion. While I hadn't often thought of myself as "fat" before that day, I certainly felt fat after shopping for a prom dress. Being big breasted and larger than a size 7, it was hard for me to find a dress in these young girls' stores. I started to hate my body for not fitting into the cute little dresses.[8]

This image of myself as fat has stuck with me since the prom. When I look back, I think of myself as a chunky and chubby teen. Recently, however, two things happened that challenged that image of myself. First, in looking at my old prom photos, and peering into them, I saw a "normal" sized girl with large breasts and big hair. Second, a friend of mine (who I consider to have a lovely shape) was admiring my dress and pointed out that it would be too small for her. How could this prom dress, bought for a fat girl, not fit this beautifully shaped woman? These two incidents clash with my perception of myself. I now imagine that other girls at my school had similar problems finding dresses. Maybe they had large breasts like me, wide hips or big bones. Did these other girls—who certainly were not obese—feel as fat as I did after shopping for a prom dress?

What causes young girls to become unsatisfied with their bodies? Most feel their bodies are too large, even those who would be considered underweight.[9] Teen magazines tell their young female readers that the most important aspect of their prom night is to look "appropriately beautiful" in the perfect dress.[10] "Appropriately beautiful" usually means thin.[11] These standards are reflected in the dresses manufactured, tailored to this image, leaving girls (like me as a teen) who do not fit into this mold feeling unsatisfied with their bodies. The prom shopping experience made me feel like I had failed, that I had not turned into a "beautiful young woman." I fell into the trap of feeling too fat, years before I actually was.

After a couple of weeks of shopping and less than a week before the prom, we finally found the dress. It happened one day when my aunt and I were out shopping alone. After looking in the last of the hip young women's stores, we decided in desperation to try a bridal shop. It turned out to be a good idea. The sales woman was used to dealing with all different body types, and she showed us some dresses that would fit the bill. Most of the dresses were either matronly or overly frilly, but there was one I didn't hate—the pink strapless one I described earlier. The sales clerk pointed out that it had boning built into the bodice which would hold unruly breasts in place. I tried it on and I must admit that it looked good—it flattered my figure and held my breasts perfectly. I still would have preferred a darker color, but beggars can't be choosers.

Settling for the pink strapless dress, I quickly fashioned a new prom dream for myself. If I was going to wear pink, I would go the whole nine yards: I would dress like a Prom Queen. This was my last chance to fit in and I would do it, if only for one night. I would be the ugly duckling that emerged a swan; my dress would transform me into the belle of the ball.[12] I thought, "I'll show them I can look like that for one night, I can conform to their (the popular students) kind of beauty if I want to."

With this goal in mind, I continued my prom preparations. Although I may not have thought of it this way, I had been preparing for this role since early childhood, listening in awe to fairy tales read to me by my grandmother. I had read *Seventeen* (in secret), and watched enough teen movies and TV shows to know how to create the right kind of costume. And I also knew that the next important step was to find the right accessories. The first thing I needed was shoes. My exposure to pop culture told me that they should be pumps, the same color as my dress. I found a pair of white satin pumps and arranged to have them dyed pink. I don't know how I ever walked in them—I usually wore converse high top sneakers or doc marten shoes!

Next, I had to pick out and order the corsage my boyfriend would give me on prom night. Traditionally the date does this, but I worried that my boyfriend might pick a corsage that would clash with my dress.[13] So my mom and I ordered a pink wrist corsage (it had to be a wrist corsage, so as not to ruin the line of my dress) to be picked up the day before the prom.

Then came the hair. On the day of the prom, I made my way to my hairdresser to get the perfect hairdo. A girl's hair is considered to be second in importance to the dress and is a very big part of a girl's prom preparation.[14] My hair had to go with my dress. I told my hairdresser Boyd* I wanted my hair big and wavy with some baby's breath flowers in it. Boyd looked at me like I had come from another planet. Boyd was a member of the same punk rock clique that I belonged to and didn't know what to think about this sudden turnaround in my attitude. "It's a girl prom thing." I explained to him. With that information, he set out about to do my hair in a way he considered very uncool. As he was finishing me, he asked with disdain, "Do you really want the baby's breath in it?" I told him, yes, if I was going to do this I wasn't going to do it half-assed. Boyd finished my hair and gave me the mirror while shaking his head in disapproval. It was perfect. My beautiful blonde hair looked like the photos I had seen of the popular girls at the winter formal.

On my way back to my apartment, I stopped at the flower shop to pick up my corsage, only to find the store closed. I had forgotten that my prom fell on a holiday—Canada Day. What was I going to do without my perfect pink wrist corsage? I ran back to my apartment and phoned my mom in tears. She called around and found a flower shop that was open. Luckily, they had a corsage left over that someone neglected to pick up the night before. It was white, not pink, but the color scheme worked out perfectly; it matched the baby's breath in my hair. I could stop panicking.

Why was I so worried about such a small detail as a corsage? It wasn't so much the corsage itself as what it represented. It indicated to all who could see it that I was accompanied by a date. An important part of going to the prom is having a date; it shows that the ultimate feminine perfection has been achieved: being desired by a man.[15] For me, having a date meant I wasn't the loser that the bullies had made me feel I was for all those years. Having a corsage was a marker of my dating status. If I was separated from my date at any time, people would know just by looking at my corsage that I had not come alone. It would show those who picked on me that they were wrong. I was not unlikable. Somebody liked me enough to take me to the prom. This was the only time I had a date for a dance, besides my junior high grad dance (and my beautiful male escort for that occasion was gay). This corsage made me feel validated as lovable.

With a corsage secured, I was onto my next step: to get my boyfriend Sam ready for the prom. Not an easy task! My boyfriend didn't share my prom dream,; he was more concerned about maintaining his image as a punk rock bad boy. The whole process of getting him ready was a power struggle, not unlike the one I had with my mom. Sam struggled to maintain his identity while I tried to turn him into my vision of the perfect prom date. After all, he had to complement the dress which, as far as I was concerned, was the star of the show. I had talked him into wearing a suit. Luckily, he had one on hand, purchased by his parents for a recent court appearance. Sam's suit was black and his tie was navy blue. I tried to talk him into wearing a baby blue shirt. This outfit would make us the perfect prom "Barbie" and "Ken" in our gender appropriate colors. He was having none of this. He would have none of that. To wear a suit was sacrifice enough for him; he was not going to compromise his image by wearing baby blue. If he was going to the prom, he was wearing a black shirt or not going at all. I begrudgingly accepted this change under the agreement condition that he let me comb his usually unruly hair.

Looking back, I'm shocked at the degree to which I tried to control his appearance. I tried to censor his sense of self. I did to him what I felt my mom had done to me when we were shopping for the prom dress. I was affected by popular cultures messages about how a prom date should look. Often, a boyfriend's appearance is seen as a reflection of a girl's sense of good taste and style.[16] What Sam wanted didn't matter to me then. He, in my grand scheme of things, was nothing more than an accessory, like my dyed shoes and baby's breath in my hair. He was a small cog in the new prom image I had created over the course of a few weeks, the image that revolved around a pink, fluffy dress.

In my rush to create the perfect prom look, it never occurred to me that this was also his first prom. Sam had dropped out of high school the year before and missed out on his prom entirely. Perhaps he had his own prom dreams too? Looking back, I also wonder if I was jealous of his black shirt—did it represent the black dress I couldn't have? He certainly could have worn that outfit if I had got my black dress. How did he get to have his way when I didn't?

Once Sam was dressed, it was time for my dad to pick us up and take us to my parents' house for final preparations with my mom. My mom and I were still trying to hold onto to some sort of "normal mother and daughter get dressed for the prom" ritual. This seemed ridiculous as I had been living with my prom date for the last six months. I liken it to women who lived with their fiancés and then spent the night before the wedding alone at their parents.

When we arrived at my parents' house, Dad and Sam went off to do something (who knows what, as Dad was not too fond of him). Mom and I went to my childhood bedroom to get ready. She helped me into my dress. It was necessary to have help, as it was one of those zip-from-behind dresses. I wonder if formal dresses are designed like that to keep women dependent on others? After the dress was on, I put on my makeup while mom sat on the bed. My makeup had to accentuate while looking natural, a look very popular at the time. Then my mom helped me with the finishing touches: a necklace my cousin had sent to me for the occasion and my matching pink wrap. My mom stopped for a moment and looked at me, and told me how beautiful I looked, and hugged me. For one moment we were that "normal" pre-prom mother and daughter.

As mentioned earlier these prom preparations were not how I had envisioned them. Too many disappointments and compromises. But it must be pointed out that it definitely wasn't the shopping trip my mom had envisioned either. The girls interviewed in *Dressfitting* often noted that their mothers were as invested as they were in their proms, if not more. My mom never finished school because of illness, so there was no prom for her. My prom was the only one she was getting. She probably envisioned us shopping for a dress months in advance and than then taking it home and modeling it for my father. When prom night came, my date would arrive in his car, and come into the house, and pin on my corsage, as my mom took pictures. He, of course, would be handsome, clean-cut, and polite. As we drove away, my parents could pat themselves on the back and be proud of what a great daughter they raised. My mom definitely hadn't envisioned having a punk rock daughter who would flout most of those conventions.

After my mom had helped me get ready, we emerged from my childhood bedroom and found dad and Sam in the living room. They both gushed about how fabulous I looked and about the heads that would turn. Then the endless picture-taking started: an activity that would take up more time than the prom itself. My mom wanted to record her version of the perfect prom memory. First there were endless pictures of me, then pictures of Sam and me together. This took over an hour. After it was over I thought we were set to go to the prom. Not Yet! My mom drove us to my aunt's apartment, so the purchaser of my dress could see how lovely I looked in it. My aunt came down to the lobby to admire me in my dress, and my mom took another series of very posed pictures. Forty-five minutes later we were on our way to the prom, with a little bit of extra cash slipped to me by my aunt on the way out. My mom dropped Sam and I off at the entrance to the Saint John Trade and Convention Center, where my prom was to be held. As we walked through the door we found ourselves at the end of a very long line. The lineup was to see the official prom photographer (see figure 5.1). It seemed to me that this night was more invested in recording the memory than living it.

I look back now at all my mom's photos of that night, most of them taken by my mother, and I see that my mom is was trying to preserve an external reality of my prom night; to be recorded as official family history for generations. The problem is that these photographs do not match my actual prom experience. When I look at my mom's set of pictures in chronological order, they tell their own story, her version of prom. If we opened her album in late 1988, here is what an outside observer would see: her beautiful blonde daughter transformed from girl-next-door to innocent princess in her beautiful pink dress. These first few photos look like they were taken before the her daughter's date arrived. Then a series of pictures with the date (who the viewer can assume has arrived to pick up her daughter). The next few pictures show her daughter, with date, stopping at her sister's house so the handsome couple could be admired more.

What these pictures don't tell the outside observer is that I was a punk rock daughter who was certainly not innocent as the images suggested, as I was "living in sin" with a boy my whole family despised. These pictures don't show the tension between my mom and I, who had recently ended three months of verbal battle about my date. These pictures would have you believe I was that normal girl going to the prom. According to Best, prom pictures organize how we remember the prom,

> The effect of these pictures is to provide a particular kind of memory of the prom. In other words, these picture inscribe within our cultural consciousness what a prom is: The girl pinning a boutonniere on her dates lapel, the boy arriving at the doorstep of his date's parents' home . . . Not just to be remembered, proms are to be remembered in a certain way.[17]

Pictures are texts that we can read and interrupt.[18] Years later, the text that my mom's prom pictures reveal is interesting. Sam and I split up (after marrying and

Figure 5.1. Photo of author and date at the prom, 1988.

going through a messy divorce), and my mom destroyed every prom picture he is was in! Her photo album now displays the innocent young girl in the lovely pink dress going to the prom alone, erasing part of my reality.

Luckily, I have the doubles in my photo album. My mom and I have recorded two different versions of the same night. Hers say, "Beautiful young daughter leaves home to go the prom." Mine say, "Former misfit proves them wrong by going to the prom with beautiful dress, beautiful date, and looks absolutely beautiful." Mitchell & Weber have argued that photographs shape our sense of the past and shape the course of our future.[19] The photos taken on my prom night certainly shape two different versions of my past and how my mom and I would interrupt it for years to come. Neither is the reality of my prom night; they represent the different realities my mom and I created for ourselves.

Once I was at the prom, the dreams I had built around this event slowly came apart at the seams. It was a rather a boring and unremarkable event. I waltzed in and paraded my dress and date around for everyone to admire.[20] Unfortunately, for me no one seemed to notice me. The music was bad; the band was middle-aged and was playing popular hits of the fifties. My few friends were not there, as they had deemed themselves "too punk rock" to go to the prom. Worst of all, two other girls had showed up in the same dress as me. Now, the dress that supposed to change my life was being sported by two others. I tried to avoid them both all night. *Pretty in Pink* this was not.

Epilogue

About nine years after my prom, I attended a second prom. This was a very different kind of event, called a prom designed for adults, specifically gay adults. It was held during the gay pride celebrations of a mid-sized east coast city. Notices advertised things like "did you not have the date you wanted for the prom? Couldn't wear what you wanted? Or maybe you didn't go at all? This is a chance to do it all over your way . . ." I was very intrigued by the idea, so I asked my girlfriend to go, but she wasn't interested. So I went with a close gay male friend.

I didn't shop for this prom. I knew exactly what I wanted to wear—a dress that was already in my closet. It was a black, sparkly minidress with a low cut back, only worn once on New Year's Eve over a year and half previous. Finally, I was going to wear my black dress to the prom. I paired it with black knee high vinyl boots and a pink feather boa (just a touch of *Pretty in Pink*). I had so much fun at this prom. My outfit was admired by many and I had many friends and acquaintances happy to see me there. After the prom we were whisked away by a limousine to a gay club downtown.

It wasn't the night of my life, but it healed some old prom wounds. I got to wear the dress I wanted and it was admired. Most important, I fit in and felt I belonged, which is what I had hoped for at my original prom. At 17, I had thought a dress would transform me and make me fit in. What this prom taught me was that I had to find the right community and people to feel like I belonged. This fitting in process was something I had to do on my own; a dress couldn't do it for me.

Don't get me wrong though, it felt really satisfying to finally have that black dress!

Notes

* All names have been changed.
1. Sandra J. Weber & Claudia A. Mitchell, *Dressfitting*, Documentary, digital video, 25 min. Directed by Sandra J. Weber. (Montreal: Concordia University, an Image and Identity Research Collective Production, 2001).
2. Ibid., see also S. R. Mazzarella, The "Superbowl of all dates": Teenage girl magazines and the commodification of the perfect prom." In S. R. Mazzarella & N. O. Pecora (Eds.), *Growing Up Girls: Popular Culture and the Construction of Identity*. (New York: Peter Lang, 1999) 97–112.
3. R. P. Rubinstein, *Dress Codes: Meaning and Messages in American Culture*. Boulder: Westview Press, 1995; A. Best, *Prom Night: Youth, Schools, and Popular Culture*. (New York & London: Routledge, 2000).
4. See Mazzarella.
5. For more on women using clothing as resistance, see Lorraine LeBlanc's *Pretty in Punk: Girls' Gender Resistance in a Boy's Subculture* (New Brunswick, NJ: Rutgers, 1999).
6. According to Rubinstein, "Elements of dress and styles of appearance that individuals chose to represent the person self are of a dialogue between self and society" (242). L. Leblanc also noted in her study of punk rock girls that they would often alter their appearance in some way to subvert society's feminine standards. But these punk girls would often retain some traditional feminine characteristics, to appear attractive to the opposite sex, for example, wearing combat boots and dress. (see L. Leblanc, *Pretty in Punk: Girls' Gender Resistance in a Boys' Subculture* (New Brunswick, NJ: Rutgers Press, 1999).
7. Best says high school proms are mediated by outside forces, such as school, society and parents, who are invested in turning out young adults who follow North American society's normative sexual order. Mothers are responsible for seeing that their daughters turn out well, that they represent our society's social norms. If this does not happen the mother is often held responsible and is viewed as a bad mother (see S. Lawler, *Mothering the Self: Mothers, Daughters, Subjects*. (New York and London: Routledge, 2000). In the case of a teenage girl going to the prom, it's the mother's responsibility to make sure that her daughter represents societies society's norms of femininity. A girl must look appealing to the opposite sex but not seem overly sexualized. The worse thing a girl can be is too sexual. "Slut" is one of the most damaging names an adolescent girl can be called (Tanenbaum, 2000). My mom was probably worried that the kind of sexy, provocative black dress I wanted would make me look like a slut and her like a bad mother. (see L. Tanenbaum, *Slut: Growing Up Female with a Bad Reputation*. (New York: Perennial, 2000).
8. The ideal body size has become increasing smaller since the sixties (Bentley, 1999). Store mannequins' measurements have always been much smaller than the size of the average

North American women, and are usually flat chested (Bentley, 1999). Clothes are made to fit these mannequins.

9. M. K. Bentley, "The body of evidence: Dangerous intersections between development and culture in the lives of adolescent girls." In S. R. Mazzarella & N. O. Pecora (Eds.), *Growing Up Girls: Popular Culture and the Construction of Identity* (New York: Peter Lang, 1999) 209–223; P. Orenstein, *Schoolgirls: Young Women, Self-esteem and the Confidence Gap.* (New York: Doubleday, 1994).
10. See Mazzarella.
11. See Bentley.
12. According to Rubinstein, clothing is a mode of expression employed by adolescents in attempt to "fit in" with their peers; they feel that if they look like other teens they will find acceptance.
13. Mazzarella notes that teen magazines remind girls that boys can not always be relied on to be as fashion conscious as girls.
14. See Best.
15. Ibid.
16. Ibid. Mazzarella also notes that teen magazines offer young women tips on how to make prom dates dress appropriately.
17. Best, 30–31.
18. Claudia A. Mitchell & Sandra J. Weber, *Reinventing Ourselves as Teachers: Beyond Nostalgia.* (London: Falmer Press, 1999).
19. Ibid.
20. Best has noted that the prom is organized around the fact that girls will be the subject of others' gaze; they will be on display as objects of feminine beauty.

CHAPTER 6

Sandra Weber

No Red Shoes

No red shoes for you, the salesman said,
They won't match your dress, don't you see?
And besides, the heels are too high
                          and the vamp's cut too low,
And you're young, much too young, for that style.

But I'm the same age as Dorothy, and *her* shoes are red
With a bit of a heel and a sparkling glow,
And I'd look grand, oh so grand,
                          and feel very proud.
Can't I have them too? Why not? Why not?

No Mary Janes for you, the salesman cried,
They've no arch support, can't you see?
And besides, they're too wide,
                          and they won't fit your foot,
And you're growing, still growing, my child.

But those black Mary Janes with their long slender straps
And the buckles that beckon and shine,
They're the ones that I love,
                          and the ones that I crave.
Can't I try them now? Why not? Why not?

No glass slippers for you, the salesman declared
They're impossibly hard, can't you see?
And besides, they're too rigid,
                and they won't do at all,
And they're not, really not, for you dear.

But those twinkling glass bows with their magical swirls
Are just what a young girl needs
To make a dress special,
                and dance the day through.
Can't I once, just this once? Why not? Why not?

No red shoes for me. Why not? Why not?

PART III

Dress and Schooling

CHAPTER 7   *Sandra Weber*

Boxed-in by My School Uniform

Tunics. The first one that I wore was the dark navy, box-pleated, shapeless sack that all young children attending public (state-funded) elementary schools in Montreal had to wear in the early 1950s. I had heard of tunics before—seen them even—long before actually starting school. I remember, for example, when I was about three or four years old, playing outside by myself on the front lawn of our apartment building, and watching older girls in the neighbourhood chatting and laughing as they walked to school in their tunics. I couldn't wait to be big like them, to go to school and wear a tunic and have friends to chat and laugh with. At that tender age, tunics represented who I wanted to become. Someone older. Someone with friends.

Of course, when the time came and my mother actually brought home the prevailing regulation school uniform for me, I hated it. Well, perhaps not so much the tunic itself, as the obligatory white "scholastic-style" teddy blouse that buttoned uncomfortably between our legs. (Thinking back on this now, I can't help shaking my head at that unwanted touching of my privates by school regulatory clothing.) And the bloomers, those flimsy, flannel, elastic-bound underpants that we had to wear over our own underwear and with the teddy blouse.[1] When we skipped or ran or bent over in our short tunics, those stupid bloomers would show. And for gym classes, bloomers and teddies were *all* that we wore, even outside! But at least for gym you got to wear running shoes and white socks. These were preferable to the hideously ugly, four-hole navy blue oxford shoes that we had to wear the rest of the time. They were sold by Buster Brown and required polishing at least twice a week if you were to pass inspection. You had to wear the whole outfit: teddy, bloomers, tunic, and laced Oxford shoes—with navy socks, of course. Not for us the lovely blue or green plaid pleated skirts or kilts worn by the girls in the private schools (called "public" schools in Britain, for reasons I've never been able to fathom).

Uniform inspection in some classrooms was a daily affair, where students stood at attention beside their desks while the teacher paraded up and down, pulling back a collar here and there in search of shameful signs of soiled "ring around the collar," glancing downwards to make sure shoes were shiny and clean and that the socks weren't slouched around the ankles (more difficult to detect on the boys, who wore trousers), and checking the hands that were held up obediently to her for telltale signs of dirt on the knuckles or grime under fingernails. For the girls, the dark box-pleat tunics with matching belt had to be spotless and pressed, no hems half-hanging down with trailing threads, no chalk dust from the day before, no signs of breakfast on the bib. Imagine the pressures this inspection must have put on our mothers, especially those who worked all day in an office, as mine did, and then had to rush home not only to feed their families and clean the house, but also to make sure their children's uniforms (and perhaps their own work clothes) could pass muster without bringing shame on them and their family the next day.

The uniform I wore was mandatory for all public schools in the Protestant School Board of Greater Montreal. Protestant. What was a Jewish girl doing in a Protestant school anyhow? I felt like an impostor, and on some level, was glad of the uniform that helped me blend in, glad I did not have to be seen in the shabby hand-me-downs from my cousins that were an important part of my limited wardrobe. We were in tough financial straits, even if my grandparents were reputed to have some money. I remember being laughed at as I trudged through the snow and slush alone to school, dressed in an old blue winter coat with the cotton insulation stuffing poking through holes, and a large diaper pin serving to keep it closed. My mother had been in too much of a hurry to get to work to sew on a button, or perhaps too depressed to care any more. My father had recently walked out on us. It was just us kids and Mummy, moved in with my aging great grandparents.

There is a photograph of my mother wearing a tunic uniform just like mine—even the blouse collar is that same floppy "scholastic" style. When I came across it as a child, the picture intrigued me, but it also bothered me, because people used to mistake the picture of *her* for one of *me*. As young girls, my mother and I looked remarkably alike—it was hard to deny. Two twins in matching uniforms. I did not want to look like my mother, I did not want to *be* like her either, I did not want her miserable life. The box tunic was boxing me in with her in a family package. The tunic became the symbol of all that I hated about schooling, about my life—the uniformity of it—a way to literally as well as figuratively box us in, mind and body.

I wonder how I would have reacted then to learn that what was a symbol of coercion and oppression to me was, during that very same time in rural Canada, a coveted or loved garment worn for very different reasons. In a play called *The*

Tunic Wars, Claudia Mitchell tells quite a different tunic tale from mine.[2] While urban children were being sent off to schools in tunic uniforms, rural children had no such restrictions put on them, something some of them actually regretted, if Claudia is an example. As long as they were clean and neat, they could wear almost anything to school. And one of the things some of them liked to wear were tunics! Your mother could order them out of a department store catalogue, probably Eaton's, and you could wear them with any kind of blouse. Tunics could be something to wear anywhere, or, if viewed as compulsory uniforms, they were something to envy because they meant you must be from a hip, big city or that you were like those children in romantic British school novels or a character in the Enid Blyton series. Uniforms meant you were classy (or from the upper class) or urban. But that was not my experience of the tunic.

On the bus to school, I would enviously eye the short, tartan, pleated skirts, elegant blazers, and spiffy ties worn by the girls from a nearby private school. They looked so stylish, so lucky . . . so . . . . rich. I would dream of wearing a uniform like theirs, imagining myself with a different family, nicer hair, a real house, and a happier life. Their uniform, I thought, was not something that would confine me, but rather free me or sweep me away into a more romantic existence. I had no idea, of course, at the time, that such uniforms are the stuff of erotic dreams for some, that prostitutes wear them for certain clients, or that school girls who wear them can be the object of mocking comments, grasping hands, and lewd looks from older men, including the bus drivers who enjoy the high hemlines, the perky look, the contrast of feminine crisp white blouse with masculine, but not-masculine tie.[3] To me, those ties and skirts were romantic and posh. The girls wearing those tartan skirts likely had quite a different take on their attire, however.

Starting in grade 5 (or was it 6?), I "graduated" to the more grown-up version of a tunic uniform, the V-neck navy blue jumper tied at the waist with a fringed sash. It was more form-fitting and was worn longer than the box-tunic. Your bloomers didn't show, which was some relief. I had actually been sort of looking forward to wearing it. But of course, even these jumpers seemed drab compared to the swank outfits worn by the girls who went to the private schools. Nevertheless, I gladly traded in my box-pleat without so much as a backward glance. I was one of the late developers in terms of breasts and so on, so for the first couple of years, I didn't have to fret the way other girls did at curves that strained at the seams of the fitted jumper. Not that I felt great about my body, what with my gangly legs, scrawny body, crooked teeth, thick coke-bottle glasses, and hair that hung limp and straight on one side, and flipped outward at an awkward angle on the other. I looked, and probably acted, the perfect nerd. I had few friends.

By high school, the V-neck tunics had lost most of their appeal. Many of the girls were becoming quite creative at finding ways to circumvent aspects of the uniform, trying to assert some individuality—taking off their socks as soon as they left school, wearing blouses that were not scholastic-style, but hiding the offending collar shapes under sweaters, sewing badges onto their tunics, varying their hairstyles, and jewelery, although there were rules about those too, and surreptitiously putting on make-up in the bathroom, when teachers and mothers weren't looking. I observed their efforts with great interest, but did not often follow suit, worried that if I did anything that might be perceived as copying them, the other girls would make scathing remarks.

By the time we made it to senior high, we were really tired of wearing the same old thing, day after day—of being forced to, of having no choice. These feelings festered and grew, until eventually, we staged what came to be known as "The Bare-Foot Rebellion." A group of senior students, girls who rarely spoke to each other, suddenly found common ground in their hatred of the school uniform. Fed up with wearing them, we decided to make a point to the school administration. None of us had ever been in trouble before; we were normally very docile. But when a girl was sent home one morning because she wore sneakers instead of Oxfords to school, things came to a boil. The next morning, a small group of us, about eight in all, took off our shoes and socks in class and acted like nothing had happened. When our teacher finally noticed, he sent us all packing down to the principal's office. He tried to sound annoyed, but the twinkle in his eye clued us to the fact that he wasn't taking this (us) very seriously. Shaking with anger at his cavalier attitude, in our bare feet, we marched down to the principal's office. The principal tried hard not to laugh in our faces, told us to go back to class and put our shoes back on, and that seemed to be the end of it. We crumpled. But just a few days later, a notice went round saying that starting in April, senior students did not have to wear their uniforms except for school assemblies and formal occasions. We were finally free.

And that's when I realized I didn't hate my uniform after all! The struggle of finding something to wear from my shabby and small wardrobe that would not make me an object of scorn felt far worse than wearing the tunic. And so, a few of us decided to keep on wearing it; we CHOSE to wear it, but with nylons instead of socks, and no scholastic blouse in sight. Graduation was at long last approaching, and I no longer cared as much what others might think. What was once a symbol of oppression, in other circumstances, became a means of resistance or an expression of individual free choice.

Afterthoughts on School Uniforms

What is the future of academic uniforms? In schools, they are being discovered anew, touted as a panacea for all that the public finds wrong with schools, a way to bring unruly children under control, to command respect, control their bodies, to instil a sense of belonging to and pride in the school, a way to free children from the tyrannical hold of advertising, from the designer shoes or jeans that many can't afford, and to put a stop to the sometimes violent taxing that occasionally occurs when children hold up their peers for a coveted item of status clothing. If everyone looks the same, the theory goes, we will treat each other more as equals, erasing class distinctions. If only it were that simple. But there is nothing simple about a uniform that is an object of erotica in both Japan and the West. What meanings do youth attribute to the popular image of uniform-as-sexy in movies and videos such as Britney Spear's gyrations in her widely played music video ". . . Baby, One More Time," where she and a host of "chorus school girls" prance about sexily in short kilt, knee socks, and tie, with blouses tied up provocatively to bare the midriff? No, there is nothing simple about a piece of clothing that can be so differently interpreted and worn.

Notes

1. Of course, I had no awareness, as a child, of the historical association of bloomers with women's activist Amelia Bloomer in America in the 1850s (although Diana Crane points out that Bloomer likely copied the design from a friend (see Crane, 2000: p. 129). Although I doubt that the knowledge of how contentious the wearing of bloomers had been for women would have changed the way I felt about wearing them at the time, looking back now, I feel a sort of perverse pride or sisterhood in having worn them.
2. Sandra J. Weber & Claudia A. Mitchell, *"Tunic Wars."* Act 2 of "Bodies of Knowledge, Knowledge of Bodies: A performance." Paper presented at the 4th Canadian Association for Studies on Women in Education Summer Institute. (Toronto, Ontario Summer Institute 2002).
3. See Gillian Shadley, "School Uniforms, Eros, and Mixed Messages," Paper presented at the Annual Congress of the Canadian Association for the Study of Women in Education, Halifax (May 2003).

CHAPTER 8

Lyse Lemieux

Tunique Desires

Figure 8.1. "2 Tuniques," 1987. Neoprene rubber. 8' × 10'. Lyse Lemieux. Courtesy of the artist.

1963: Chez les soeurs blanches d'Afrique[1]

Il y a un calme lourd
dans la salle de classe où
Je suis seule où
les pupitres vides fixent le tableau où
les nuages de craie blanche embuent les âmes grises

L'autel des soeurs à la gauche de mon pupitre
passionne, effraye—appel.

J'ouvre le ciboire symbole d'un enfer certain.
Sainte Marie mère de Dieu priez-pour moi et mes péchés
brûlez mes jeunes mains avec la chaleur du désir.

Sous le pied de cette femme le serpent me défie
Il veut mon enfant.   Il veut mon âme.

Je ne suis pas confessé. J'ai le péché originel.
Mes doigts retirent le couvercles de la coupe rédemptrice

Je suis en troisième année et je porte ma tunique bleue.

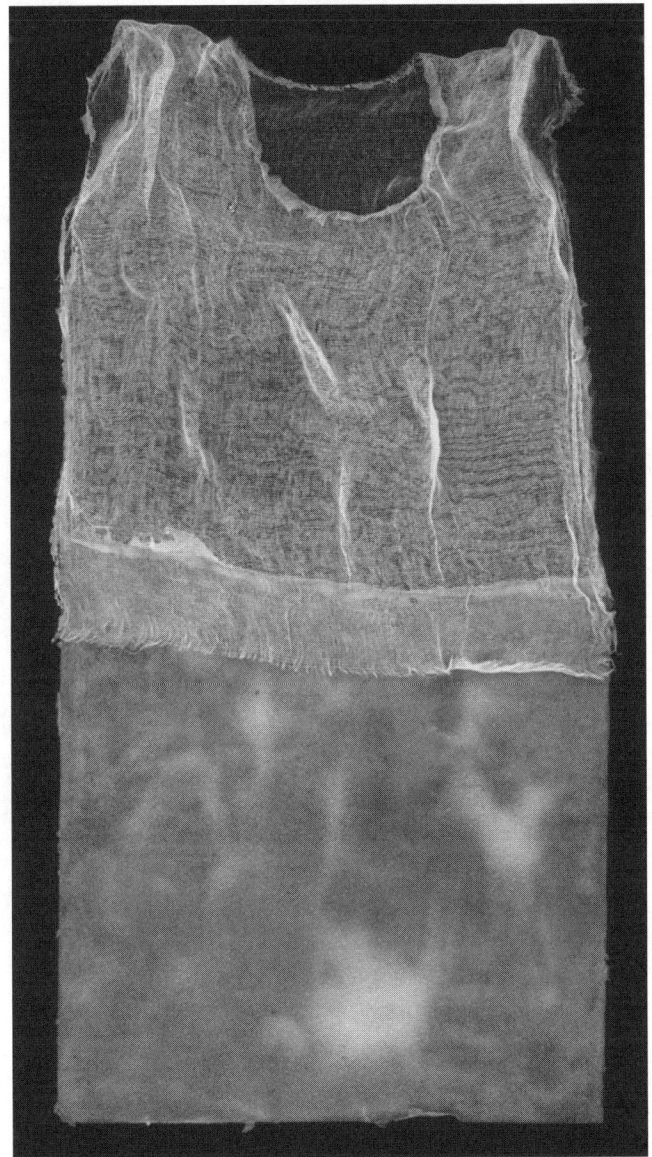

Figure 8.2. "La peau de Mme Ives (mère) 2," 2003. Latex rubber gauze, 22.5" × 47". Lyse Lemieux. Courtesy of the artist.

1963: With Our Lady of Africa

there is an eerie calm
in the classroom where
I am alone where
empty desks stare at blackboards where
clouds of white chalk stain grey souls where
to the left of my desk stands
the White Nuns' altar.

Thrilled and frightened, I cannot resist the call
of that forbidden sanctum,
and remove the ciborium
ensuring thus the time
I will spend in hell.

Mary mother of God pray for my sins
burn my young hands with the flame
of desire

Under her foot the serpent defies me
wants my child   wants my soul.

I have not yet been confessed. I am the original sin.
My fingers uncover the redemptive cup.

I am in grade three and I am wearing
my navy blue tunic.

Notes

This poem is based on a real event that happened in grade 3 in a very small French Canadian Catholic school in Ottawa. Grades 1, 2, and 3 were combined in the same classroom and we had recess in the basement or outside in the summer. One day I found myself alone in the classroom. I did what I had always wanted to do . . . I went into that little altar set up in the classroom to find the secret (the host) that was inside this sacred place. For years I thought I was damned. Who knows . . . maybe I am!

1. The elementary school I went to was run by the White Nuns *(Les soeurs blanches d'afrique)*—missionary nuns who inundated us with images of Africa: little black students also wearing our tuniques, Africans suffering from leprosy (the price they no doubt had to pay for not being Catholic!) and of course the white nuns themselves. White flowing gowns with a sky blue neck and face piece. It left me with incredibly strong images of costume/dress/vestment/clothing—which has never left and which I continue to work with in my sculpture.

CHAPTER 9   *Candis Steenbergen*

In Front of the Closet: (Ad)dressing the Academic

> ...it was not only that I had read Foucault and Althusser (they had said nothing of gender) and Woolf and MacKinnon (they had), but also that I had absorbed as my experience (through my own history and engagement in social reality and in the gendered spaces of feminist communities) the analytical and critical method of feminism, the practice of self-consciousness.
>
> TERESA DE LAURETIS[1]

1999

A week before my MA thesis defense, I called my advisor in a panic—apprehensive about my introductory statements and the committee's reactions, worried about the unknown and wanting desperately to troubleshoot whatever was to come. Should I reread it all, again? Should I integrate so-and-so's work into my presentation? I wanted guidance: straight-up information about what I could expect, the best and worst-case scenarios, how I could best prepare. "Relax," she said. "You've done all that you can possibly do with your text, it's out of your hands. Concentrate now on the things you can control. Go to your room, open your closet, and start figuring out what you're going to wear on Friday."

That practical advice was probably the very best I could have received—perhaps the best I've *ever* received since my academic journey began.[2] It kept me, my mind and my nerves sufficiently occupied, got me through the week and to my defense in one piece. It was also far more difficult than I expected. I wanted to look—at once—like the funky yet relaxed, together but layered, sassy and serious young feminist academic. I wanted to embody the third wave feminist politics I had attempted to write and would be defending. I recall going to my room and looking into that sparse closet full of thrift store clothing and my (younger) sister's hand-me-downs thinking, "What *am* I going to wear?" A challenge that rapidly became more daunting than the upcoming defense.

Shopping for something new (or even new to me) wasn't an option; my teaching assistantship rewarded me barely enough for the basics of rent, utilities and food. My wardrobe wasn't very accommodating to the look I wanted to achieve either: I had worn most of the items throughout my undergrad (and some, admittedly, through high school), and many were worn thin or frayed or stained. I remember calling one girlfriend for suggestions ("wear pants—not jeans—and a neutral coloured, long-sleeved, button-down top"), another to learn what she wore during hers (a dark, fitted business suit with a knee-length skirt, "classic and professional but still slightly casual") and inviting a third over to help me mix-'n'-match ("What about this?" she asked, holding up a (very retro) black lycra catsuit and a floor-length, crocheted dress to match). I'm almost certain that I eventually went with one of my "good" outfits—most likely purchased or sewn by my mum (who has the gift of pinpointing both fashion *and* style) as Christmas or birthday gifts—but I'm not entirely sure.

The defense went well and I left with my degree in hand. Funny thing is, no matter how hard I try, I can't recollect what I eventually decided to wear that day.

2002

When the letter arrived I was ecstatic. It was official: acceptance of both my part-time teaching application and my course proposal. My second year as a Ph.D. candidate, and I would be making the transition from what felt like perpetual-TA to Lecturer the next fall term. I felt the role change was going to be a relatively smooth one and in many ways, I was fortunate: I would teach a course of my own making on a topic I was already well versed in and intensely passionate about, in a discipline I treasured, at a location I had already grown familiar and comfortable with, and with a class size enrollment cap of twenty-five. All the TA facilitating, moderating and marking, topical guest lectures, and conferences under my belt made me feel prepared and ready.

I called my mum the moment I received the news. Not long into the conversation, she asked, "What do you wear for a position like that?" Clothes. Right. I'd forgotten. As a TA, it was "understood" that I was still, in essence, just another student—albeit one with slightly increased authority and responsibility. I hadn't worried about what I wore then; I dressed for style some days, comfort on most. But this new role seemed more tenuous: I would be both teacher *and* student. As an instructor, I was not only moderating discussions, I would be lecturing; in addition to increased responsibility, I would be accountable.[3] As a student, I remained very much like most of the undergraduate students I would be guiding: young, with shared tastes and similar argot, and broke.

After organizing, revising and preparing the syllabus and assembling the assigned readings, I revisited my former advisor's suggestion. Approaching my closet with more than a little trepidation, I found little deviation from the wardrobe I peered into years before at a different school in a different province. A few Christmases had passed and I was a couple of years older, but limited selection still peered back at me. The (more than a) few pounds I had gained in the interim made the collection even thinner.[4] I shut the doors and started thinking. Where will the course take place? What's the temperature of the room? What do other instructors in the program wear when they teach? And when they don't?

The logistics were easily-identifiable and instantly useful: I learned that my course would be held in the Institute's lounge; a comfortable, intimate, and open space featuring couches and chairs, not desks. Everyone would be at the same level, seated, and at close range. The room was set a little below ground level, making the space damper and cooler than most of the school's classrooms. The AV materials—television, VCR, chalkboard and overhead projector—were all on swivel casters. Outside, Montréal weather was volatile at best, and autumn could be as hot as mid-summer or brisk, and as winter approached it would turn bitter cold. Taken together, dressing for comfort should be priority: nothing too constricting, definitely nothing that pinches at the waist, clothes that move. Layers, perhaps. Yes, layers could be the answer: loose, relaxed layers—long sleeve T-shirts or button-down shirts with big collars over jeans or long skirts with tights under soft loose-knit sweaters—would provide movement and alleviate temperature gauging; smooth enough to fit under my winter coat, bulky enough to hide the bulges.

As diverse as the courses they taught, my colleagues' dress wasn't as straightforward. The two tenured professors very much wore their profession on their sleeves: one, an activist sage, wore clothes with stories and history, dressed primarily in solids, and always looked prepared for teaching, media interviews, or a protest; the other wore a subtle glamour, a serious style with pragmatic but alluring accessories: a loosely draped textured scarf, a chunky pendant, or a sleek, silver watch. The part-timers ran the spectrum: athletic and hip, conservatively functional, loose and flowing, practiced nonchalance. One is a friend who, as she says, wears clothes that "gotta speak." Through them, I read—volumes—into her style, influences, age, and her pedagogical practice. To me, she is the irony she theorizes, an embodiment of the pop culture complexities she teaches, and she wears both her "grrrl gear" and her approach to pedagogy every day.

My work situates itself within frameworks of paradox, of contradiction, of identities and of feminisms: the messy spots that sometimes link and sometimes separate theory and practice. My course, "Feminist Generations," was an extension of that, and sought to simultaneously deflate popular myths about "feminism" and "feminists," engage with feminisms' diverse and not-so-distant past, deconstruct the "generation gap," and to problematize and explore the concept of "generations" by scrutinizing the "waves." In short, it aimed to examine the historical roots and contemporary dimensions of feminist identities. As a course, it was challenging enough. As a teacher, I wanted to push the boundaries and disrupt assumptions, to provoke, to stimulate, to enrage, and inspire.

How do I dress that? Was I already wearing it?

My colossal naïveté of what was to come helped most of all. Time was an enormously significant factor in how I dressed on Wednesday mornings throughout the term, and rapidly became an even more precious commodity as assignments came due, marking began and my own deadlines approached. The slim pickings (of what still fit comfortably—or, more realistically—what *fit*) in my closet worked overtime and were recycled over and over again. One week of missed laundry meant going tight or going wrinkled, and the latter usually won. An inability to forecast the day's weather often meant wearing my jacket through the duration of the class or leaving with a bag full of extras.

Ironically, the introduction to the course syllabus read:

> Each person will approach this material with a different background and a different set of experiences. This course is premised on the belief that there is no *one* feminist approach, and that all of us are creating, shaping, and transforming feminist theory and practice in our own ways. As Geraldine Finn has noted, "Feminism does not speak with one voice."[5]

Of course, feminist teachers—and teachers of feminisms—do not dress in a precise fashion either.[6] One of the major objectives of the course was "to (try to) situate our current historical moment." As a young, optimistic, very green feminist instructor (and still a student), I wore my role insofar as I was it.

1985–1997

I was that student in high school and undergrad who scrutinized teachers' appearances from my partial view back row seat as they spoke way, way down at the front of the room. I watched the performance of their every move during class, from week to week, all term, all year. During particularly dreary lectures, I examined their hair (the cut, style, highlights, dye-jobs, *au naturel*), their footwear (sneakers, loafers, pumps . . . scuffed or shined? laced or zipped?), and, especially, their clothes. I noticed when the same outfit was worn two weeks in a row, how separates were combined and reassembled, if hems were cut too short, color schemes, patterns and textures, what worked, what didn't—the lot.

Slouched, taking notes, and doodling in the margins, my mind wandered as I ruthlessly—and aimlessly—studied skirts, scarves, golf shirts, power suits, blue jeans and cowboy boots. I could be callous; cattily examining and evaluating their selections, noting wrinkled shirts, soiled sweaters and outdated slacks, silently "tsk, tsking" what I deemed an unfortunate combination or an outright fashion faux pas. I would associate garments with politics and make mental notes, equating the consistent single-breasted suit or Laura Ashley flower print with conservatism, the dark blazer with brevity and gravity, funky and/or mono-black with verve and high theory, denim with the left. My papers would often dress accordingly.

Through their clothes I idly tried to imagine their wardrobes, their lives. It not only successfully passed the time; it allowed me to imagine the life of a teacher outside the classroom, the professor outside the academy—as well as inside. Who was she trying to be when speaking to/at/with ten, twenty-five, two hundred students? Who was he outside of that space? Were they the same? And on a different level, my inspections permitted me to quietly pass the teacher/student divide: Does he have children? Pets? Is she straight? Does he like his job? How old is she? Vegetarian? Is she happy/ lonely/(virtually any adjective)? However unsubstantiated and imaginary, their clothes spoke volumes and my stare translated and read both the attire and accessories.

My gaze was indiscriminate; it targeted whoever happened to be at the front of the room at the time (but in retrospect, my political science program paraded significantly more male apparel). There was one gendered exception: the watch. I'm not sure when it happened; at what moment my fixation centred on the functional adornment of my female instructor's wrists, but the timepiece—a very particular kind of watch, no less—achieved monumental significance during my in-class scrutiny. Hers was silver (never gold), analog, shiny and slightly oversized: a combination of chunky metal and sleek simplicity. It fit her wrist loosely, but didn't dangle; it settled on the base of her hand comfortably and peeked out modestly under her sleeve. To me, it was the ornament of true scholarly success, conveying intellect, confidence, minimalism, efficiency, value, and style. She wears it only when she's made it.

I have difficulty recalling clear snapshots of the clothing worn by those who would come to be my mentors (most unwittingly); the scholars I wanted to become, the teachers I wanted to be. When I try to envision the details of their dress, the "stuff" that made up their physical presentation, I can only bring fleeting images of movement to mind: a brush of a hand smoothing a shirt, the swing or swoosh of a skirt in stride, the click of a heel, the adjustment of spectacles. I remember their words, their writing, their advice, and their selected reading lists most vividly. My mentors—all older, most tenured—*had* made it. I couldn't possibly imagine their wardrobes; let alone how to emulate them.

2003

I had taught a university class before, but this one would be different. I would be teaching in the Department of Education, a course called "Sex Role Socialization in the School," just one term following my appointment in women's studies. I had to face a large class (with projected enrolments as high as 140 students), in an unfamiliar faculty, in a traditional lecture hall, teaching a course I had worked on as a teaching assistant just one year prior. I knew the material well and had adapted the syllabus to my own strengths, so I wasn't overly concerned about my articulation of the core concepts or detailing examples or descriptors. This time around, it was clothes that I was worried about; particularly on the first day of class.

In its content, the course specifically targeted and interrogated sex, gender, class, sexuality, and race—and their relationships with and in institutional schooling. Unlike women's studies, most students in the program would be learning the theory and its vocabulary from scratch, and many would be thinking about situations—in the school as well as in their everyday lives—as *gendered* for the very first time. As future teachers themselves, they would be examining the complexities of being raised and schooled as "female" or "male," deconstructing stereotypes, and investigating their potential complicity in defining what gender means and how it can be expressed in their own classrooms.

I would be speaking throughout the year about Goffman's vision of social life as a stage, the everyday as a performance of multiple scripts, and his separation of onstage (the visible, the interpretable) and backstage (the place "where the impression fostered by the performance is knowingly contradicted as a matter of course").[7] We would be discussing social mores, rules, and codes in institutional spaces. We would address gender and its intersections and the axis of difference as performance. We would speak of outward appearance as an active process; one constructed by the presentation of the wearer and interpreted by their viewers, and then reconstructed. We would acknowledge that this all gets complicated by class, race, sexuality, ability, and age. As well, the former professor of the course would be guest lecturing on "Prom Night"—a talk that would inevitably speak to gender coding via dress (and dresses), the connotative and denotative meanings of clothes, and the constant material re/invention of identity in particular contexts. If they hadn't considered that appearances communicated meaning before, they certainly would early on in the term.

I had scoped out the space ahead of time, and the classroom itself was sizeable. A LOT of people would be in the room. Many of them would be close to my age. Fear of maintaining order crept in immediately (as did anxiety about my youth) and a desire to appear authentic, credible, and authoritative soon followed. Once again, I went back to my closet. I began a process of elimination: nothing flashy, nothing intricately decorated or oddly cut, nothing trendy, and no concert shirts. Nothing that would even hint at my tattoos. I wanted to command attention; not draw it. I wanted the focus to be on my words, not my style. The students' seats were elevated and splayed, movie-theatre style, and I would be speaking at the entrance level; a sort of inverted pyramid with the lecturer at the bottom. A podium equipped with a microphone and technical equipment stood at stage left and was at breast-level, the only obstruction of gaze. No matter where I walked, I would be in full view of everyone in the room for almost three hours per week. And so would my attire.

The prospect of that kind of prolonged attention to my physical body gave the selection process significantly more import: mismatched colors would be immediately pinpointed, bad hair/skin/face days noted, discomfort and insecurity with my personal presentation painfully obvious. Students would be watching me, and just thinking about that potential inspection made me nervous. Returning to my closet, I continued the cuts with a new goal in mind: alleviating potential attention-grabbers. I immediately disqualified half of the clothes for no longer—and perhaps never again—fitting. Everything white or light-colored went next; bottoms because they accentuated size, tops because they emphasized what I wanted to preemptively avoid: sweat stains, and (lacking fabulous lingerie) transparency and headlights. It narrowed the selection noticeably, showing what I had to work with.

Contrasting this experience with teaching women's studies, I suspected that many enrolled in the class would hold stereotypical ideas of what a "feminist" is and looks like—images, mostly negative, fueled largely by popular media. Knowing full well that I would be teaching the course with a strong (but unnamed) feminist lens, I was afraid of tipping them off—and, consequently, *turning* them off—too early in the year. I revisited my wardrobe again in an attempt to defuse my women-centered politics from my form.[8] Everything with a feminist slogan was deemed ineligible for wear, and activist buttons were removed from jackets, sweaters and hoodies (save two: "I am a rabble rouser," from rabble.ca and *pretty, porky & pissed off's* "joy to eat"). Hyper-aware of how my body wears a very particular feminist brand by sheer virtue of my color, age, and education, I didn't want to be misconstrued as a proto-post-feminist—more concerned with baubles and glitter than political principles—either. I wanted my dress to serve as both armored protection from stereotypical assumptions and as an obscured but theoretically powerful weapon.

My final consideration as I stood in front of my closet, for what I hoped would be the last time before the first day of school, was of femininity.[9] How "girlie" did I want to go? I knew that gender was a process, an active development that shifted according to moment, and that the students would soon be reading me with that lens. Should I be practicing what I teach? Should I make use of that awareness and seek to intervene and disrupt the performance? In my "real" life, I saw myself as a woman who sometimes rejects and sometimes participates in prescribed models of feminine presentation. I also knew that both the indulgence in and parody of those could run the gamut from fun to complicit to downright threatening—depending on who was doing the reading. To me, dressing was a personal choice (based largely on my own confidence and mood) *and* a political decision (what statement do I want to make?) and I felt the responsibility to my future students weighing on me heavily. I wanted to break down stereotypes and point out and tear down barriers to the performance, instigate a little gender play, while at the same time convey the message that there was absolutely nothing wrong with being—and dressing—the girl. I was left standing there, in front of my closet, thinking and looking; not entirely pleased with what the garments that stared back at me had to offer. I made no clothing selections or cuts. Was it the wardrobe I was frustrated with, really? Or was I more unnerved with what my clothes were saying out loud about my own sense of self? About my own complicity in self-(re)creation?

Less than three hours before addressing the class for the very first time, the most important time, the intro class, I scrambled to the closet and pulled out three items with nary a thought: an ankle-length "dirty" stretch denim skirt (my sister's gift to me last Christmas) that not only fit but had room to move, and an oversized, bright red, fleece hoodie with a zipper up the front (a gift from my mum the same holiday). They were, at that moment, my "good" clothes, my still (as yet) baggage-free clothes, and they were warm, moderately concealing, and comfortable. The only decision left was what to wear under the sweater. I looked through the hangers of T-shirts that had met my meticulous criteria up to that point. Unhappy with what I found—a bland row of plain *blah* colors, shirt after shirt—I reached back into the disqualified row and pulled out a black *Le Tigre* concert tee. Pulling it over my head and adding the bulk, I headed for the front door of my apartment, stopping only to pull on a pair of clunky, thick soled, black leather lace-up boots. Armed and ready, I left for school.

Standing in front of the closet, negotiating fiercely with myself and my clothes, has forced me to realize—and sometimes resist, and sometimes accept—my own body, rife with contradictions. It is a private, intersubjective negotiation of self-representation, and my closet and I have developed a close, almost empathic relationship as a result. Its contents, the garments of varying ages, styles and colors, afford me the possibility of agency and self-determination, and remind me that my performance of self is a gendered, classed, and raced act, as well as a pedagogical, political, and feminist undertaking. Together, we work to eke out a coherent space; a network of puzzles that can be navigated regardless of how daunting everything else might seem. Some days, it is the lens through which I see and am seen. On others, it's a game of pleasure and indulgence and play. Now and then, the fragments of patterns and designs expose my complicity (and complacency) with the status quo. But every day, it is a negotiation of multiple meanings that I cannot avoid.

Reading the encounters I've had with various closets over the years, I recognize myself. I negotiate with my closet as if—somehow through the collaboration/tension—I can control the way my self-presentations and performances are executed and received; as if I can defend my research, run a seminar, sit in the back of a room, or stand in front of a classroom and guarantee that my ideas, my words, my sharing of theory, my feminism, and my politics will be greater, more commanding than the performance signified by my adorned body: wrinkled, faded, stained, or worn.

Notes

For invaluable comments and advice on earlier drafts of this paper, I am very grateful to Nina Karhu and Ernest Harris Jr.
1. Teresa de Lauretis, *Technologies of Gender: Essays on Theory, Film and Fiction.* (Bloomington and Indianapolis: Indiana University Press, 1987) 20.
2. Special thanks to Katherine Arnup, Carleton University, for her words of wisdom.
3. For more on "dressing the part" in academic culture, see E. Green, "Suiting Ourselves: Women Professors using Clothes to Signal Authority, Belonging and Personal Styles." In A. Guy, E. Green, & M. Banim (Eds.) *Through the Wardrobe: Women's Relationships with Their Clothes* (Oxford and New York: Berg, 2001); S. Kaiser, et al., "Minding Appearances in Female Academic Culture," in *Through the Wardrobe;* and A. Schneider, "Frumpy or Chic? Tweed or Kente? Sometimes Clothes make the Professor: Academic Wardrobe Selection can Involve Ideology, Discipline and Job-Hunting Strategy," *The Chronicle of Higher Education* (January 1998) 23, 17–19.
4. See, for instance, M. Banim & A. Guy, "Dis/continued Selves: Why do Women Keep Clothes They No Longer Wear?" in *Through the Wardrobe.* They write, "For example, women felt they could not wear certain clothes because of a changing body shape but the clothes were kept in the hope that the body would be able to wear them again one day" (205).
5. Angela Miles & Geraldine Finn (Eds), *Feminism in Canada: From Pressure to Politics.* (Montreal: Black Rose Books, 1982) 299.
6. For a hilarious and "Fond Look at the Fab, Funky world of U.S. Feminist Fashion," see *Ms.* (July/August 1992) 3.
7. Erving Goffman. *The Presentation of Self in Everyday Life.* (New York: Doubleday, 1959) 22–24.
8. Peter Dickinson's coining of the phrase, "the hats-backward syndrome," is called to mind here, although he is describing a kind of "dress up" that connotes inclusion to a marginalized or historically disenfranchised group for increased credibility in academic circles. He describes it as a "sense in which the performative . . . translates into a kind of critical cross-dressing, a process of self-fashioning, or refashioning, to which anyone can subscribe merely by donning the appropriate apparel. . ." See *Here Is Queer: Nationalisms, Sexualities and the Literatures of Canada* (Toronto, University of Toronto Press, 1999) 187. At the same

time, Keenan notes that while they offer "assurance and reassurance," for the wearer, "clothes are a flimsy disguise for our naked ambitions and inhibitions." I'm almost positive my "neutral" façade barely prevented—if at all—my feminist roots from showing. See "Introduction: 'Sartor resartus' Restored: Dress Studies in Carlylean Perspective." In W. J. F. Keenan (Ed.) *Dressed to Impress: Looking the Part* (Oxford and New York: Berg, 2001) 19.

9. Leslie Minot targets, negotiates with and then (almost) reconciles the "girlness" of her clothes as a potential "way out of gender" in her article, "Girl Clothes in a Box," *Bad Subjects: Political Education for Everyday Life,* Issue 10 (December 1993). Available online: http://eserver.org/bs/10/Minot.html.

CHAPTER 10　　　　　　　　　　　　*Claudia Mitchell*

Was It Something I Wore?

Was it something I wore? How do you prove the existence of the often intangible aspects of "unwanted sexual attention"—what, since the mid-seventies, has come to be defined as sexual harassment: a leer, a tone of voice, a certain suggestiveness? The accused might protest: "She was asking for it." "It was all in the way she walked across the front of the room." "It was the way the top three buttons of her blouse were left undone." "It was the rustle of her dress against her hose." "She walked across the yard in her short summer frock, bare arms. . . ." These are the very intangibles that the movie director, modelling agency, fashion photographer or portrait artist try to capture, aren't they? For me, in real life, it went something like this:

> "You're not one of the student teachers, are you?" is what I think he said. Or did he say, "Are you one of the student teachers?" I can't actually remember now although either way it must have been the way he said "you're" or "you." But the surface structure—the exact words—of what he, Mr. J. the cooperating teacher from "Eastern High" one of the local high schools in Montreal, said, doesn't really matter. It wasn't so much what he said, as *how* he said it, what I heard him to say, or rather, how I understood him to say these words, once I realized that he was talking to me and not to one of the gathering of five or six student teachers with whom I was touring that first day at the school. This was to be the school where they would be practicing to be teachers for the next six weeks, where I, the representative from McGill University would be supervising their teaching, and where Mr. J. would be what is called the cooperating teacher. It is hard to avoid italicizing the words practicing, supervising and cooperating since they are so euphemistic. Student teachers don't like to think of themselves as "practicing" and the teachers in the schools think that those of us from

the university are hardly in a position to "supervise" since so many of us haven't taught in schools for years and in any case have no responsibility for the classrooms in which we are apparently supervising. As for Mr. J, the "cooperating teacher," well, I'll leave you to draw your own conclusions.

Mr. J.'s words went something like "you're not a student teacher" and one could have taken it as some sort of age thing—like the two of us—we're the adults in all of this and you know what adults do? It felt like some sort of "wink wink nod nod" sign: adults watch adult movies, read the plastic encased adult magazines displayed on the top shelf in the local Multimags shop, participate in adult entertainment. Or, maybe when he said "you're not a student teacher," he meant "We're the real teachers; we're experienced and not just students." Somehow real teachers in this context seem to refer to the kind of people that you'd find in a *Carry On Teacher* movie or referred to in songs like "Teach Me Tonight" or are referred to on bumper stickers like "teachers do it with class" or "English teachers are novel lovers." The real thing. You might think he was flattering me—"*you're* not one of the student teachers," but even though you are forty-plus, you could be! The term student teacher conjures up all those sixties and seventies film images of "the interns," "the student nurses," "summer school."

Was it something I said? Was I standing a certain way? Was it something I wore—a plunging neckline, a short skirt? "This is highly unlikely," most people who know me will say. Or was I wearing something so totally unsuggestive that Mr. J. was going "show me a good time"? Women teachers—let your hair down: *The Prime of Miss Jean Brodie* and *Rachel, Rachel*. Think of all those images of women professors in movies you know, like Barbra Streisand in *The Mirror Has Two Faces*.

We all know how these scenes are supposed to go. She is committed to her students and her scholarship, and resigned to being called a spinster. Childless, never child-free, forced to pay the single supplement on bus tours of Santorini during her summer vacation. Then *he* comes along—he doesn't even have to be a professor. According to an article I read in *The Economist* about a meeting of the Romance Writers of America, the new hero in the various romance series these days is no longer "the brooding English Aristocrat." Rather, in a post–September 11th world, "cops, firemen and blue-collar workers are incredibly hot."[1] He removes her glasses and gently releases her long locks from the confinement of the classic bun, and lo, the audience is transfixed by her transformation. *Pretty Woman* and *My Fair Lady* in reverse.

But in this case, my glasses are merely figurative, and my hair is way too short. Nothing to let down—just a short-haired woman who wears no make-up? Ah, a feminist who needs some jollying, perhaps. I don't look woman enough but that's because I am probably a man-hater—but capable of being converted and reformed. And maybe he has worked out that I actually *am* a dyke, but instead of writing me off, he's going to rise to the challenge. What I need is the attention of a *real* man. He is going to "cure me."

I didn't answer his "you're not one of the student teachers, are you?" since by the time I even realized that he was talking to me, the moment had passed and our little group—the student teachers and I—had already begun to make its way down the corridor. And by the time I arrived home that evening, I wasn't quite sure that I had really heard what I thought I heard anyway. I mean, no one would say what I thought he said to a female McGill professor, over 40 and in front of five student teachers—though whether it was my institutional affiliation, my age, or the professional situation that was the most inappropriate factor still isn't clear. But then, if he didn't say what I thought he said, what did I hear? And what evidence did I have that this even happened? Now that I am writing this so many years later, I can't be certain at all what else I thought or felt that night. There is a blankness that may be more than just challenges to memory. This is something that I have also found when I have spoken with other girls and women about sexual violence.[2] Somehow it is as though the silence *at the time* sets in motion a whole series of silences.

The very next day, though, one of the student teachers who was in the group of five students handed in to me her reflective journal in which she was required to write about her school visit. I couldn't believe my eyes. She writes about the incident. *She saw it. It did happen.* I don't remember exactly what it was that she wrote; but it had to do with a description of her visit to the school. She had managed to insert something about the event, something like "I can't believe what I heard." I didn't make a copy of what she wrote although I do know I wrote back to her in her logbook. I think my response was something almost the same as what I have just written: "Did I really hear this? Did this happen? It did, didn't it?" Did we ever speak of it again? I doubt it. Did we both just imagine this? After all, there was no visual evidence.

When I perform this "was it something I wore" scenario in front of a live audience that is made up almost entirely of female educators, I sense the nods around me that pick up on many of the collective (and cumulative) tensions of our lives as women. This scenario is part of a collection of short vignettes called *Wardrobe Moments* all based on autobiographical clothing episodes in my life: the role of the little black turtleneck in distancing myself from being "just a teacher," my love/hate relationship with suits, the politics of dressing for interviews, and so on. When I perform these scenes on stage I also include slide projections of photographs from my picture album. There's one of me, for example, looking very self-satisfied as a first-year teacher in my horn-rimmed glasses and artsy black turtleneck. The caption reads "I am a writer, perhaps and not 'just a teacher.'" Then there's another one of me dressed-for-success in my 1980s-version grey flannel suit, and another of me in my not-quite-suit denim ensemble but with matching top and bottom.[3] The "centerpiece" of these wardrobe moments—for me, at least—is "Was it something I wore?" the only scene for which there is no photograph and hence no visual evidence. There is only my testimony, and maybe that's the real point in trying to understand sexual harassment.

When I construct this particular scene with its "you're not a student teacher, are you?" opening line, I find myself considering where best to place this scene within the overall performance of *Wardrobe Moments,* which is made up of four short scenarios. I decide to start with *Little Black Turtleneck* as Scene One, followed *by Dressing for the Interview* as Scene Two. *Was It Something I Wore?* is Scene Three, and *Suit Yourself* is the Fourth. The first scene, I feel, must do double-duty, since I need to establish the genre. In the performance, each scene is a short monologue marked by a change of photograph on the slide projector, and my movement on stage. Each is also meant to operate like a very short short story, crafted with the intention of creating some sort of self-study or questioning on the part of the audience.

Little Black Turtleneck is a good opening scene. It is the shortest and it is personal, but not *too* personal, and it takes up a theme common to many teachers: "I am not really sure that I want to be a teacher." *Dressing for the Interview* is a little longer and more complicated, but it is also more humorous. The many possibilities for what can happen when you try to dress for an interview are just that—complicated and often, at least in the re-telling, quite funny. But I worry that the same people who would have laughed *with* me at my rendition of *Little Black Turtleneck* or *Dressing for the Interview* will think that *Was It Something I Wore?* is just one more piece that is meant to be humorous. The audience, if they laugh, will be embarrassed as the piece unfolds and they realize that it is dead serious. I can't let that happen. In theory, it's a difficult bit of pedagogical work: It's up to me, the writer and performer, to direct the audience, through my voice, my stance, my presence on stage, to "will them" in a sense, right from the very beginning, not to laugh. In practice, however, no one laughs, although I hear a solitary hoot of recognition from the back of the room during one of the performances. I take the ease of rendition as testimony to the collective years of experience that I, and most of the women in the room, have had with the practices of the unspoken ("I can't put it into words") as well as with the practices of being coy, of being expected to say "no," of being misread, of protesting at not being believed.[4]

"Was it something I wore?" Say it aloud. Listen to yourself utter the same line as "Was it something *I* wore?" "Was it something I *wore?*" That line, which so many women are used to saying, sounds as though it comes laden with agency and intentionality—but think of when you are mostly likely to say it, or to hear it. There is always doubt. It is one of those tag-end questions that we as women are supposed to be famous for.[5] Similarly, this expression, while not strictly speaking a passive construction, nonetheless carries with it an absence of agency.[6] Maybe we aren't necessarily "read" the way we think we are, but in our intentionality we attempt, at least, to "write ourselves" a certain way: *"I wore the glasses or the little black turtleneck sweater so I would be taken seriously." "I wore a suit because I wanted to be 'dressed for success.'" "All the manuals on power dressing say 'wear a jacket.'" "This outfit is a little too casual, or it is a little too severe."*

As for my dilemma on that day at Eastern High and the reading back to what Mr. J. *might* have meant, you probably have no difficulty in appreciating my distress at how to now tell it. When I look at what other academic women have written about clothing, it is all there:

> . . . Senior women are acutely aware of the need to guard their embodied appearance, lest they invite sanctions or unwanted attention as sexualized bodies within the academy. Most avoided what they perceived as embodied "sexual display."[7]

> . . . it's wanting not to have any hint of sexual display so I wouldn't . . . Wear anything that was low-cut . . . I don't want to feel that X across the table is trying to peer down my cleavage . . . I just don't want to be on display in that kind of way.[8]

Kate Gillen lays out the map of "not too" much: Avoid appearing to be sexually available—"since this will cost them respect"—but at the same time, look attractive or "suffer loss of respect."[9] In *Reinventing Ourselves as Teachers,* Sandra Weber and I cite the case of Ellen, a teacher who, in taking off her jacket when the classroom becomes too hot, receives wolf-whistles. Her male counterparts, she observes, would just "naturally" take off their jackets in the middle of class without inviting comment or reaction.[10]

Was it something I wore, you might ask? Indeed, what was I wearing? On the morning in question when I was dressing for Eastern High, I doubt that I put on something that didn't somewhere fall into my "McGill-professor-going-to-visit-student-teachers" genre. It was not quite what I might have worn in my "back-to-the-land" days of teaching in the early 70s, or the 1980s grey flannel suit. I met Mr. J. in the early 1990s, and I am almost certain that I was wearing some version of a full-length, down-to-the-floor, flowered paisley dress from *Cache-Cache,* or a long skirt and vest. It would have been late fall, so I would have worn full-length sleeves, probably a shirt buttoned right to the neck, or most likely a loose and flowing garment that revealed very little of the contours of my body. And almost assuredly, my legs would be fully covered. Now, more than ten years later and writing about what I might have been wearing, even I find it excessively modest.

Was it something I wore? Did this even happen? After all there was no visual evidence.

Notes

1. "True Love Returns: American Rediscovers Its Heartland," *The Economist* (27 July 2002) 364, 31.
2. Here, for example, I am referring to the work on gender-based violence in South African schools and the development of the module on gender-based violence. See O. Mlamleli, et

al., *Opening Our Eyes: Addressing Gender-based Violence in South African Schools—A Module for Educators*. (Pretoria, South Africa: National Department of Education, 2001. See also M. Mak, *Unwanted Images: Addressing Gender-based Violence in the New South Africa*. A video documentary, Directed by M. Mak, Produced by C. Mitchell (Montreal: Canada South Africa Education Management Program, 2000).

3. C. Mitchell & S. Weber, *Knowledge of Bodies/Bodies of Knowledge,* Staged as plenary session of Education Graduate Studies Society Conference (November 2–3, 2001); C. Mitchell & S. Weber, *Knowing Embodiment,* Staged as plenary session of the Canadian Association of the Study of Women in Education (CASWE) (Toronto, May 2002).

4. For a more extensive discussion of the role of performance in self-study, see our chapter on visual approaches to representation in self-study: S. Weber & C. Mitchell, "Using Visual and Artistic Modes of Representation for Self-Study," In J. Loughran, M. Hamilton, V. LaBoskey, & T. Russell (Eds.), *International Handbook of Self-Study of Teaching and Teacher Education Practices.* (Kluwer Press, in press).

5. See, for instance, the linguistic analyses of Deborah Tannen, *Gender and conversational interaction* (New York: Oxford University Press, 1993).

6. See Julia Penelope's work on patriarchy and language. J. Penelope, *Speaking Freely: Unlearning the Lies of the Fathers' Tongues* (Toronto: Pergamon Press, 1990).

7. Ellen Green, for example, calls it "managing the professional body" in "Suiting Ourselves: Women Professors Using Clothes to Signal Authority, Belonging and Personal Style." In A. Guy, E. Green & M. Banin (Eds.), *Through the Wardrobe: Women's Relationships with Their Clothes* (Oxford: Berg, 2001) 97–116, 110.

8. Ibid., 110.

9. K. Gillen, "Choosing an Image: Exploring Women's Images through the Personal Shopper." In A. Guy, E. Green & M. Banin (Eds.). *Through the Wardrobe: Women's Relationships with their Clothes.* (Oxford: Berg, 2001), 71–96, 86.

10. Hanson, quoted in C. Mitchell & S. Weber, "Dressing the Teacher," In C. Mitchell & S. Weber, *Reinventing Ourselves as Teachers: Beyond Nostalgia* (London: Falmer Press, 1999), 124–163. See also: A. Hansen, "The day the heat went on," In J. S. Kleinfield, & S. Yerian (Eds.), *GenderTales: Tensions in the Schools* (New York: St. Martin's Press, 1995) 131–7.

CHAPTER 11

Madeleine R. Grumet

My Green Robe: Scholae Personae

> *A thousand winters*
> *Will strip you bare as death, a thousand summers*
> *Robe you life-green again.*
> The Foresters, TENNYSON

It's odd that I don't like the term "the personal." In my field, curriculum theory, that's what I'm known for. For twenty years I have drawn on autobiographical accounts of educational experience, reading them through lenses of phenomenological, psychoanalytic, and feminist theory. Related to that work is my effort to study the relationship between reproduction and education and to build discursive bridges between home, where we were children and raise our own children, and school, where we work with other people's children. Nevertheless, throughout these years I have systematically avoided the personal as an emblem for my efforts. Now academics don't often write about the material that we wish to avoid. And unless someone asks us to address these issues that make us anxious or annoyed, we usually don't think about them much at all. They just don't seem to crop up.

I will start this discussion turning to the place I would avoid, the thing I would not think about and would not choose to show you, my green robe.

When I think about the personal, I think about my green robe. It's not jade green, although that's what it wants to be as it becomes a robe that I am starting to write about. It begins to lean toward the kind of robe that Joan Didion would write about in "On Keeping a Notebook," with a black satin tuxedo collar and black curlicues embroidered on a slightly iridescent brocade, the kind of robe her aunt Miss Lucy Farnsworth would have brought back from the Orient.[1]

My robe is what some would call kelly green. I don't remember buying it. I could blame it on a relative, but that would be cowardly, and a betrayal. It is warm and thick, Orlon probably, often coffee stained, and it is good for writing in on cold Rochester mornings, and afternoons for that matter, if no one drops by. It is not a robe for entertaining.

It can go in the washing machine and dryer, its synthetic fleece indestructible, but it works best when slightly soiled, worn with unwashed hair, a flannel nightgown, clogs, and Gerald's grey socks. When I think about it I remember my body.

It is a green cocoon. After a while words fly out of it.

Maybe if I were younger and thinner, the green robe would be jeans and a sweatshirt. But I grew up in the forties when mothers wore housedresses that were not really robes, but were not really dresses either. You wouldn't wear one to the store, but you were dressed if someone rang the bell. When I would come home from school for lunch, my mother would be wearing a housedress covered with small flowers, and I suspect that even if jeans suited me they would not surround me with morning light and kitchen smells.

When it was my turn to keep house, I would sit at the word processor, in the green robe, until the school bus rolled down the block. Then, as I saw my kids coming up the walk, I'd dash for the shower, protecting them from the sight of my literary decadence, for, unlike my mother, I was not dressed if someone rang the bell.

It is a robe I write in, not about. It is strange to see it move into the yellow letters on my screen.

It is my robe, it has my smell, and as I present it to you, it becomes my costume. I may never write again.

My ambivalence about this word, "personal," sends me to the OED which reveals the historical incarnations of my present perplexity. Call me the Shirley Maclaine of etymology. "Person" is traced to the Latin verb "personare," to sound through, later falling from act to object as a mask, the thing through which one sounds as in a play: dramatis personae.

That is the first meaning of person, one that the OED admits hasn't made it into English. It offers many more, among them this pair: "The living body of a human being; either a) the actual body as distinct from clothing, etc, or from the mind or soul, or b) the body with its clothing and adornment as presented to the sight of others."

A-flesh, or B-fashion?

And so I deliberately choose fashion over flesh, to argue that the personal is a performance, an appearance contrived for the public, and to argue that these masks enable us to perform the play of pedagogy.

Now that I have opened the door to my pedagogical wardrobe, I propose to recapitulate a series of responses that I have made over the years to one of the most consistent and absorbing problematics in modern pedagogy: what to wear.

Convinced in the mid-seventies that students of education required a greater selection than what was available to them in a field dominated by positivistic social science, behavioral objectives, and standardized tests, I started asking them to write autobiographical narratives of educational experience. Even then I did not refer to these narratives as "personal" writings. Perhaps the avoidance of the personal was merely strategic. In the mid-seventies I was eager to distance this work from humanistic psychology's hip huggers and Nehru shirts. And from the start we had to defend this approach from accusations of bourgeois subjectivity levied by colleagues wearing leather jackets that signaled their Marxist and working-class identifications. In 1975, when Bill Pinar and I published *Toward a Poor Curriculum*—a year before the publication of *The Mermaid and the Minotaur*, and two years before Gilligan's "In a Different Voice" in the *Harvard Educational Review*—the personal still signaled lingerie.[2]

Nevertheless, facing rows of students at Hobart and William Smith Colleges—all of whom wore clothing designed to conceal all ethnic and class stigmata, all attired so that they would look exactly like each other—I asked for autobiographical narratives: seeking the specificity, the material, the lost shoe, the dead rabbit that would return studies of education and them and me to the world.

Single narratives were frightening. Written against the background of a curriculum that disallowed the first-person pronoun, these narratives could take on the status of revelation. But then thrilling disclosures and declarations would slide into a sickening puddle of objectification. Long before postmodernism exposed the pretensions of a unified consciousness, there were Nietzsche and Freud to steer us away from deadly coherence.

James Olney's wonderful 1972 text, *Metaphors of Self,* rescued us and our students from these objectifying sentimentalities by portraying autobiographies as metaphors for the self providing representations of subjectivity for the public world.[3] Olney's autobiographer was hardly static, for he often transformed his own self-understanding through the act of narration, like Sartre, wriggling out of his self-representations as a snake sheds old skins. Rather than the hand-me-down determinism of the Polish playwright Witold Gombrowicz, whose characters' identities and fates are determined by a prop or piece of clothing that accidentally touches their person, I chose Sartre's approach, window shopping.

I avoided the personal, just as I avoided "authentic" and "sincere" as descriptors for this prose and for this process, and turned to multiple narratives to invite the range, the contradictions, and all the robes—silk brocade, orlon, rayon (packs well), terry, seersucker, velvet, leather, feather—that students could find for this academic procession.

I would ask the students to write three narratives of educational experience, right at the outset of a course in the philosophy of education. Asking for only two narratives would have invited primordial pairs: mind/body, individual/community, boy/girl, leisure wear/formal dress. Three separate narratives made things hard to match.

I asked students to think of the stories that come to mind when someone says, "That was a really educational experience." I told them that the truth of autobiography was embedded in its detail, not its generalization, and asked them to eschew moralistic propositions. They were instructed to type each narrative and were told that I would read and respond to them and that they would also be duplicated so that other students could read and work with them as well. William Earle's *Autobiographical Consciousness* and Didion provided philosophical and literary frames.[4] At the same time that students were thinking about the stories of their lives and how they would tell them to me, that telling was also being framed as a way of knowing.

Then came the three-week winter break, and I took all the stories home to read. I can still see them, sitting there in the study, next to the computer, waiting for me. I couldn't pick up just one or two and stick them in between trips to the store, or dash off a few before going out to the movies. Each set of three held a green world, thick with vegetation, and the only way I could make my way through it was in my green robe.

Green-robed, I would crawl under their leaves, feel the rhythm of their sentences, move to the places they skipped over. A semiotic reading, if you will. I hated entering those texts, giving up my world for theirs, but once I had migrated, I started speaking in their tongue, I became a citizen, started taking notes, started speaking back, asking questions. Like Kristeva's baby I would become mimetic.[5] The echolalia is subtle, but it is there in the style of response that jokes with the jokers, is tentative with the defended, discursive with the loquacious. And then at the end I would surface with a paragraph suggesting the philosophical questions implied in the narratives as well as readings that might inform further pursuit of these issues.

I denied the intimacy of my reading by abstaining from writing on their papers. I would place a number next to the sentence or word to which my comments referred and type them on a separate sheet of paper, sequenced by corresponding numbers. I read them in my green robe, but I typed my responses on the word processor, deliberately interposing the machine, the type of our texts, between our bodies. We made ourselves up in typed face. Masking our handwriting in type endowed our exchange with formality, intended to bring student stories into the legitimated discourse that constituted the knowledge of this philosophy of education course. I do confess that I signed my name, my first name, Madeleine, in black ink, at the bottom of the page. Nevertheless this correspondence was not to be a set of confidences exchanged behind the closed door of the office; in fact, I hardly ever met with students to discuss the narratives, per se, but I remember how I felt, handing back the papers after vacation, each with a typed sheet of questions and responses appended. See how much I love you?

As I remember the years of this work it is clear to me how it moved across these spaces, their places and mine, and then dressed itself up to appear in the classroom. If the classroom was my stage, then my study was my green room. The OED does not tell us why the color green is used for the place where actors relax, prepare, and gossip before they go on stage, but it does tell us that in a warehouse or factory the green room is used for the reception of goods in a green state: such as cloth fresh from the weaving factory, undried pottery, autobiographies, etc.

I don't know where the students were or what they wore as they wrote. I do know that the educational experiences they wrote about rarely took place in school. The classroom was our scene. Their stories shifted our view to yet other scenes, and my questions and their reflections often moved beyond the scenes of the narratives to scenes that they disguised or elided, the scenes against the scene, the obscene. Herbert Blau suggests that the obscene threatens every scene:

> There is in every performance an aggression against the scene of the performance as a value, a derealization. . . . In the history of theater itself, the scene invariably tends toward fragmentation, closure, loss of outwardness and a sense of infinite behind . . . the pressure toward a surface makes you wonder what's behind. The scene remains obscene. The obscene submits what should be kept private to public scrutiny. In that act, the value of the private may be reduced.[6]

Behind the scenes, I was raising three children, and raging at my field for refusing to acknowledge the primal scene. At conferences of education researchers and theorists, children rarely came up. Few admitted to living with children, having children, knowing children, or ever having been children. Nevertheless, so-called reproduction theory was the order of the day. In this tale of procreation, factories and corporations and schools come together to make people in an industrial version of the Immaculate Conception. There was no acknowledgment of the possibility that our original experiences of reproduction, of being children, of having children, might influence our relations to other people's children. *Bitter Milk: Women and Teaching* was the book I wrote to portray a dialectical relation between reproduction—as we experience it as parents and children—and education.[7]

Contradictions between the projects of reproduction and the patterns of gender identity provide a space that invites our exploration and transformation. For if the father's project is to claim connection against an epistemological presupposition that assumes separation, and if the mother's project is to foster separation against an epistemological presupposition of attachment, then we require a system of schooling where the fleeing mothers and the finding fathers can meet to make the switch.

But what of the teaching mother?

Let me reread my reading of my student's stories, no longer wearing the green robe, but keeping it in view. Here are four stories written by Catherine Fisher. They are my favorite stories, for they are wonderfully economical and full of the world. They were published in an issue of *Liberal Education* where they were read and responded to by teams of liberal arts and science and education faculty from Brooklyn College to demonstrate the ways that autobiographical narratives can be used to ground and frame interdisciplinary discourse in education. Here are Catherine's stories:

Catherine's Stories of Educational Experiences

Story One

There was a woman who lived in my old neighborhood. She had grown-up sons and a dog. I don't remember the dog's name or even that I liked the dog—I just remember it was a blond Pekinese with a pug nose. I used to take the dog for walks. It was something different to do. I never thought the walks were for the dog's benefit, I always knew they were for mine.

One day I decided, after getting permission to walk the dog, to go to Hummels. Hummels was an old, dank store that was full of treasures. It was pretty far away but it was more than the distance that made the walk exciting: Going to Hummels was an adventure because it was in the opposite direction than I usually walked. When I think about this day, I picture myself alone, although I'm positive either my sister Melinda or my friend Donna Baggott was there. Melinda claims it was herself, but I'm still not convinced.

We were about half way to Hummels when I noticed that the leashed Pekinese had slowed down and that his mouth was covered with foamy white stuff. I remember thinking that he must have had milk for breakfast. Within seconds after this thought passed through my head, the dog began rolling around strangely on the grass. I realized something was drastically wrong. Next I remember screaming at the top of my lungs—FASTER, FASTER—to my companion, who was running furiously towards home and was almost out of my sight. A woman appeared. She picked up the dog, placed it on a hill and fanned it with a rug. Her own dogs were standing behind her watching the scene. I went inside the woman's house to call my mom. I had a hard time remembering my phone number, and then my mom could not understand what I was saying—she thought I was telling her I lost my change purse. Within a few minutes my mom and the dog's owner drove up in a car.

The dog was dead. No one yelled at me, but I wasn't consoled, either. I felt really sorry the woman's dog was dead, but I don't think I ever talked to her again.

Story Two

Fourth grade—Girl Scout trip to the Smithsonian . . . June Smith's mother was the chaperone. We were all gathered around the balcony looking down on the big moving clock. Someone explained, "The pendulum moves as the earth rotates in its axis . . . Hmmmmmm, I thought about this, and when I looked up the entire Girl Scout troupe had disappeared. I wasn't particularly concerned, and I found them a while later. I thought the issue was a dead one, but June Smith's mother was mad. As I was getting on the bus to go home, she announced that "Catherine Fisher should not be allowed to go on any more trips because I was careless enough to get lost." I felt betrayed, mad, and helpless, but I said nothing. I knew I could never change her opinion of me.

A few years ago I saw June Smith's mother for the first time since the incident. She recognized me as "the one who got lost in the Smithsonian!" She didn't believe me when I told her my version of the story. Her opinion hadn't changed.

Story Three

One evening when we were very young—young enough for my older brother, younger sister, and myself to fit in a bathtub together—we did just that, we all climbed into the tub and had some fun. Our parents were gone—the grandparents from Texas were staying with us. We filled the tub too high. I remember looking up at the wet ceiling in the room beneath the bathroom. Everyone was mad. They were pointing to the wet spot, telling us to get dressed and come back downstairs to get spanked. We all raced upstairs scared to death. We thought frantically about how we could protect ourselves. We decided to put on as many pair of underwear as we could and hope it wasn't noticed. We raced around the room looking for underwear. The memory ends with the command, "Pull down your pants," and a feeling of inevitability.

Story Four

A big black dog that lived behind our house had caught a baby rabbit. With the help of Mom we somehow got the rabbit away from the dog. We put it in a shoe box and fed it with an eyedropper.

I don't know what I was doing in the dark foyer at night or how the rabbit got on the floor. I stepped on it, though. My mom was there. She took the rabbit upstairs to the lighted kitchen and placed it on the cabinet. Looking up at it, I saw that blood was coming out of its nose—I knew it couldn't live.

I reread the stories; I see the scenes, imagining, remembering scenes behind the scene, our dead hamsters, and the white rabbit we had who died after lapping up the milk from the broken milk bottle. I remember and imagine spankings as well as that photo of my girl scout troop and my mother taken at the Statue of Liberty I remember what I typed on the page then and there, in my green robe, and what I didn't.

Over and over again the stories portray separations and isolation. "When I think about this day, I picture myself alone." Educational experience is portrayed as the realization of the betrayed and lonely consciousness, suggesting that whatever is shared in common escapes the distinction that makes it memorable. Educational experience differentiates and separates Catherine from her friends Melinda and Donna Baggot, from her mother who cannot understand what she is saying, and from the owner/mother of the dog. In my green robe I remember the repudiations of my children telling the stories of their lives as if they belonged to them alone, the fiction of their singular identities. I am the listening mother. What happened at school today? It was a long time before anybody asked me that question. Eclipsed, at home, the listener, not the storyteller, I point out to Catherine her apparent investment in her narrative solitude.

In my green robe, I read the Smithsonian story as Catherine's complaint against the maternal arrogation. She has moved into space and time, into science. The Girl Scouts (a paramilitary expression of ambivalent female solidarity if there ever was one) leave her alone to contemplate the universe until she is rebuked by June Smith's mother, frozen forever in her characterization as the one who got lost in the Smithsonian. Falsely accused. Years ago I suggested that she read Sartre's *Saint Genet*.

Story three: infantile sexuality overflows all bounds. Brothers and sisters in the bath together, the water overflows the tub, flows through the floor and ceiling below, leaving the stain. As inevitable as the dog's death, as June Smith's mother's indictment, is the humiliation; yet for all its declarations of fear, the tone is playful, for all its sadism, delighted at its exhibitionism. Or at least, that is how it seems to me, reading in the green robe.

Story four returns to death, a struggle of species that makes the shoe box, eyedropper attentions of the would-be savior poignantly insufficient. In this story the observer and putative victim of stories one to three becomes the killer. In my green robe I read it as the killing of her own babiness, a death which even Mom cannot prevent. Life keeps leaking out in these stories, and the knowledge, communication, and plumbing at our disposal are dreadfully inadequate to the task of containment.

What do I write to Catherine? I point out the contradictions, the inconsistencies, and the leaks: the companion that appears and disappears in story one. The shift from third person to first in story three: "Catherine Fisher should not be allowed to go on any more trips because I was careless enough to get lost." And then I leave loss and love to germinate in the deep pockets of the green robe among the chewing gum wrappers and address those themes in the terms of the course. I invite Catherine to think about her stories and to relate them to questions about education. Is education about discovering what knowledge denies? Is rational knowledge the fallacy that permits us to hide from the unavoidable recognition of our own mortality? Where is the lonely cogito of idealism in the compulsive sociability of progressive education? And I do ask her how June Smith's mother learns to see another woman's child as static when her own body must remember the sequence of changes that she has danced with her child. Catherine will choose. I offer more than she can use.

Whatever is too close or too distant is ignored. If she wants to talk to the green robe, she may work with Winnicott's or with Chodorow's texts.[8] Or she may stick to Plato and Dewey or try Norman O. Brown. My hope is that I have met the furry, bloody, sudsy presence of her text with mine, and that I have offered linguistic connections between her world of rabbits and Girl Scouts and the complex contradictions in the work of teaching and education that fascinate me.

Do I work with other people's children to separate from mine or connect to theirs? The green robe is no negligee. I wrap myself as a maternal body as I relinquish my definition to its green indeterminateness, tactile and cozy, rounding off eroticism. Let my children go.

The teaching mother recovers herself and her children in this discourse. Differentiation is not desertion. In Freudian and Lacanian theory separation from the body of the mother is the loss of her. In Lacanian theory the living body and its semiotics are sacrificed to desire and are swallowed into the sign. But Kristeva offers us a sense of the sign that does not entail utter loss of the mother. The mother looks over her shoulder. The baby follows her gaze. The baby is interesting, even fascinating, to the mother, but so is the news, the novel, talking to grown-ups. In Kelly Oliver's reading of Kristeva, access to the symbolic offers a reunion with the maternal body that is experienced as loving something other than itself.[9] My students stories are interesting to me and so is Kristeva and so is Lacan. The gaze that passes between us includes them. In Oliver's reading the mother's love enacts the transference from the mother's body to the mother's desire. The mother's love provides the needed support for the transference to the site of maternal desire. I am interested in the world. They, sometimes, follow my gaze. They want it because I love it.

With words I am disrobed and articulated. As text, in the typed responses to Catherine and the others, I re-present myself as the object of desire, dressed up in the words of the world. In the mise-en-scène of the classroom, *scholae personae* simultaneously conceals and reveals my leaks, my denied dependencies, my fantasies, my desires.

The green robe stays in the green room.

Notes

A version of this chapter was originally published as M. R. Grumet, "Scholae Personae: Masks for Meaning." In J. Gallop (Ed.), *Pedagogy: The Question of Impersonation* (Bloomington, IN: Indiana University Press, 1995) 36–45.

1. Joan Didion, *On Keeping a Notebook: Slouching toward Bethlehem*. (New York: Dell, 1961) 131–41.
2. Madeleine Grumet William F. Pinar, *Toward a Poor Curriculum*. (Dubuque, IA: Kendall/Hunt, 1976); Carol Gilligan, *In a Different Voice: Psychological Theory and Women's Development* (Cambridge: Harvard University Press, 1982); Dorothy Dinnerstein, *The Mermaid and the Minotaur: Sexual Arrangements and Human Malaise*. (New York: Harper, 1976).
3. James Olney, *Metaphors of Self: The Meaning of Autobiography* (Princeton: Princeton University Press, 1972).
4. William A. Earle, *Autobiographical Consciousness* (Chicago: Quadrangle, 1972).
5. Julia Kristeva, *Tales of Love*. Trans. Leon S. Roudiez (New York: Columbia University Press, 1987).
6. Herbert Blau, "Letting Be Be the Finale of Seem: The Future of an Illusion," *Performance in Postmodern Culture*. Ed. Michel Benamou and Charles Caramello. (Madison, WI: Coda, 1977) 59–77, 75.
7. Madeleine Grumet, *Bitter Milk: Women and Teaching* (Amherst: University of Massachusetts Press, 1988).
8. Nancy Chodorow, *The Reproduction of Mothering. Psychoanalysis and the Sociology of Gender* (Berkeley: University of California Press, 1988).
9. Kelly Oliver, *Reading Kristeva: Unraveling the Double-Bind*. (Bloomington: Indiana University Press, 1993).

CHAPTER 12   *Sandra Weber*

Curse You Descartes! My Academic Gown

My academic gown usually hangs somewhere in the back of a closet—dusty, seldom used, and out of sight. After more than 25 years in the Academy, I still don't even really think of it as *mine* or as something I would ever *choose* to wear. This reluctance is perhaps understandable, considering that, much to my mother's dismay, I categorically refused to wear an academic gown or even attend convocation to pick up my first university degree, a B.A. in Psychology at McGill. It was the 1960s, and I suppose I was simply acting the self-respecting, establishment-hating, pseudo activist, aspiring intellectual, like so many other university students of my era. If someone had told me back then that one day, not only would I eventually routinely wear an academic gown, I would even own one, I think I would have cringed at the thought of wrapping myself in the trappings of grandeur and power, of selling out! Not that I actually went out and bought the gown I now own. It was an unsolicited gift twelve years ago from my second Alma Mater for services rendered. Nonetheless I did keep it—and even said thank you.

To further unravel my ambivalences, I recall now that although I refused to attend my first university convocation, I did allow my mother to convince me to have a graduation photo taken in the academic robe provided by the McGill-approved photographer, Jostens. It wasn't fair of me, my mother said, to deprive her of the pleasure of seeing me walk across the stage. She insisted that the very least I could do to make it up to her was to have a graduation picture taken to put on display.

The photograph was thus duly and hastily procured and entrusted to her maternal custody, along with the diploma written in Latin that was later mailed to me, attesting to my degree. There they remain to this day, stuffed somewhere in the jumble of her basement. I don't even remember putting on the robes for the rushed

Figure 12.1. Photo of the author. University graduation, 1969.

pose, but I *must* have, it's *in the photograph.* So although I stuck to my activist convictions (or what some might label pretensions) by not attending convocation, in sitting for that photo I was nonetheless complicit in the family fiction of a compliant scholar and new member of the Establishment.

Setting idealism and self-delusions aside, the fact is that nowadays I dutifully trot out my academic robes on those occasions when I resign myself to being part of the platform party at convocation ceremonies. I doubt that they would let me up on the stage without it. And you're not supposed to wear just any robe, you are asked to wear one that conforms to the colors and style regulations of the university from which you obtained your last degree.

I never know what to wear *under* the robe (at the University of X, there are strict rules about what to wear underneath, but that is unusual). Should I wear dark pants as I usually do, like the men do, seeking to blend in, first and foremost, as a scholar, showing that women can wear the *pants* as well as the robes of the Academy? Or, should I stress and celebrate my womanhood, standing out from the sea of male scholars by wearing what *they can't* (although perhaps a few of them secretly would like to)—things like nylons, high heels, silky underwear, and a skirt or dress? Should I dress all in black, my habitual choice, so that it is the Academic Robe that is featured? Or, for once, should I wear something silver or gold or bright red that distracts from the gown and features my fondness for fashion eccentricity?

Oh, what does it matter, anyway? Whatever I choose is mostly hidden by the bulk of the robe. And so is my body, for that matter, something I am increasingly grateful for as the pounds slip on and the flesh sags and bulges in ways I had not anticipated when I was younger. Yes, to be honest, I sometimes find myself quite content to hide beneath the gown. And, I hate to admit this, but I think my gown is rather nice. It has beautiful wide blue velvet stripes on the puffy sleeves and blue velvet borders on the front vertical edges. I unobtrusively stroke the soft velvet while seated on stage, a way to calm and distract myself, I suppose.

Robed *nudity* in not an option that ever occurs to me, well, at least, it didn't until writing this piece. It can get so hot up under those stage-lights, that little or no clothes underneath might be a sensible choice if the darned robes weren't so scratchy and flappy. But of course, in Western culture, nudity would not be read as a practical decision, would it?, but rather as . . . as what? An erotic or exhibitionist act? A political stance? A way of privately subverting or mocking the whole meaning of the ceremonies? A thumbing not of one's nose, but of one's privates at the Academy? Perhaps there are some who entertain romantic or erotic notions of the naked academic (male or female) coyly reposing half-robed on a worn leather couch in a twilight wood-panelled office, perhaps with a fire glowing in the stone hearth that seems requisite to such fantasies but so absent in the ugly, modern serviceability of our real university digs.

To each her or his own, I say, but frankly these are not the sorts of preoccupations that occur to me as I stand before the mirror. It's the covering over—not the exposing of the body that concerns me. Never mind my body—look at my Beautiful Mind! In writing this, I am startled, finding myself complicit in that ubiquitous Cartesian myth of Body as separate from and subjugated to Mind. How can that be? Me?! I am thoroughly opposed to that devious dichotomy! Why I have even been known to imagine giving that bastard Rene Descartes a swift kick in the balls and telling him "Think on *that*!" I doubt that I am either the first or the last academic to discover that my theoretical convictions and my practical actions are not always in sync . . .

In the faculty changing room before the ceremony, we struggle to put on our cumbersome gowns, borrowing pins to hold the hoods in place, twisting and turning to make them hang right or, more often than not, just giving up and shrugging them on in any old way. It is mainly the women who peek in mirrors, making a desperate swipe, perhaps, with a comb or a tube of lipstick. And then we march, a straggly line of aging bodies, covered and gowned—men and women alike—robes flapping or gaping, caps, if we wear them, askew, and trying not to trip as we mount the stairs onto the stage.

I hate sitting up there on those hard chairs under hot lights for hours, listening, or pretending to listen, to speeches that are usually too long and often quite boring, trying not to fidget too much . . . And not being able to avoid overhearing the occasional whispered commentary as people parade across the stage:

"Look at her, wearing sandals and green toenail polish on stage, for heaven's sake. That's no way for a professor to dress for convocation."

"Those chemistry professors. They're such flakes."

"Look at her! What a sweetheart—lovely girl."

"Why does he insist on wearing that silly cap? We're not required to any more. It makes him look ridiculous."

"How did he ever make it through the program? One of the worst students I've ever taught."

"What happened to her hair, sticking up all over the place like that—did she forget to comb it?"

"What a lovely gown his university has. I wish my degree was from there."

"Sequins before noon. Whatever is that girl thinking?"

"Turquoise hair! And I thought he was such a mature student!"

These seem rather strange comments when you pause to think that The Academy is not exactly known for its sense of high fashion (!), or if you consider that the stereotype of the absent-minded professor has, for so long, been the image of a lumpish or emaciated, greying or balding male body clothed in ill-fitting and patched jackets, clashing pants and rumpled shirts, with mismatched socks to complete the sorry picture. Although alternative caricatures exist—for example, jeans and lab coats for the scientists or science wannabes, or the de rigeur black-on-black for the deconstructionists, artists, and feminists—the general, and perhaps actively cultivated impression is that we have no time or patience for fashion, no interest in the presentation of our bodies—No, our Cartesian minds are elsewhere, occupied with intellectual matters of great import.

And so, at convocation, covered up as we all are, students and professors, in academic gowns, it thus amazes me to see how often the focus shifts to the bits of body parts and clothes that stick out or that are momentarily "flashed" when a robe gapes open unexpectedly. We seem determined to note the differences, seeking the individual body under the sea of robed sameness. With our eyes and comments we disrobe each other. Are we seeking areas of vulnerability under the armor of our uniforms?

What is the academic robe meant for anyhow? To hide our bodies lest they attract notice or offend or distract from the scholarly mission of our fictive and disembodied Minds? Or are they meant to be a democratic uniform—a safe exemption from fashion's tyranny—a level playing field where differences of size and shape and curves and sexuality and color and tastes do not matter when they are hidden under the robe. I would like to think so, but I don't think history would support such an interpretation.[1]

Perhaps the gown is more accurately viewed as an historical relic—a dress code meant to signal our elite status as supposedly superior knowers, a marker of entitlement—pomp and circumstance and all that. Or, in some symbolic way, the robes may still serve, as they did more literally in twelfth century Britain, as a protection against the dirt and cold of the world—a way of keeping our clothes and bodies warm and clean, part of the stereotypical ivory tower world where we supposedly live in the realm of pure ideas, unsullied by the untidy practicalities of daily life and social struggle.[2] No need to pay heed to the stain of stale coffee or semen or wine or food crumbs or unpaid bills or frayed mismatched clothes or discarded lovers or petty jealousies or fragile egos or failed dreams—just sweep them under the robe!

Is the academic robe the last refuge of scoundrels, or an expression of reverence for learning, continuity with traditions, and a commitment to higher learning? It depends on who wears it and why, doesn't it? In some colleges and private schools, instructors are required to wear academic robes in the classroom. Do we need a material symbol of power to command respect or inspire reverence? Is the gown meant to let others know who the teacher is, so there is no confusion when you walk into a lecture hall? Or, ironically, is the wearing of the robe an egalitarian gesture to put teachers and students in the same confining garb? To "dress up" knowledge? To give in to Descartes, perpetuate the myth of mind/body duality, and continue to cover over the body, cover over our differences, and deny that we learn through our bodies, that we *are* our bodies? Who decides what a robe, a simple piece of cloth, means? Whose "reality" are we dressing?

Notes

1. With "femmage" to the work of Madeleine Grumet and due apologies to René Descartes! (See, for example, W. N. Hargreaves-Mawdsley, *A History of Academic Dress in Europe until the End of the Eighteenth Century* (Oxford: Clarendon Press, 1963).
2. G. W. Shaw, *Academical Dress of British and Irish Universities* (Chichester, U.K.: Phillimore, 1995).

CHAPTER 13

Lorri Neilson Glenn

Basic Black: A Wardrobe Primer for Seasoned Academic Women

1. On the Feet:

   birks sandals (well, yeah—granola, hormone-free, left-wing, high on fruit & veggie-intake index), long-serving official footwear of many women's studies faculties, a safe bet;

   thick-soled clogs (kinda funky, give extra height for gatherings, convey soft, non-threatening authority, stability, and, like the birks, a whiff of the European, but not, you hope, in a Western colonial androcentric sort of way);

   ankle-length boots, lace-up, best with black tights & long skirt or slim dark pants & leather jacket—both jacket & boots required for urban academic enclaves where vestigial Marxism mixes with multi-syllabic discourse—you look good, even while making propositions no one can understand;

   pumps, low, sensible heels, say "I am conservative, dependable, I follow through," good with knee-length slim skirt or casual suit if you can wear tights and avoid nylons, perfect for interviews & talks to community groups, shoes you thought you'd grow up to wear more often but don't, or hardly ever.

2. On the Top:

   tank, in heavy cotton, washable but fade-resistant, for under casual jackets & large shirts (no, not "blouses"), says: "I aim to co-ordinate, can layer, am prepared for varying room temperatures and body fluctuations"—downside is potential for exposing flapping upper arms, so keep over-shirt on anyway;

tee shirt, also in washable cotton or a poly-mix, great with jeans (black, yes, but not too faded), together they lengthen the line, hide ten pounds, say maybe butch, maybe not, but don't mess with me in any case;

turtleneck, cotton or wool, large enough to cover hipline and rear inflation, worn as honorific of the early beats from the late Fifties, but now, in your own fifties, you know that all women were allowed to make for the revolution then was love, oh, & the coffee, but still, great item to hide wattles, chicken neck syndrome, disguise a flat chest or ample one. Cool. Arty. Thrifty. Potential for irony, with a certain self-parody. A kind of you know I know, but, like, whatever.

3. On the Bottom:

jeans, faded blue and slightly ripped (with lone tank, above, to show your sculpted arms) if you're a single-digit body, black denim in all sizes for the majority, but choose your label carefully: since Vogue ads and the female work force of developing nations don't mix, try second-hand stores & discount houses so your conscience doesn't bite more than the zipper;

leggings, stretch pants, biking shorts, & other all-purpose bottom slimmers, early morning easy choices since there is too much to think about—124 emails & 14 letters of reference & overdue grades & a lost independent study portfolio & you can't find your keys & your son forgot to give you the release form to sign & the bus leaves in three minutes—great with shirts, long sweaters & vests, tunics (no, not your old school ones, although with a few piercings & the right coloured hair, say, fuchsia, for example, & a pair of old Docs, you could get away with it), perfect for most climates in the far north or the Antipodean far south, can be bundled with thick socks for a retro Flashdance effect, or at least to keep your busy feet warm.

4. Beneath the Surface:

underwear, no bra, or a sturdy functional one, not like those you saw at twelve in Photoplay ads for Frederick's of Hollywood, D-cups like the head of the Tin Man in Oz, lace that promised full-bodied unravelling some time in her future (but good lord, not your future, you were not going to be one of those women, you vowed to your friend as you flipped pages for the story on Eddie & Liz & Debbie, secretly hoping you might be, maybe once or twice in a hotel room in a large exotic city), yes, a good serviceable bra for everyday with straps that don't peek out of the tank top, layers that cover your punctuation in the cold air, perhaps a push-up one too for nights you plan on having more than one glass of scotch but without the lace—on the bra, that is—because you have a mind, after all, and know we're all female impersonators, all in drag, dress-up, the human carnival and all that;

and speaking of, yes the final, must-have: the brief—
(you have found it hard for your lips & tongue to articulate "pantie"—it sounds so ditsy, so girlie-girl yet you regret using—okay—*appropriating* the male term)—all cotton, if possible, but cotton gusset mandatory, mid-length or bikini, smooth elasticized trim barely perceptible under your jeans or skirt as you reach for a reference book or bend down to pick up your pen in the hall when you run into the dean. Comfort is the key here, room to move, to breathe, the first covering on your body in the morning, the last off at night. Simple, affordable. A bite of zest, hint of passion. And private, for your eyes only. But no safety pins (remember what your mother said). No iron, no irony. No comment, no commentary. At least not outside your own bedroom, nor outside that hotel room off Bourbon Street one night years ago, the scotch—no, was it Jack Daniels?—and you were late for your keynote the next morning, wore a too-tight outfit & a too-loose grin,

but that's another primer, another field of semiotics, one in which your needs for all of the above were fewer, and your desires not greater, perhaps, but different. Ah, those days, rolling in the seasons of your skin, in the sartorial splendor of glistening, feral flesh. You—raucous, ravenous. Primal. Basic.

PART IV

Dress Rituals and Mothers

CHAPTER 14 *Annette Kuhn*

A Credit to Her Mother

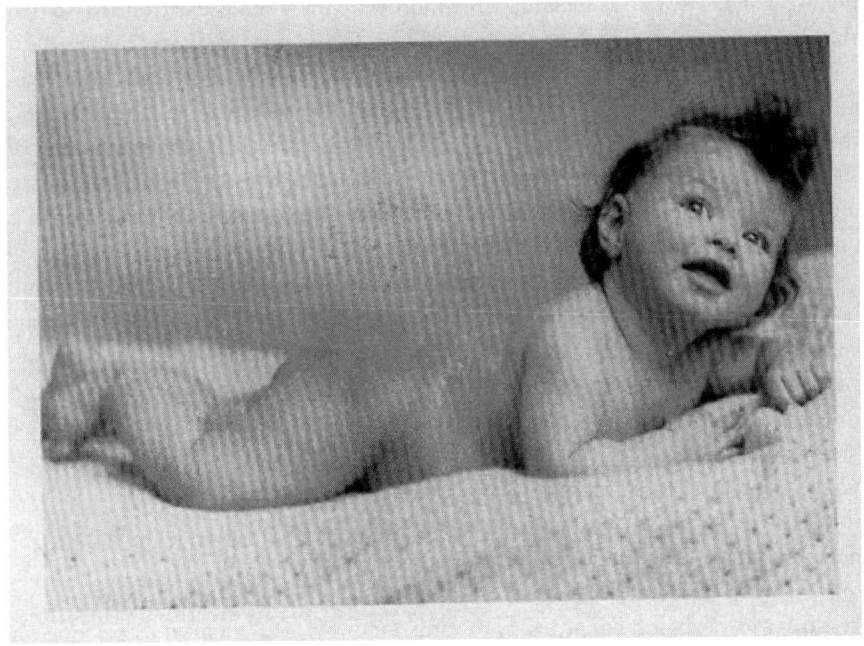

Figure 14.1. Photo of author as infant.

My family photograph collection includes two copies of the same studio portrait of myself at four months of age. The baby is naked, lying tummy-down on a blanket, facing camera but looking upwards to a point somewhere above camera level. This, as far as I know, is the earliest photograph taken of me; and one of my copies of it accordingly features on the very first page of the photograph album I began putting together when I was eight, in an effort to make both a family and a life history for myself. The other copy, sent to me by my mother long after I had left home, grown up, and broken contact with her, bears a lengthy inscription on the reverse:

> Thought perhaps you might like this. You were a beautiful baby from the minute you were born. I loved you and you were always immaculate and well cared for. Your hair was very dark and there is a great resemblance to Marion and Samantha. Written in pencil, you may want to erase.

This inscription, pointing up a likeness between my infant self and my two nieces, the only daughters of my two much older half brothers, was obviously written at the time the picture was sent to an adult and estranged daughter. The copy of the picture which carries this message—my mother's copy—has been trimmed, so that the area of the image which had been background and not baby is cut away.

Two copies of the same photograph, then, but embodying very different uses and meanings at different moments for the various people with investments in it: the parents of the newly born baby, the child herself as a little girl, the mother of the adult daughter, the daughter as an adult. In itself, the image carries meanings outside these immediate contexts, too, revealing a great deal about how infancy is understood in a particular social and cultural situation.

The baby's nakedness, suggesting newness, naturalness, innocence, is set within particular conventions of photographic portraiture, which in turn mimic high art conventions—notably, but not exclusively, those of the (adult, female) nude—suggesting that this is no mere snapshooter's effort, but a professional piece of work. In the process, babyhood in general, a particular baby, and a specific image are made special; lifted out of the ordinary, the everyday. My photograph is in these respects no different from the thousands, the millions even, like it: it speaks volumes about the cultural meanings of infancy, the desires our culture invests in the figure of the newborn child. But while such meanings are certainly present in the specific contexts in which images like this are produced and used, every image is special, too: gesturing towards particular pasts, towards memories experienced as personal, it assumes inflections that are all its own. My photograph, then, is the same, and yet it is different.

On the surface, the family photograph functions primarily as a record: it stands as visible evidence that this family exists, that its members have gone through the passages conventionally produced in the family album as properly and necessarily familial. My photograph thus records the fact that a particular child was born and survived. But recording is the very least of it. Why should a moment be recorded, if not for its evanescence? The photograph's seizing of a moment always, even in that very moment, assumes loss. The record looks towards a future time when things will be different, anticipates a need to remember what will soon be past.

Even for outsiders, family photographs often have a poignant quality, perhaps because they speak all too unerringly of the insufficiency, the hopelessness, of the desire they embody. Time has passed, time will pass. The image of the infant, innocent in its nakedness, naked as the day it was born, cannot so much fix that moment of innocence as testify to the inevitability of its slipping away, of a slippage from grace. Hence the sadness, the sense of loss and longing, I read in my mother's words. "You were beautiful," she says; beautiful, pristinely, "from the minute you were born." Her choice of the word immaculate here is telling: I was, she recalls, spotless, unsullied, free from sin or stain; precisely in a state of Edenic innocence.

Perhaps the mother's recollection speaks a degree of identification with the baby—a desire that she, the mother, might partake of the newborn's innocence; that in giving birth she too will have been reborn, granted the gift not just of innocence but of a fresh start. More specifically, the immaculate may be read back to the baby's very conception; as an expression of my mother's wish (which might well have been retrospective—written into the past constructed by her inscription, that is) to have been my only begetter, for me to have been hers alone. The reference to my nieces, my brothers' daughters (one of whom I have never met)—in effect negating the role in my conception of the man I knew as my father, who was not the father of my brothers—would certainly support this reading.

It seems, then, that the mother's love for her baby, not least in its retrospective assertion, is far from unambivalent. "I loved you," she tells the grownup daughter who has left her. Loved me once, that is, in my immaculate, unspoiled state. Which suggests that this love had a hard time, and very likely failed, to outlive the loss of innocence, to survive the baby's growing older and the mother's learning the hard lesson that life carries on much as before, except that now there is another mouth—and one that talks back, into the bargain—to feed.

In readings which shift back and forth across contexts—from the cultural to the familial to the individual to a specific constellation of family relations—the notion constantly re-emerges, in different shapes and forms, of infancy as spotlessness, innocence; and of the figure, the image, of the newly born child as embodying at once a desire for return to innocence and a knowledge of the absolute impossibility of such a return.

It is also clear, though, that the naked and immaculate body of the newborn Annette figured for my mother as *tabula rasa*, an empty slate, on which her own desires could be written—in an endeavor, perhaps, to repair lacks of her own. Born fourth in a family of seven, the fourth daughter of a man who desperately wanted a son, she felt she had never been wanted, loved, or cared for enough, certainly by her father (in her account a violent man and a poor provider) who despite—or perhaps because of—his absence at war figured overwhelmingly in her childhood memories. (In a book-length memoir written when she was in her sixties, my mother recalls her father's first return home on leave from the war:

> [I]t was in 1915, and our Dad seemed to have been away for ever. But one day during the Summer holidays when we were playing on Moor Mead, a girl came running up to us and said, "I think your dad's come home. A soldier went in your house." Without waiting to hear the last of what she was saying, I was on my way home, my bare feet hardly touching the warm pavement . . . There in the kitchen was my dad, sitting in an armchair near the fireplace. I wanted to climb all over him, but before I could reach him, he said in a very stern voice, "Where's your shoes? Put them on at once! . . . ")

It seems clear to me today that my mother's love for the "immaculate" baby Annette was marked very much by a quest to love the abandoned and unloved child she felt she had been: in other words, that this maternal love involved a work of identification; identification then subjected to threat through that erosion of the ideal that comes with the inevitable loss of the innocence attaching to the figure of the baby. My mother's inscription on, and indeed within, the photograph, made when her baby had grown up and to all intents and purposes had decisively separated herself, speaks with some eloquence of these investments, their failure, her disappointment.

In the Eden myth, the moment of the fall from primal innocence is marked by Adam and Eve's covering their nakedness; and, significantly, in the family album nakedness is admissible only in photographs of babies and very young children. My mother tells me that not only was I beautiful in my natural state, from the minute I was born; I was always well cared for, too—well cared for, of course, by her: well turned out, in another favorite phrase of hers. Immaculate here then partakes not only of the natural but also of the cultural: the newborn's primal innocence is overdetermined by—is perhaps even subsumed to—the mother's labor of care for her child. When my mother says I was well cared for, I know quite well that she is referring as much, if not more, to a public presentation of a well turned out child ("a credit to her mother," she would often say of Marion, the niece whom she maintains I resembled) as to any less outwardly apparent caring or maternal love on her part. Or rather, perhaps, that for her the two things are inseparable: one loves one's baby, of course; and the evidence and the guarantee of that love lie in the labor of care evident in the child's appearance. But there is more to this than mere display. The baby's body is here quite literally a blank canvas, screen of the mother's desire—desire to make good the insufficiencies of her own childhood, desire to transcend these lacks by caring for her deprived self through a love for her baby that takes very particular cultural forms.

In my mother's account, her childhood was deprived materially as well as emotionally, and for her the two types of lack were inseparably intertwined. In this context, loving becomes synonymous with having—or rather with being given—enough to eat and decent clothes to wear (the detail of the unshod feet in her memory of her father's homecoming is, I think, significant). This perhaps explains the enormous investment, in all senses of the word, in my appearance: not just in my clothes, but in my hair, which for special occasions, and with huge effort on her part and much discomfort on mine, my mother would tie in rags to make the ringlets she herself had worn, or would have wanted, as a little girl. As I grew older, she took an interest in my body language as well, trying to get me to stand straight and not slouch: "Back up, tummy in!" For if I failed to be well turned out, that failure would surely be hers, and she would be exposed as a bad person: not just an unloving mother, but—worse, perhaps—an unloved and unlovable little girl.

I am my mother's only daughter, and her youngest child, always to my irritation referred to as her baby. My childhood was none the less punctuated by many births in the family, of the children of my two brothers and of numerous extraordinarily fecund cousins: births of babies and talk about babies were, it seemed, endless. Among the favorite topics of conversation, especially among girls and women in the family, was the sex of a forthcoming baby: will it be a boy or a girl? And which would be preferable? There was a solid, perhaps an overwhelming, body of opinion that girl babies were on the whole the better deal, because you can dress a little girl up.

On this conscious level, at least, a mother's attention to her baby's appearance has everything to do with gender: her love for a girl infant will be legitimately expressed in ways different from her love of a baby boy. Significantly, my mother's description of my niece Marion as "a credit to her mother" was never applied to Marion's two younger brothers.

In the summer before my fourth birthday, a photograph was taken (possibly by my father) of my mother and me on the front lawn of our ground-floor flat in Chiswick, West London. It is the only picture I have of myself as a small child with my mother. In this one, I am seated on my mother's knee as she grips me firmly in the crook of her left arm and rests her right hand across my ankles. We are both looking at the camera, and I am clutching a doll and wearing a tartan dress with puffed sleeves and matching underpants, and a bow in my hair. On the back of this photograph my mother has written: ". . . Chiswick. She was nearly 4 years old. Dress and knicks by me." Again the picture has been trimmed, and part of the inscription cut away as a consequence.

This picture disturbs me somewhat: a feeling, I think, which has a lot to do with my mother's uncharacteristic presence in the image. On the surface, it seems a

Figure 14.2. Photo of author as a child.

commonplace and happy enough example of family photography. But beneath the sunny facade lurk shadows: the mother-father-daughter triad the picture (assuming it was made by my father) points to was not in fact a real family. The child being held so tightly was an intrusion. If I put myself in the position of my mother as she was at the time this photo was taken, somewhat younger than I am now, all sorts of ambivalences surface.

She holds on firmly to this little girl who is hers, whom she perhaps desires to be hers alone. But children, as she would often remind me, tie you down. When I came along, unintended, her younger son was thirteen and she thought she was finished with childrearing. Life had not been easy with the boys and their father, and now in her late thirties she was hoping, at last, for a good time. If she did find a bit of fun with my father, though, she had been thrown back to square one by its consequences: me. Trapped in a situation she had not bargained for, my mother was tied for the foreseeable future to a child she had neither planned nor wanted to have, and (in days when the concept of the single-parent family had yet to be invented) to a man she would grow to despise.

But if the child was a mistake, she was not entirely a misfortune: she was a beautiful baby from the minute she was born, her mother's only daughter, who would always be her baby. The care and pride that have been lavished on the little girl's appearance are visible in this picture, which is readable—and, I would contend, was certainly read by my mother—as evidence, proof of that care. This is underlined in the statement, seemingly addressed to no one in particular, that the little girl's outfit was of her, the mother's, own making.

Children are a costly commodity: their upbringing calls for hard cash, as well as a good deal of labor of various kinds. This, though (we are told), ought to be a labor of love, entered into freely and without reservation. Counting the cost is not appropriate. Sure enough, the family as it is represented in family albums is characteristically produced as innocent of such material considerations, above price: to this extent, the family album constructs the world of the family as a utopia. And yet I feel sure that my mother, whose own childhood had been so marked by poverty, must have known, or even calculated, the exact cost—to herself, at least—of having and keeping me. Perhaps in my earliest years her economic and her emotional investments measured up to each other, so that her identifications—of her baby with the unloved little girl in herself—could proceed unchecked. In these honeymoon years, being the mother of a well turned out baby must have provided enormous pleasure and emotional reward.

Keeping up appearances could not have been easy, though. From my earliest years, perhaps right from my infancy, both my parents worked outside the home. When I was very small, they shared responsibility for cleaning the public areas of the block of flats where we lived and of which my father was caretaker. They also worked together in my father's photography business, and both had jobs as bus conductors. While I do not know whether these jobs were simultaneous or consecutive, nor indeed whether there were any periods when my mother was actually at home full-time, it seems clear that a lot of hard work was being done to earn the means to keep the household going; and that there would have been little by way of leisure time for my mother to pursue dressmaking as a hobby. Since, however, clothes were still on the ration, in common with many other items during the years of postwar austerity, she would simply have had to find the time to make do and mend. In this climate, making clothes for herself and her baby was probably a necessity more than a hobby.

Whatever the case, though, keeping the baby immaculate and well cared for, while a source of pride and pleasure, must still have cost a good deal of effort. Hence the ambivalent feelings of a mother whose life and circumstances had been, indeed remained, far from easy toward a baby born into a world which held out the promise of new opportunities for the children of ordinary working people; a baby, moreover, who seemed to be the object of all the love and attention she herself had been denied; a baby, none the less, who would one day grow into a woman in a society still unkind to those of her sex.

Thus may a mother's investments in her baby daughter, inflected by particular circumstances of time, place, culture, and class, meld the social with the psychic. This mother's ambivalent identification with her baby daughter already contains the seeds of overidentification, of difficulties of separation. If a daughter figures for her mother as the abandoned, unloved, child that she, the mother, once was and in some ways remains, how can mother and daughter disengage themselves from these identifications without harm, without forfeiture of love? How can mother and daughter learn to acknowledge that they are separate people, to respect their differences from each other?

Any resolution, it seems, must come with very great difficulty: there will inevitably come a moment when it is no longer possible for the mother to sustain the fantasy of her daughter as *tabula rasa*, of the daughter's body as screen of her own fantasies of plenitude. The child will one day start answering back, refusing the mother's gifts, along with the vision of the perfect, immaculate, well turned out little girl. At this point, matters of appearance, including clothes, may well cease to be a source of pleasure for the mother, and even become a site of struggle between mother and daughter.

You can dress a little girl up is one of those statements, certainly in the context in which I quote it here, whose truth is assumed to be perfectly self-evident. It points to one of the obvious and most important pluses of having (and not, it should be noted, of being) a baby girl. As a piece of conventional wisdom, it condenses a range of commonplace and generally unremarked cultural associations between dress and gender. But it also asserts a good deal more than that, say, there exist distinct forms and styles of dress which are very much tied to gender. It implies as well that the ways in which we actually relate to clothes and to matters of appearance in general are a ground, as much as an outcome, of sexual difference.

If, for infants themselves, sexual difference is hardly yet an issue, it certainly figures very prominently, and often in unconscious and contradictory ways, in adults' attachments to babies and very young children. Dressing a little girl up is held to be an occasion of rightful and proper pleasure, and reward, for its mother; the unspoken corollary perhaps being that while a boy will obviously have to be clothed, this is more of a functional necessity, and that to dress him up in a way that goes beyond tidiness or smartness might be inappropriate. In this particular social, historical and cultural context, at least, the investments in a mother's dressing a boy baby and dressing up a girl baby are assumed to be quite distinct. In this context it may well be inadmissible for a mother to claim, by word or deed, any pleasure in dressing a little boy up, as opposed to merely dressing him. For this in effect would be a confession that she was disturbing the natural and proper order of gender difference: making a sissy of him.

But even such a forceful prohibition as this cannot account for the positive pleasure a mother may take in dressing up her little girl. For the mother, the labor of attending to the appearance of a girl baby is surely of a very particular kind: it is caught up in that series of investments and identifications at play in general in her care of her little daughter. Dressing up a baby girl is a socially sanctioned opportunity for a woman, in caring for the little girl in herself, to love herself; while at the same time providing her with the opportunity to display, for the public gaze, the praiseworthy qualities of an adult who puts the needs of others above her own: a good mother, in other words, and therefore a good woman.

In a number of ways, therefore, having a baby girl she can dress up might be intensely rewarding for a mother. However, distinctions between dressing and dressing up on the one hand and between having and being a baby girl on the other signal areas of potential contradiction, and are thus perhaps worthy of further exploration. Dressing up as opposed to mere dressing implies, as has been suggested, a more than purely functional attitude towards clothes: it points to the element of display, of performance, inherent in certain relations to dress. Clothes are what you put on and take off, and consequently various identities may—sometimes quite consciously—be created across the surface of dress. This element of performance holds within it the potential of prying apart the gender/dress association, and this in turn can disturb the order of gender difference naturalized in certain clothing styles.

The naturalized order of gender difference rests on more than just the forms and styles of dress, on differences as it were in the content of clothing: it is a question of forms of relation to personal appearance more generally, to the entire realm of bodily adornment. Dressing up—like its cognate activities making up and doing one's hair—suggests a relation of fabrication, construction, production. Herein lies an interesting paradox: dressing up a baby is possible, indeed socially acceptable, provided—and because—the baby is a girl; while (less consciously, perhaps) dressing up will also actually produce any baby, male or female, as feminine. As long as one baby in its clothes could look much like any other, outwardly visible marks of gender (the colour coding of baby clothes, for example) acquire a certain importance. In this context, while dressing up is part of the production of gender, it also gestures towards the very artifice of that production.

A mother's attention to the clothing and general appearance of a baby girl, then, is part of the social, cultural, and undoubtedly also the psychical, construction of gender; specifically, of course, of femininity. It fabricates something we are supposed to believe is natural, already there; and so reminds us that femininity is not in fact a given, but a product of labor. But in the specific instance of a mother's dressing up a baby girl, the labor involved is also imbued with particular investments of desire, fantasy and identification; with the body of the baby figuring as pretext for what will be experienced as an enjoyable creativity. In this sense, the baby girl becomes its mother's muse, its body her canvas, the dressed-up little girl her mother's very own work of art: to be looked at, admired, photographed, and hailed as a credit to her mother.

The often arduous and time-consuming work of producing a well turned out baby girl then becomes an end in itself, its results apparent, its use value palpable. This is visible and unalienated labor, whose product bears, for all the world to see, the signature of its maker: indeed, the most satisfying sort of work. The end product becomes identified with, reflects back on, the worker herself, the mother, just as it constitutes the baby as a little girl. As, through this labor, femininity is produced in and through costume, through masquerade, so a mother's investment accrues to her own credit. Clothes, as they make the little girl, also make the grown woman.

The mother's fantasy of identification (in which she cares for her little daughter as she would be cared for herself, and produces the baby in herself as a beautiful little girl worthy and deserving of love) rests upon a degree of projection, the baby its object, its screen. In the processes of projection and identification, the baby is fantasized as part of the mother—who can then simultaneously have, and be, the baby girl. In both senses, the baby becomes her mother's possession, and the play with femininity involved in dressing her up part of the mother's own involvement with femininity and its paradoxes, its ambiguities, and its masquerades.

In this respect, the mother's pleasure in dressing up her baby girl may not be entirely unalloyed. Aside from the possibility that her care for the child could be an attempt to repair, to compensate for, deprivations in her own childhood—in its very nature a highly problematic project—the mother must on some level also be aware that the femininity she is calling forth in the masquerade of the dressed-up little girl is not without its complications and contradictions in the world beyond the mother-baby dyad.

Related to this must be the virtual inevitability of the mother's fantasy of oneness with her baby girl coming unraveled: for as the child grows older the fantasy of the baby as the screen of its mother's desire will become increasingly difficult to sustain. It is here that the distinction between having a baby girl and being a girl child comes into play. What happens when the child herself intervenes in the dressing up process, perhaps to assert her own wishes about her appearance? How, in such a circumstance, can a mother protect her investment? How can the child continue to be a credit to her mother? And what sort of story might the little girl herself have to tell about all this?

One of the manifestations of my own mother's involvement with her daughter's appearance was a passion for fancy dress. My photograph collection bears witness to the fact that, until I was around eight or nine years old, I took part in numerous fancy dress competitions. This was entirely my mother's idea: she entered me in the contests, made the costumes, and exhorted me to display them to best advantage. A frequently expressed conviction of hers had it that costumes she called original (which for her meant conceptual as opposed to mimetic) stood the greatest chance of winning; and that if an original costume did fail to net a prize, it was still far superior as fancy dress to the obvious, and perhaps more acceptable, sorts of costumes little girls might be dressed in for these occasions—nursery rhyme characters, fairies, princesses, brides and suchlike. While I cannot in truth say I would have preferred any of the more conventionally little girlish costumes, in what I did wear I nevertheless did feel exhibited, exploited, embarrassed. Even if I won, there was little pleasure in competing in this way—in being put on display, scrutinized, weighed up, given points, judged. As I grew older, I grew less willing and no doubt decreasingly compliant.

A photograph of me wearing the costume for what I believe to be the last fancy dress competition I entered shows me, aged about nine, wearing a long shift to which are attached empty cigarette packets, drinks cartons, ice-cream containers, drinking straws, matchboxes; with a head-dress comprised of one waxed Kia-Ora orange juice carton flanked by a pair of ice-cream tubs. On my right arm rests a placard explaining the costume "Cinema Litter"; and on my left a jigsaw puzzle, presumably my prize. It is difficult to put a precise date to this photograph, partly because, like the others, it has been trimmed down: the background is consequently minimal, offering no clues as to location; and whatever had been written on the back of the picture has been almost completely cut away.

(I find myself extraordinarily, perhaps excessively, troubled by this habit of my mother's of cutting photographs down. The historian in me objects to the tampering with evidence; the critic to the lack of respect for image composition. But the strength of the feeling really has to do with the fact that these acts of my mother's seem to me to be crude gestures of power, at once both creating the evidence that fits in with her version of events and destroying what does not; and also negating the skills and aesthetic choices of the photographer, usually my father. This particular photograph certainly looks like one of my father's efforts: if so, it must be among the last pictures of me he made, for by this time he had more or less given up what was in any case by now no more than a hobby.)

In the context of my own memories, I see this photograph, which I find very painful to look at, as a cusp image, marking a transition. It must have been made

Figure 14.3. Photo of author as a child.

around the time of our move; away from my first home in Chiswick to live in the house of my recently deceased Granny, my mother's mother. This move was highly traumatic for me, in large part (as I now construe it) because although they remained together, leaving Chiswick marked some decisive rift between my parents.

Our new home was very much my mother's territory: it had been lived in not only by her mother, but before that by one of her brothers. Over the following few years she saw to it that both her sons moved with their families into other houses on the same street. In all this, I believe my father must have felt increasingly marginalized: illness—he suffered from bronchitis which later became emphysema—by now dominated his life and isolated him from those closest to him. This, along with his abandonment of the hobby of photography, which had been a source of such pride and pleasure, must surely be symptomatic. I, too, felt displaced: in my new school, corporal punishment—completely alien and shocking to me—was practiced; I was mocked by the other children for my posh accent; I even caught head lice and had to have my plaits chopped off. Desperately unhappy, I started putting on weight.

It was around this time, too, that I started answering back, embarking on a lengthy and bitter struggle with my mother over issues of separation—issues which would never finally be resolved. I recall feeling unhappy about being put into this particular costume and into the fancy dress competition, and had doubtless let my objections be known in the various overt and covert ways of the uncompliant child—whining, sulks, refusal to smile and a general slouching on parade. If the photograph itself reveals nothing of all this, neither, though, does it seem to me to present an entirely untroubled surface.

The girl looks neglected and slightly scruffy, a far cry from the immaculate three-year-old. Little effort seems to have been put into her hair, badly cut (could this have been soon after the head lice episode?) and all over the place; her smile seems slightly doubtful; her eyes are closed. The costume is even more illuminating. In itself, it is certainly a clever idea: but more remarkable is the fact that the child wearing it is being displayed as a figure for the detritus, the discarded byproducts, of a pursuit whose pleasures hold a distinctly erotic appeal. The implications scarcely need spelling out: it is fortunate, perhaps, that this was to be the last of my fancy dress costumes.

My mother's passion for fancy dress can be regarded in certain respects as an extension of her earlier investment in dressing up her infant daughter: though there is undoubtedly more to it than that. As a cultural form, fancy dress gestures with some urgency towards the performance aspect of clothes. Indeed, it renders this aspect entirely overt: for the whole point of fancy dress is that the masquerade is there, self-evident, on the surface. Fancy dress partakes of the carnivalesque, a turning upside-down of the everyday order of hierarchies of class, status, gender, ethnicity. A bus conductor's daughter can be queen for an hour—or even, indeed, king, for girls can be boys and boys girls, and either can be neither. A fracturing of the clothes/identity link is thus sanctioned—at once permitted and contained, that is—by the cultural conventions of fancy dress.

Also, and relatedly, there is clearly a fantasy component to fancy dress: indeed, the word fancy itself derives from a contraction of fantasy. But whose fantasy? In the case of "Cinema Litter," as of the other fancy dress costumes my mother made for me, certainly not the little girl's, certainly not the daughter's. Costume which presents itself so unequivocally as performance or masquerade will often—and certainly in the case of "Cinema Litter"—beg for a symptomatic reading. But while an interpretation of "Cinema Litter" reveals meanings tied specifically to a particular costume and context, taken together with all the other fancy dress costumes my mother made for me (and certainly if it is accepted that one of the issues at stake here is a mother's identification with her daughter) this can be seen as expressive also of fantasies of a rather different nature: the desire of a working woman, no longer young, to be noticed—seen, applauded, rewarded—as someone special, different from the rest, out of the ordinary, precisely an original. The daughter in fancy dress, attracting attention, winning prizes even, becomes a vehicle for the mother's desire to transcend the limitations, dissatisfactions and disappointments of her own daily life.

But given the conceptual and/or the androgynous quality of the costumes she favored, it seems to me that at this point my mother's fantasy had little to do with femininity as a site of redemption, and much to do with a wish to overcome the limitations femininity imposes. To this extent, the unconscious aspect of the fancy dress project either runs somewhat counter to the earlier project of producing a "well turned out" little girl, or underscores the contradictions and ambivalences around femininity that were already, perhaps, lurking in the latter.

While all this might bespeak resistance, or signal the (limited?) liberatory potential of certain cultural practices for individuals and social groups who lack power in the public world, it should not be forgotten whose fantasy it was that drove these particular practices of dressing up and the fancy dress. For the little Annette, her mother was all-powerful; and it seems never to have occurred to her, the mother, that her daughter could possibly harbor genuine feelings or wishes or hopes or ambitions that in any way diverged from her own, the mother's.

What, then, of the daughter's story: the daughter put on display, exhibited to the public gaze in a quest for rewards from strangers for costumes, for outward appearances, that by nature and intent cloak, occlude and subvert—as well as create—identities? What if the daughter was not entirely comfortable with such identities, with being the site of another's investments, the vehicle of another's fantasies? What of the daughter who refused to smile prettily at the judges, refused to want to be picked out from all the others as a winner, and yet who found utterly unbearable the humiliation of losing? What of her? That little girl got fat, looked terrible in everything she wore, and answered back. What a disappointment to her mother.

Note

Originally published as a chapter in Annette Kuhn, *Family Secrets: Acts of Memory and Imagination* (London & New York: Verso, 1995) 40–58.

CHAPTER 15   *Jennifer Musial*

Fashioning Pregnancy: The Maternity Dress in Clothing Catalogues

As a woman who has never been pregnant, the embodied experience of pregnancy has always struck me with what French psychoanalyst Julia Kristeva calls, a "fascinated rejection."[1] The inhabitation of the female body has consistently reminded me of a parasitic alien, waiting to break out of the body through the violent process known as childbirth. On the one hand, while I understand pregnancy in scientific language, it still remains an embodied enigma to me—how *does* something seemingly just materialize inside a woman? On the other hand, there is a certain repulsion, a cultural construction I have come to discover, to the protruding pregnant body. The seemingly small layer of tissue separating a fetus from the outside world is not an adequate buffer for someone such as myself who is sometimes-squeamish about bodily processes. Yet, as a woman, pregnancy is thought to be my biological imperative, the only way I will be truly accepted as "woman" in contemporary Western culture. So, why *is* pregnancy such a mystery to me?

Most people look at me with interest when I say that my research examines representations of the pregnant body in popular culture, with specific emphasis on how this potentially transgressive corporeality is contained through dominant ideology in media products. This subject ultimately leads them to question whether I secretly desire to be pregnant myself. This assumption is telling: obviously, thinking about pregnancy assumes an inner desire to be pregnant. If anything, I have become more firm in my wish to remain childless. This decision is arrived at through the examination of how pregnancy is contained in contemporary Western culture, treated more like a disability than an everyday occurrence.

I began my query into maternity clothes in 2000. Why do women buy them? When? How do women who cannot afford the expense make do? What options are available in terms of clothing styles; and, importantly, how do images of the clothes represent dominant ideology while marginalizing women who do not fit the social status quo? When I tell women that I'm writing about maternity clothes, more often than not, they're excited to discuss their experiences. Surprisingly, most women offer their insights without any prompting; it is as if they have never been asked about the subject and are excited to share their stories with someone. At a conference in Toronto, I began talking to one woman about my project and as another woman joined into the conversation, they began to commiserate with each other about buying and wearing maternity apparel. Overall, what I have found is that women really want to talk about this phase of the pregnancy experience. There are many stories to tell, and it is a neglected area of pregnancy discourse and gender identity theory. So this project represents one way of looking at the relationship between the liminal experience of pregnancy and "fashioned" social identity.

Clothing acts as both signifier and signified of gendered embodiment. What is worn on the body is meant to be a reflection of identity, but this relationship becomes problematic when that identity is in flux, or in a liminal state. Pregnancy is one embodied temporality that traditionally necessitates a change in a woman's wardrobe. However, the decision to purchase maternity clothes is not without negotiation; once a woman chooses to wear said attire, she publicly announces her pregnancy, and, in effect, her embodied experience becomes public discourse. Many first-time pregnant women recount their experiences shopping for maternity clothes as a rite of passage, and a time when they reflect on their lives pre-pregnancy and look forward to their new social role, and identity, as "mothers."

Pregnancy is as much a social experience as it is a personal one; a time when dominant ideology dictates the proper pregnant subject, and prescribes what is acceptable for a "mom-to-be." As a liminal body, pregnant corporeality is threatening because it refuses categorization. This potentially transgressive embodiment is diffused through maternity wear, either through infantilizing or matronizing the wearer. This method of containing the body can be seen not only through garment styles, but more importantly the representations of pregnant models as they appear in maternity clothing catalogues. Catalogue shopping fosters a particular lifestyle in an attempt to appeal to a target consumer. Through examining the representations of pregnancy in the JC Penney and Pumpkin Maternity catalogues, class differentials can be deciphered to understand how dominant ideology works on the working–middle-class consumer, while the message presented to the middle–upper-class woman is more subversive in tone.

Originally, I was looking for a representation of the pregnant body that went beyond the dreaded "cutesy" bows I had heard so much about. I thought that design was a thing of the past; this was the year 2000, surely there must be more progressive clothes for pregnant women now? The first catalogue I picked up was the JC Penney spring/summer 2001 maternity collection.

Figure 15.1. "Front Cover." JC Penney Maternity Collection Catalogue. Spring/Summer 2001.

My response was one of consternation with the white, Madonna-esque connotation of this picture.[3] While it is common to find a white woman representing the beauty aesthetic in Western-European culture, I was startled by the Aryan nature of this image—the blond, blue-eyed, white child accompanied by the blond, white woman reminds that the Caucasian standard of beauty prevails, even in maternity catalogues. There are two things happening simultaneously in this image—the pregnant model appears both childlike and maternal. In looking at other images, I found these seemingly discordant personas occur frequently in tandem. This led me to conclude that pregnant women are infantilized and matronized in maternity catalogue representations.

Figure 15.1 depicts a young woman with a child resting on her pregnant belly. Of the other images in the catalogue featuring women and children, there is only one that does not depict the woman nurturing or guiding the child. Through the child, the woman appears more youthful and innocent while at the same time, maternal. Infantilization is also achieved through the image's color scheme. The woman advertises JC Penney clothing: a white T-shirt, blue jeans and beige checkered collared shirt. While the visual representation itself is not a particularly infantilizing image (minus the "cutesy" bow on the T-shirt), the catalogue's other graphics make the model look more youthful. Specifically, the use of pink in other places, such as the child's shirt, the JC Penney logo and the word "maternity," recalls the phrase "pink is for girls" (as opposed to adult pregnant women). The color scheme alongside the model's pose reinforces traditional femininity.

In addition to the dominant ideology associated with conservative femininity, the JC Penney catalogue reinforces the status quo. Of the ten pregnant women used as models, only one model is not wearing a wedding ring in any of her pictures. The ideology maintained in these representations is a heteronormative discourse as the wedding ring signifies a heterosexual coupling sanctioned by religion and/or state. The wedding ring combined with the presence of young children in the JC Penney catalogue also maintains the "ideal" of a nuclear family. Interestingly, although some of the clothing could be worn in a workplace, most of the photographic settings in the catalogue are markedly domestic outdoor settings such as a child's birthday party and in the garden. In the images advertising business attire, the women are posed indoors in what looks to be a house foyer. Ultimately, notions of conventional femininity are upheld in the JC Penney maternity catalogue.

I contend that pregnancy is a troublesome embodiment because it challenges traditional notions of space and boundary. In context, I began to understand why pregnant women were being represented in this way—it was a form of sanitation. If this transgressive corporeality resists ordered categories, it must be contained in dominant discourses so as to appear less threatening. By infantilizing and matronizing the models, they are made more consumable to the general public.

Julia Kristeva's notion of the "abject" is helpful in understanding why the pregnant body is such an enigma. In defining the abject, she writes:

> We may call it a border; abjection is above all ambiguity. Because, while releasing a hold, it does not radically cut off the subject from what threatens it—on the contrary, abjection acknowledges it is to be in perpetual danger.[4]

Abjection is both a source of fascination and repulsion; it is like the car accident that mesmerizes other drivers. The abject is a constant reminder that danger is lurking around every corner, and that the body can be corrupted without forewarning. Kristeva includes Mary Douglas' work on body fluids to further her theorizing about the abject. Kristeva's use of Douglas, as well as Elizabeth Grosz's, is important to looking at how the pregnant body is a unit for containment as well as something to be contained—in this case, within particular clothes. Therefore, Kristeva helps to illustrate the cultural fear of the pregnant body as one that threatens "normal," acceptable boundaries of representation.

Abjection explains why the pregnant body is stifled within discourses of infantilization and matronization—these are acceptable versions of femininity. Infantilization is achieved through both the design of the garments and representations of the models. Often, these clothes have childish patterns such as bows, polka dots or flowers, and are frequently only available in pastel colors. The majority of women I spoke with lamented these designs. When asked to describe their maternity attire, many of these women crinkled their noses in disgust, often followed by a recounting of the "awful" patterns and styles that made these women look "girly." The infantilized design of clothing makes sense in light of the fact that recently the maternity buyer at Sears "was promoted from the junior department to draw from the youthful fashion sensibility."[5]

There are rarely bold, dark coloured clothing except in business attire where power-dressing is appropriate. Patterns reinforce femininity because they are light, airy and unobtrusive—as women are supposed to be according to the beauty myth. It is not surprising that the most popular cut for a maternity dress is an A-Line, commonly referred to as a "baby doll" dress. This style de-emphasizes the protruding tummy while re-emphasizing childishness. With this fashion "choice" presented to pregnant women, it is not surprising that many women are apprehensive about shopping for maternity wear. The degrading nature of the clothing makes it difficult to find attire that accurately represents a woman's sense of *adult* identity and agency.

Infantilization appears not only in the styles and patterns of clothing, but also in the representations of the pregnant models. Often, the women are shown to be with children. Here, women are made childish by association—they appear playful, cute and innocuous. One explanation of infantilization of pregnant women relates directly to sexuality. By appearing youthful and innocent, the pregnant body is desexualized. Since it is assumed that a woman has been sexually active to become pregnant, making her look like a child erases adult female sexuality—a sexuality that is threatening in Western culture. A pregnant woman is further thought of as asexual because her body has now become that of a mother's. Her body is claimed by the fetus she carries and in a form of projection, the pregnant woman's body becomes that of "her" child. This reveals the pronatalist bias seen in maternity clothes' representations since pregnant women are assumed to be carrying their biological offspring and will in fact become a mother to this child. These discourses marginalize adoptive mothers and surrogate women who are left out of the equation. As well, women who have miscarried or aborted are effaced because although they were pregnant, they are not mothers. There is a heteronormative context here as well, as the pictorial representations of maternity clothes nearly always feature models wearing wedding rings.

If pregnant women are not infantilized through clothing representations, they are matronized instead. Pregnant women should "look the part" and "dress appropriately." Many women report "feeling old" when they become pregnant. In this way, the attire marketed to pregnant women reinforce pregnancy as a temporal period of maturation—such clothing marks a new stage in life when a woman is assumed to go from being independent and childless to enacting her role as mother. These two stages are generally mutually exclusive.

Victor Turner's concept of "liminality" illuminates pregnancy as a transient period during which a pregnant woman is neither childless nor a mother. Applying Turner's theory to pregnancy, cultural anthropologist Robbie Davis-Floyd explains liminality as "strange-making—making the commonplace strange by juxtaposing it with the unfamiliar and symbolic inversion . . . [Pregnancy represents] the physiological process of becoming a mother . . . Pregnancy is both a state and a becoming."[6] The experience of pregnancy is comparable to Alice in Wonderland—the physical changes occur at such a rate as to make the body unrecognizable. In fact, many women report they do not recognize their own bodies while pregnant.

Interestingly, some women I spoke to talked about the process of shopping for maternity clothes as an exercise in realizing their embodied state. The point at which a woman chooses to purchase, and wear, such garb represents a right of passage because she accepts her body as changing. The recognition that pre-pregnancy clothes no longer fit necessitates a change in attire. Therefore, wearing maternity apparel reflects not only a particular biological stage in pregnancy, but also a shift in personal identity because when a pregnant woman "breaks down" and buys these types of garments, it signifies her letting go of the "old self" and the acceptance of the new embodied state.

Liminality is characterized as being "betwixt and between."[7] Pregnant women, then, occupy a space betwixt and between discourse, often embodying a space of simultaneity. This state of ambivalence is identified as both/and as opposed to either/or. Because pregnancy does not fit into any one category, it is important to consider sometimes-contradictory discourses. This work is set up according to such opposition because culture continually attempts to contain the unlocateable pregnant body. To continue, maternity wear occupies that ambivalent state because it acts to both infantilize and matronize pregnant women through representations found in maternity apparel manuals, clothing advice texts, and through the clothes themselves.

Visiting the local maternity store at the shopping mall, I was quite surprised at the conservative clothing available. But what disturbed me was the majority of mannequins sporting pearl necklaces and scarves, which have come to signify motherhood or grandmotherhood. So, for pregnant women who choose to buy said clothes, the matronly look is still a popular style. These types of outfits, or accessories, reflect a pregnant woman's impending "status" as mother-to-be. A particular line of Tommy Hilfiger t-shirts also struck me. While the t-shirt was a traditional dove grey cotton garment, the Tommy logo frames text reading "tummy girl." This shirt reminded me of other maternity tops I have seen which read "baby" with an arrow pointing towards the womb. It is as if a pregnant woman's adult identity is effaced and she is reverted back to her prepubescent-girl stage.

Class discourses also develop when talking about purchasing maternity clothes. According to pregnancy manuals, what is most important for a woman in choosing clothing is to maintain her sense of "style." However, style often comes with a hefty price tag, which many cannot afford. For purposes of class analysis, I compared the JC Penney catalogue representation to a smaller clothing company, Pumpkin Maternity, because each relates to a target consumer who is positioned within a specific class status. I wanted to know if the ideology would be the same when addressing a working-class pregnant woman as it would be with an upper-class pregnant woman. What I found is that the representation of working–middle-class women in the JC Penney maternity catalogue reflects the status quo for traditional femininity. Conversely, Pumpkin Maternity presents images that challenge conventional femininity, instead presenting an aggressive version of pregnant identity. Whereas JC Penney is a department store that targets working–middle-class consumers because the clothes are "reasonably priced" and reflect imitation designer styles that are somewhat conservative in appearance, Pumpkin Maternity is a company that appeals to women with more money to spend.

I came across Pumpkin Maternity's website when conducting an online search for pregnancy clothes companies. Often, if there is no local maternity outlet or section of a department store that sells such clothing, women are forced to shop via the internet. When I found Pumpkin Maternity's website, I was enthused with how women are represented differently than in the JC Penney catalogue. Here seemed to be the progressive pregnant woman I had hoped to find originally.

Created by Pumpkin Wentzel, Pumpkin Maternity was conceived in the fall of 1996 as [Wentzel] toured Europe with her rock band in a converted fish truck. She thought of her sister and her best friend back home, both pregnant and complaining that they had nothing to wear. She knew exactly what was needed—a fresh, simple line of maternity clothes for the practical as well as fashion-savvy woman.[8]

According to Wentzel, "Pregnancy should not require a radical break from personal style." Located in New York's Soho, Pumpkin Maternity sells clothing aimed at "chic" women with money to spend.

Figure 15.2. Pumpkin Maternity Catalogue. Fall 2000.

What is interesting about Pumpkin Maternity is the representation of the pregnant woman in both its advertising and website. The models pictured here are neither infantilized nor matronized, as in other publications. The model appears without (born) child. She sports a grey sweater coordinate with black stretch pants. In contrast with the JC Penney model, the Pumpkin Maternity model is clearly pregnant as her form-fitting shirt reveals. Also, the Pumpkin Maternity model looks aggressively at the camera (whereas in the JC Penney image, the model looks downward smiling, a traditionally feminine pose). Further, she assumes a seated posture associated with men, one arm between her open legs while her other arm rests on the chair.

The picture is somewhat recuperated, though, with the attention paid to her high heels—a reminder of her femininity. However, her aggressive pose and look at the camera defiantly asks, "Yeah I'm pregnant, do you want to make something of it?" What is unfortunate is that Pumpkin Maternity is a small-scale retail outlet with one shop in New York that sells clothing to a middle-to-upper-class consumer. The pictorial representation of the pregnant model is progressive in that it does not rely on traditional femininity, infantilization, or matronization. Nevertheless, perhaps it is the case that these images reinforce the class divide by asserting that only women in the upper class can afford to be transgressive.

Women who choose not to purchase maternity wear may opt to make their clothes. One book, entitled *Great Expectations,* is devoted to teaching women how to make pregnancy attire. It was the only pattern book I looked at that presented positive images of belly-baring women enjoying their ever-changing bodies. Since *Great Expectations* is outdated by contemporary style standards, I wanted to find a maternity clothes manual that resonates with 21st century pregnant women. I discovered the same trap in terms of class disparity—the only books available praise the search for "style," a fashion sensibility that targets financially successful women.

Ultimately, I was disheartened to find positive images for pregnant women in specialty catalogues or pattern books only. It seems maternity clothes are a problematic contestation where women must negotiate infantilization, matronization, and traditional views of femininity. In addition, pregnant women contend with the beauty myth that contributes to negative self-image. In *Great Expectations,* Leigh Adams and Lynda Madaras write:

> Most of us have enough vanity to enjoy the way we look dressed up in clothing we like. It's especially important to support your vanity when you're pregnant. Our self-images depend at least in part on the messages we get from those around us.[10]

Since the marketing of maternity clothes is a one-and-a-half billion dollar industry, it is crucial to reinforce positive representations of pregnant women and create mature, and affordable, apparel to clothe them.[11]

Notes

1. Elaine Hoffman Baruch, "Two Interviews with Julia Kristeva," *Partisan Review*, 51.2 (1984) 120–132, 124.
2. Trademarks associated with JC Penney Maternity Collection are registered © 2001 J.C. Penney Company Inc. and/or JCP Media L.P. Used by permission.
3. It must be noted I have consciously chosen images that represent dominant ideology, which in contemporary Western culture means white women are the "norm." Popular representations of the African-American and Latina pregnant body are the *social* abject, embodying social moral panic. However, this discussion is outside the scope of this work which looks at the construction of normalizing images.
4. Julia Kristeva, *The Powers of Horror: An Essay on Abjection,* Trans. Leon S. Roudiez. (New York: Columbia University Press, 1982) 9.
5. Jennifer Steinhauer, "The Maternity Blues: What to Wear." *New York Times* (29 June 1997) 34.
6. Robbie Davis-Floyd, Birth as an American Rite of Passage. (Los Angeles: University of California Press, 1992) 19, 23.
7. Victor Turner, The Forest of Symbols: Aspects of Ndembu Ritual. (Ithaca, New York: Cornell University Press, 1967) 97.
8. Pumpkin Wentzel, Pumpkin Maternity Online. <*www.pumpkinmaternity.com*> (March 29, 2001).
9. Thank you to Pumpkin Wentzel for the use of this image. © Pumpkin Maternity Fall 2001. Used by permission.
10. Leigh Adams & Lynda Madaras. *Great Expectations.* (Boston: Houghton Mifflin Co., 1980) 4.
11. Chris Murphy, "Maternity Creates a New Identity Online." *Information Week.* (October 16, 2000).

CHAPTER 16   *Ardra L. Cole*

The Christmas Doll

Figure 16.1. Photo of author age 4, Christmas doll photograph courtesy of the Cole family album.

Each year, as a child, my mother eagerly awaited the arrival of her new Christmas doll. I have been told that on Christmas mornings she would stand in front of the splendidly decorated tree and direct her gaze skyward, careful not to touch anything until the rest of the household had awakened. Craning her neck she would see it perched on the treetop nine feet away. Only able to discern the general size, appearance, and dress color, she would spend the next twelve days, until the tree came down, gazing longingly upward, imagining details of her new doll's every feature, and planning their first moments together—moments that seemed a lifetime away.

One of those dolls, a Highland lass, sits each year on a branch of my Christmas tree. Age reveals itself on the clothing and body of her small 10-inch frame. In full Highland dress—tartan kilt, white blouse, navy velvet jacket with matching tam, white knee socks, and tiny black single-strapped shoes—her brilliant blue eyes and wide dimpled smile are undeterred by the small chips in her plaster face. The mass of unruly chestnut brown curls that frame her face is tamed only by the oversize tam pinned to her head. She has her own special storage box—the same box she came in I expect—a now-faded green heavy cardboard box exactly her size with a lid on which is written in my mother's stylized script, "Handle with Care. Contents Very Special."

My mother loved to tell doll stories—of the long hours she and her best friend spent playing with their dolls, dressing and undressing and dressing them again, changing their outfits to suit the many and varied occasions they imagined. She would describe in great detail their extensive doll wardrobes and how delighted they always were when a parent or relative added to their collection—"What one got, the other got." They took great care of and pride in their dolls, primping and preening them by the hour so that they were always picture perfect. They imagined themselves as mothers fussing over their own real live little girl dolls.

My mother's childhood dream followed her into adulthood. She desperately wanted a little girl to dress up, fuss over, and primp and preen. After two baby boys, she had all but given up hope. Then, one December, I was born, my mother's real live Christmas Doll.

As promised, I was primped, preened, and fussed over. I had a wardrobe that would rival any doll's. I was dressed and undressed and dressed again, always picture perfect. To my mother how I looked mattered much more than anything else. I wore dresses of Viyella flannel with intricate smocking, taffeta with wide sashes tied at the back in perfect bows, soft velvet with organza accents, authentic Highland tartans, wool outerwear with coordinating accessories—hat, shoes, gloves, and basket or purse—even a fox fur neckpiece at age three; everything matching and meticulously detailed.

Throughout elementary school every night before she went to bed, my mother laid out my next day's clothes and, every morning while I dressed, she stood over the kitchen stove, slowly drawing my hair ribbons, carefully chosen to match my outfit, across the spout of the steaming kettle. The ever-present hair adornments—most often ribbons, bought by the piece from spools in the department store where my mother was a cherished customer, sometimes barrettes, sometimes both—were attached to the ends of my long, perfectly braided hair. "Does this go, Mummy?" I would ask every once in a while in an attempt to exercise my free will and wear something of my own choosing. As I got better at discerning what went and what didn't, I earned the right to choose my own clothes—selections which, of course, reflected my mother's teachings.

Tartan kilts had either a matching vest or coordinating cardigan with a tartan ribbon accent. Blouse color depended on the tartan but was usually white or pale yellow so as to enhance, not detract, from the colors in the particular tartan—Black Watch, McNab, Stewart, Nova Scotia, Cape Breton. Knee socks were chosen to pick up one of the darker colors of the tartan, usually navy or hunter green; occasionally the socks, too, were matching tartan. And hair ribbons of course followed suit, usually chosen to match sock color. I learned that hair ribbons, socks, and waist sashes were key to tying an outfit together. For outerwear, this rule applied to hat, gloves, purse, and shoes.

Every occasion or event demanded a new outfit. Wardrobe was as much a part of the ritual and tradition associated with special occasions as were each occasion's social, cultural, or religious customs. Donning a new nightgown preceded the hanging of the Christmas stocking; Christmas dinner could not be eaten in anything but a new dress; a birthday girl couldn't start a new year in last year's attire; Saint Patty was happiest when the green being worn was new; church on Easter Sunday was really about parading a new bonnet. It was unthinkable to start a new school year without new shoes. And, of course, new shoes shone brighter when an accessory to a new outfit. Summer got off to a better start with a new bathing suit; a new parka somehow made each winter seem more bearable. And then there were school functions such as parent visits, concerts, field trips, annual fairs, Tea and Sales, and graduations all of which required new attire for both me and my mother (because she was usually involved). On the home front, my wardrobe grew whenever company came, when my mother took me visiting with her, or when I accompanied her on any of her numerous volunteer activities.

I grew up with years of lessons about what went and what didn't, about how appearance speaks louder than words, and about how you look affects how you feel, about pride in appearance. My mother was so committed to her rules about clothing and appearance that she occasionally found herself at odds with some of my teachers—the "fuddy duddies" who, according to my mother, were blind when it came to fashion. (One of my mother's [and my] favorite teachers was one who had quite an eye for fashion herself.) When the opinion was conveyed to my mother that my skirts were too short or that I should be wearing a more appropriate kind of leg covering or more casual attire my mother threatened to keep me home from school until the teachers learned to mind their own business.

From her very modest socioeconomic position, I think that my mother used clothing as a mask. To see her parade down the street, daughter in tow, both of us looking as if we had stepped off the cover of a fashion magazine, no one would have suspected that we had hardly a penny to our name. To the outside world we had worth. It was written all over our bodies, from impeccably coiffed and behatted tip to stylishly adorned toe. My mother had learned from her mother that clothing was cultural capital.

My grandmother was reputed to have spent (some might say squandered) the best part of my grandfather's meager earnings on clothing, hats, and jewelry. My mother had apparently learned at an early age that a woman who wore a hat, especially one with flair perched at a sassy angle, received a different kind of attention, was treated with more respect. She liked that. In her early years, what she learned from her mother she practiced on her dolls. Later my mother's keen eye for fashion and taste for quality demanded financial support and she got a job—at a department store. She spent most of each paycheck on fashions purchased from her employer's company.

War time in a port city meant a busy social life: handsome, young naval officers, keen to distract themselves from their tour of duty, offered a free arm to the white-gloved hands of attractive, unattached women; volunteer relief efforts brought women on the home front together for a common cause; band concerts in the public gardens; Saturday night dances at the Officer's Mess; hastily planned weddings to secure ties before overseas departures; not to mention the regular shopping and afternoon tea outings. All of these were public occasions. All of these demanded attention to fashion and appearance. That was in the '40s though, when young women were expected to give up their social and financial freedom for marriage, babies, and domesticity, which is what my mother eventually did, her reluctance somewhat bolstered by the naïve expectation that her wardrobe would continue to grow. Perhaps she was also heartened by the prospect of eventually having a little girl to dress, a live doll of her very own.

My father, a handsome, dapper young man with a flair for style himself, was never financially supportive enough of my mother's fashion needs, at least not from her perspective. Times got tougher with each new baby; eventually she was dressing for four. But luckily, the last baby was a girl—me—her Christmas doll, her companion. She had much to show me; I would learn to be shown.

Before it became socially permissible again, now that the war was over, for married women in our community to be gainfully employed outside the home, my mother devoted herself to volunteer work. She gave days of each week to our schools, church, the veteran's hospital, a long-term rehabilitation facility, a community day care, and the Canadian Red Cross Society. She convened Tea and Sales each Christmas and Spring raising money for the church, the Home and School Associations of our elementary and high schools, and the hospital. Hardly a week went by that her photograph didn't appear on the social page of the local newspaper. And in no two photographs did she, could she, wear the same hat. Each hat reflected the latest fashion trend: white pillbox with small black patent bow accent; black felt fedora-style with long feather plume; large, high-crowned navy straw with wide upturned brim; smaller, tightly woven beige with upturned brim trimmed with narrow ribbons of orange and brown. In desperation, to uphold her reputation and public appearance, she resorted to skimming money off the top of the meager household allowance my father gave her.

When my mother eventually did return to paid work, it was part-time at first. The social politics of the time demanded that domestic responsibilities and volunteer work take priority. Her limited income gave her back a small measure of autonomy and enough spending money to keep our closets full and our appearances picture perfect. The measure increased when she eventually returned to full-time employment at a—you guessed it—clothing store. For the first year or so her responsibilities were general and light—serving customers, handling cash, and keeping clothing displays tidy. Then, gradually, she took on more specialized responsibilities as manager of different departments—lingerie, children's wear, hats and wigs, bridal wear. This role also meant that she was the first to be informed by head office of end-of-season "mark downs." These reductions, along with her regular employee discount, enabled my mother to stockpile gifts and wardrobe items. Later, my mother's attention to fashion earned her the role of window and mannequin dresser and for years she orchestrated an annual spring fashion show. The last few years before retirement my mother was put in charge of receiving and ticketing store inventory, a job that gave her a preview of each season's line-up and an opportunity to set aside for later purchase items to be added to the next season's wardrobe.

Working in a clothing store put my mother more directly in the public eye. She had to keep up appearances—which she did, daily. Working in a clothing store also meant that she would keep up my appearances—which she did, relentlessly. Did I mention that my mother's affinity for dolls never left her? Think for a minute about the proverbial kid in a candy shop. That was my mother, set free (a good discount was close enough) to acquire all the clothes she wanted for herself and for her real live doll.

Each payday, for as long as she worked, my mother left behind more money in her employer's coffers than she took home. Her wardrobe became so excessive that she also had to purchase a couple of the store's clothing racks to accommodate the overflow. This occurred after she had already commandeered the closets my brothers had vacated when they moved away from home, and after she had outfitted the storage closet with rods to hold what wouldn't fit in her own closet. Storage was an ongoing problem for me, too. And so I rotated clothing each season, packing summer away in suitcases and boxes stored under my bed to give closet space to fall and then winter. I installed extra shelves and rods for hanging in an already overcrowded wardrobe. I regularly donated shopping bags of very slightly used clothing to the Salvation Army.

My mother continued to use every occasion as an excuse for gifts to me of new items of clothing. And, when the number of gifts exceeded the number of the usually celebrated events, she made up new ones. She also had a litany of rules that governed public appearance and justified each new display of fashion. She would never appear in public without earrings. She would never be seen in church on Easter Sunday without a new hat. It was bad luck to return from any outing without a parcel. She would never allow any of us to leave the house "looking like someone's poor relation." For my mother, it all came down to the social and cultural capital of appearance.

Did I also mention that my mother was manager of the hat department at one point? Just imagine . . . Oh, and did I also add that I worked in the store with her on a part-time basis all through high school and the first few years of university? Need I say more?

At the nursing home, decades later, my mother sat slumped in her wheelchair, dressed in a two-piece polyester track suit stained where the bib had missed errant bits of food or drink and wrinkled from the intense heat of the industrial dryers. White polyester socks and vinyl, Velcro-fastened track shoes replaced the nylon and leather of her past. Her gray hair, cropped short for easy care, fell straight and limp across her forehead. A vacuous stare and an occasional unabashed toothless grin reminded me of how difficult it was for staff to keep track of dentures and eyeglasses. Although I could well appreciate the institution's need for efficiency in the provision of care, I was struck by how much of my mother's physical transformation was a result of this. Her wardrobe was chosen for convenience—synthetic and tailored for easy dressing and undressing. Fashion was no longer a concern, jewelry was too hard to keep track of, and there was little time for attention to appearance. I felt somewhat relieved that my mother, in the late stages of Alzheimer's disease, had lost touch with her self-image. She would have so strongly protested the way she looked. Clean and warm wouldn't have mattered to her if the colours didn't match. What would people think? As I gazed intently at her, I wondered about the connection between vanity and dignity and whether the former had been lost as the latter diminished. I also wondered whether, without the sassy hat, she was treated any differently.

I had come "home" for Christmas, to be with my mother; the Christmas Doll now all grown up—a busy and hardworking professional. There was no family home to come home to anymore. This institution, with its disinfected character and stainless steel ambience, was her home now. A few family photographs, the only remnants of her history, were on display in a corner of the room she shared with another Alzheimer's victim. From evidence alone it would be virtually impossible to create a portrait or story that even approximated the woman my mother once was and the fashion-centered life she led. I had come home to be with her because I didn't know how many more Christmases I would have with her. Even now it was hard to tell whether she knew I was there or who I was.

It was Christmas Eve and a carol sing was about to begin around the Christmas tree in the large common room. It was a social event and, regardless of my mother's level of cognizance, a persistent voice inside me reminded me that she needed to be presentable for the occasion. It was up to ME to dress my shrunken, frail, and delicate doll for Christmas.

I wheeled my mother up to the bathroom sink, where I washed her face and hands with warm soapy water, and then back over to the large mirrored dresser that she shared with her roommate. I positioned her so that she could watch while I fussed over her although, from a glance in the mirror, it didn't appear as though her eyes registered anything. Rummaging through my shoulder bag I pulled out my cosmetic case, face cream, and hair brush. My mother's skin, dehydrated from the controlled climate of the institution, absorbed lotion like a sponge and began to take on a rosy glow; a dusting of face powder, a dab of rouge, and a bit of color from a tube of lipstick smoothed over her dry, cracked lips enlivened her complexion, restoring some of its natural lustre. With each stroke of the hairbrush she purred with contentment. My strokes were soft and careful; her fine, limp hair lay flat against her scalp. I moistened two fingers on one hand and swept her bangs to the side away from her eyes. With no time to change her clothes I could at least dress up what she was already wearing. Rifling through her dresser drawer I found the beads and matching earrings I had bought for her last Easter. I fastened the necklace and clipped the earrings in place. The Christmas corsage I had brought her lay unforgotten in her lap. I picked it up, passed it under her nose, and pinned it close to her left shoulder so that she could smell the carnations—her favorite flowers—if her head happened to move in that direction. Perhaps she would be drawn to them of her own volition. I stood back to assess her image in the mirror. Our eyes met, seemed to connect. Was it my imagination or was she sitting just a bit straighter, holding her head a tad higher? Did she feel differently about herself than she had only minutes before? Did she know that her appearance had changed?

As I wheeled her through the doorway I glanced back at the colorfully wrapped parcels on her bedside table. I would help her open them later: the cozy flannelette nightie that she would wear to bed tonight and a new dress for Christmas Day. After tomorrow the dress would likely hang in her closet along with most of the other clothes she brought with her to the nursing home. They simply required too much care or time to put on and take off. It simply didn't matter anymore. Or did it?

※

It is eight years since my mother's death. It seems more like eight days or weeks at most. I cherish that. I don't want her memory to fade. I want her with me although I know that I couldn't let her go even if I wanted to for the simple reason that every day I get dressed. And every day I hear her in my mind's ear commenting on my wardrobe decisions. She'd adore the sassy little vintage hat I recently purchased to wear to a wedding and she'd be especially pleased to know that I was the only one in church wearing a hat. She'd have a great chuckle over the disparaging comment I overheard someone make about my affinity for leather clothing. She'd love the fact that I fuss the way I do about what goes with what and the time and care I take to achieve a certain look. She'd nod approvingly at my collection of unusual earrings.

I write this from my front deck, a stone's throw from the Atlantic Ocean on Canada's east coast where I grew up. It's where I do my "best" thinking and most of my writing, away from the all consuming demands of urban, university life. I am on an island, a rugged little fishing community with dirt roads, a general store, a post office, and one restaurant open only for the summer season. Not a lot goes on here yet the days are full. I move rhythmically between the tools of my academic trade and those housed in my tiny garden shed, carrying ideas and words back and forth between the two. I work the land and enliven my body, mind, and spirit. It is hard not to think of this life and place as idyllic; and it is, almost.

The other day a friend, who was visiting from out of town, asked if I planned to retire here. I thought for a while about my response—not my answer but how I would convey it. I chose my words carefully, trusting that this friend would understand. "Well," I said from underneath my layers of old clothes that make up my wardrobe here, "part of me wants to but there's another part of me that would wither here. Despite the fact that my rubber boots are purple, my earrings big, and that I knit colorful socks, fashion possibilities are limited." Before continuing I sneaked a glance to gauge my friend's reaction. Her sincere expression and nod prompted me to go on. "You see, a big part of who I am—my history, my identity—is wrapped up in what I wear. When I stand in front of my open closet door each morning, deciding on which jeans and t-shirt or sweater (often both) to put on, I think of my mother in the nursing home dressed for comfort and convenience in clothing that covered up who she was. Dress mattered to my mother and it matters to me."

CHAPTER 17   *Gary Knowles*

Constraining Mother: Corsetry, Control, and Comfort

> *The corset is probably the most controversial garment in the entire history of fashion.*
> VALERIE STEELE[1]

I lay in bed, breathing quietly, alternately dozing and pretending to be asleep. In the faint, breaking light of a March day in a hotel in Sydney, Australia, I watched her as she arose from the adjacent bed. She moved with purpose but not with certainty. A slip in confidence, perhaps? Anxious to board a mid-morning flight home over the Tasman Sea to New Zealand, she methodically showered and prepared for dressing. Frailer, now, than on my previous visit with her, I marveled at the changes in her body and, especially, her movements; acknowledging they were each imbued with a sameness yet a perceptible difference. Over the previous days I noticed that her close attention to garments remained—considerations of their fit, cut, color, and texture were still important—but the clothes were less complex and their fall on her body telling.

"Gary, come here, help me! . . . Now, hurry up, I haven't got all day."
Barely up and awake, often half dressed, I'd race to her bedroom. There, standing in front of the mirrored dresser, beside the window—in full view of passers by, I imagined—she waited.
Always impatient. In control.
Every morning. Before school.

Several days before, we had witnessed the marriage of her oldest grandson—my son—a man for whom she has great affection and pride. With trepidation and some physical difficulty, my 86-year-old mother traveled from her home to the wedding. With me as her companion, she negotiated the journey. Traveling by car, then plane, then car again, we spent close time together. Sometimes talking, sometimes silent, lost in thought, awkward, the years apart inducing a loss of immediate, intimate knowledge of the other. When words bridged the gulf between us they were of distant memories and places associated with my childhood home and hometown, of my son and his new wife, of other family matters, and about sports events of the week—especially the New Zealand–Australia cricket test matches playing out as we traveled and celebrated the wedding. I was reminded of her once youthful, athletic prowess. She talked cricket statistics as only she could—bowling averages, runs, LBWs, wickets, and innings—and she conveyed brash, informed opinions about key cricketers and their actions on the oval. This was her talk. Cricket was her lifelong love, not mine.

I moved to North America in 1982. In the intervening two decades many changes in her body and posture became apparent. Each yearly visit to New Zealand over this period found her, first, slimmer; then more recently, frailer. Clothing began to drape on her, then sizes decreased—gradual morphing for an athletic, well-formed woman. The dominant memories I have of her remain those from the days of my childhood and early adolescence.

> Cartwheel after cartwheel, she rolled across the lawn, skirt or dress tucked into her "panties—bloomers" she called them sometimes. Her strong arms and legs, like spokes on my grandfather's wagons, supporting and propelling her, connected to broad shoulders, well endowed breasts, and constrained waist. Bending, bending, but only so much. Breathing deeply. Sometimes, wanting more flexibility, more breath, she'd rush inside and "remove the foundations." Then, on returning to her rare playfulness, "Ah, relief! Glad that's gone," she'd exclaim.

In the motel room, I watched her dressing. Deliberate, slow movements. Her underwear. Simple. Now, obviously awake, I spoke morning words, ones we'd uttered for years. "Good morning! You're up early. Sleep well?" Still inclined to the harsh and antagonistic—despite mellowing over the years—she replied in her typical fashion, in the ways I remember from my youth. "Get up . . . Get cracking! We haven't got all day!" So easy. The words roll off her tongue into my ears with the force of breaking Tasman Sea waves. Second nature—her words, that is. I was still the adolescent, the 14-year-old. Then she surprised me. "Give me a hand," she demanded. Or was it a gentle request? Perceptions are sometimes conditioned.

Visions of a lazy start to the day—after all, her flight was still more than five hours away—were vanquished with her words, just as my hopes for the release of responsibility were dashed early each morning of my youth.

"Give me a hand," she ordered.

"Where's Dad?" I replied, "Can't he do it?"

Well, mostly he couldn't. I knew that. Still, I had to protest.

Dad left home early each morning. At 7:05 AM precisely. On week days. He began work 30 minutes later, across town, opening the family's motor vehicle business seven days a week. On the weekends he left home just a little later and I was often relieved of my responsibility. When I was 13, sometimes I opened on a weekend and that meant, for sure, that I was off the hook. Oh, did I say there were lots of hooks—and eyes as well?

The rest of her clothes were now carefully laid out on her already made bed ready for dressing. "Can't let the maid know that we slept in the bed, now, can we. . . ?" she could have said, but did not. But when did she make the bed? I must have dozed! Laid out, also, was her silver and marcasite jewelry that she has worn for decades. Elegant yet resilient pieces. Memories of her long-departed husband, my father, still lingering with them—he's been dead, now, for over three decades. Memories of a more youthful time. Memories of her mother as well.

My mother took pride in her appearance. Like her own mother, she dressed with care, given a certain frugality, displaying a moderated attention to detail that has remained with her over the years. Vibrant colors are now her preference, emphasizing her glossy, white, wavy hair and Celtic complexion. Her modest wardrobe witnesses her late life disinterest in shopping for clothes, and I speculate that her selections are an expression of her aging body. Outer garments, now, are a necessary covering, not a cherished, vain indulgence. Still, she looked glorious and happy—despite her aching limbs—days earlier at the wedding. That she still took pride in her appearance was obvious to all. Now, in the motel room with the brightening light, she laid out a finely crafted, simple, two-piece suit in a non-crush, synthetic fabric. Turquoise, her favourite color! Her organized preparation for air travel reinforced my thoughts about her as I reflected on my long-held experiences with her.

So what occupied her life? My mother was a busy woman: never frantic, just organized. Between regular volunteer work for "Meals on Wheels" and the Plunket Society,[2] responsibilities at the family business, keeping home and maintaining the house and yard (especially the garden), and sports and leisure activities, she was always on the go. A powerful work ethic, inherited from both maternal and paternal sides of her family, governed the days of her life. She also fully participated in the affairs of Parent-Teacher committees and events, knowing most of my teachers on a first name basis—indeed, one was a neighbor, some were my parents' customers, and their close relationships were always a source of potential embarrassment or concern to me. (What on earth *did* they talk to one another about?) My mother was also well known. Many of the town's 6000 residents knew her from either the business or for her athletic achievements—she had represented the province in both women's cricket and basketball.[3] In my youth she was a prominent golfer. Never still! An active woman.

> The label on the garment declared "For The Active Woman." I'd sneaked a peek, one day, as it hung inside out on the clothesline down by the cherry tree. I checked it out. It was pegged there, hanging upside down for neighbours to see, all pink and fleshy—one of several models she possessed. Awful! Embarrassing! I imagined over the course of my primary school years that the garment was especially tailored for my mother—after all, it fit her like a glove. She epitomized The Active Woman and I wished to God, and for all my ungodliness, that she'd not be so active. If she slowed down maybe I'd get some rest. I'd not have to work—all the time, every spare moment, or so it seemed. In the garden, yard work, housework, delivering this or that, newspaper run, working at the business, and whatever.
>
> "Do this . . . and this, too," she'd point, "before you go off gallivanting around the place with your mates." And she'd order more! But even as she ordered I knew she'd work just as hard on the tasks as she'd expected me to do.
>
> Idleness was ungodliness in Mum's view although she never went to church, publicly prayed, read the Bible, or did anything to suggest her god was other than the Mammon of Action. She practiced the religion of The Active Woman. So, what did inactive women wear? I wondered.
>
> My aunt lived next door. "She's spoiled you rotten," so Mum often said of her. Auntie didn't make me work when I visited her. "She'll make you soft," Mum said. My aunt was more refined, physically inactive and especially leisurely, playful, took long visits to the podiatrist and the hairdresser, had long, frothy baths, read interesting books, bought magazines from half way around the world, played idle games of cards, puzzled over crosswords and jigsaws, fussed tentatively in the garden, went on long shopping sprees, frequently buying useless "modern household gadgets," and wore the latest, frivolous fashion. You name it, she wasn't like my mother. Diminutive, slight, all 60 inches of her—if that. Small boned, breasted and hipped, slim arms and Highland Dancers' legs, she was—in physical and emotional qualities, as I later realized—all that my mother wasn't. Linked by marriage, there was nothing else which united them in spirit or deed. Opposites! And, she didn't wear one! Auntie was an inactive woman. So there.

The closeness of the motel room made watching my mother seem, at once, voyeuristic and normal, familial. To see her in modes of undress and preparation to dress was one of those fundamental and defining elements associated with my early years. Neither did she flaunt her body nor exhibit discomfort at her revealed nakedness or state of undress. She simply was! Perhaps it was an expression of comfort with others—me, in this case. Comfortable with herself and without embarrassment. Even with in-laws and their offspring she showed little change in her morning rituals and her dressing conduct at home, her home. Even when away, staying with family or friends, she acted little differently! Now, beside me in the room, close to the bed, it was the same.

I responded to her request for assistance. As I did so she quietly and apologetically stated, "My arms are tired." Her legs also pained her, and deeply so, as evidenced by rippling, knotted, blue varicose veins on the surface of weathered skin. She handed me her slip, a fine silk garment, and I flipped it over her head, over her undershirt. (Always the undershirt.) As it fell, it skimmed her loose fitting brassiere. She hardly needed one now. She gingerly passed me the blouse and I slipped it, too, over her head, its tight-woven, opaque, white surface hinting, beneath, of her undergarments and sun-damaged skin. "Thanks. Get about your business now." Without further comment she accepts my assistance.

> Oh, I longed for a sibling. Actually, I specifically wanted a sister. She'd be good with hooks and eyes. I knew it. A sister'd be more ambidextrous, more helpful with Mum and her garments.
>
> It wasn't as though I was the girl surrogate. Indeed, I often imagined that she'd preferred a boy over a girl. We all knew "boys could work harder than girls!" Sure! Her own mother had worked her hard through the lean years of the Great Depression and, with the absence of my father's earnings, she'd survived four, scarce, rationing years during the Second World War. I figured that a sister might mean that I didn't have to help with doing or pegging out the laundry, or working in the flower beds, or assisting with grocery shopping, or . . . These were things that, as all my mates knew very well, girls could do better than boys. And, a sister could help Mum in the mornings I imagined (never wondering about the evenings)?

With her undergarments adjusted I helped my mother with the two-piece suit. She stepped into the skirt and flipped the front-buttoned top on, arms first. She was more confident, now, in her actions. Not needing more assistance she moved to the bathroom out of sight.

> Entering the bedroom I'd usually find her with the garment half on—she'd be wriggling into it or wrapping it around her midriff or hitching it up under her ample breasts. Sometimes, she'd just be standing there in her singlet. Waiting for assistance. The task of putting it on varied with style and make. The beige coloured one, with the long vertical ribs—"whalebones," she called them, although I knew they were made of metal—and long dangly bits, for example, wrapped around her body, fastened by eyelets and hooks. The awful, fleshy pink, For The Active Woman one, she'd have to step into, given its rear, laced fastenings.
>
> ". . . No need to gawk, you've seen me before!" Of course I had but always the same response—or some version of it—whether I looked more closely or not! The undershirt, with close, fine holes from a delicate factory knit, and slim shoulder straps, bulged over her breasts, nipples puckered, prickling the surface—a fact about which I later became embarrassed when I thought about it at high school.

... Throughout the 1950s and well into the 1960s, most women wore some sort of body-shaping foundation garment. Corsetry was not limited to women trying to deal with a heavy figure. It was widely believed that the right foundations could "preserve" a youthful figure. "An uncorseted body is prone to fatigue and even if slim, with taut stomach muscles, it is wise to guard early against future 'spread,'" declared one fashion writer. "This isn't something you can afford to be slack about."[4]

"Here, take it. . . . Now don't mess around." I don't know whether it's real or feigned impatience she displays. (She talks like this with family but not with customers.) There's no time to think too much. No use objecting. Her attitude doesn't hint of self-consciousness.

I fumble for the two tie-up laces of the pink fleshy one. The foundation of her outer attire? Or, is it her body? The pink fleshy one, I think, is her favorite. She's never told me this as fact and nor do we discuss it, but, when I'm in her room, helping her, she positions herself in front of the dresser mirror, gazing sideways, half out the window to the street, half aligned with the mirror. An oblique view of herself and the world. Perhaps even seeming "big town sophisticated," as she might say, posing in a way that resonates with little of the woman I know from my other, everyday, experiences of her. But, the reality is, I don't understand this stuff. Kids never do—even though I've gazed inquisitively at pages of pictures of women in underwear contained in Auntie's magazines. Ads for Formfit and Maidenform and Excelsior. Sleek, shinny, seamed and stretched garments fitted over slim, shapely (even sexy) women—different from the Playboy pictures I found under Uncle's chesterfield but none the less intriguing.

So it is I have little knowledge of my morning role beyond the immediate, obvious one. I don't even know of the real purpose of the garment. Sure, I see that it holds her in. Makes her smooth. But that's it. The foundation—the awful, pink fleshy one and the beige coloured one, with the long dingle dangles for holding up her stockings (actually, they're like the clips on Dad's suspenders, the ones used to hold up his socks, a fact I discover later). Anyway, she calls it "corset" in the bedroom. Yes, she calls it that when I'm there with her. Other times she says it's "The Foundation."

I struggle to get the laces taut, starting at the top, high in the middle of her back. Wrapping the laces tightly around the hooks, then holding the pressure, while moving on to the next hook in sequence is a feat that takes some practice. (It's only when I'm finally nearing high school that Mum acknowledges my expertise.) So, there I am, all seven years of me, when my morning job first began. I weave the laces alternatively over and around the hooks, moving down Mum's back, on the weirdly stitched, lined, and ribbed "corset thing" with the different kinds of fabric. It looks like it's been made out of scraps of material!

The fleshy pink one and the beige colored "corsets" cover her boobs. (Of course I never use the boob word in her presence. Come to think of it I never called them breasts or anything else when she's near. Actually we never talk about our bodies at all.) But she has a couple of other "corset things" which don't—cover her boobs, that is. Then she wears a "wired brassiere," as she calls it, to support her breasts. (Heavy breasts, too, it seems, given their size. I asked about an indentation on her shoulder one time when she was about to go swimming. "Mind your own business," she replied.) But these words, the names for her clothing! I used the b and the c words one time in class—we were in a game and doing something like naming clothing for the letters of the alphabet—and there was a hush and giggles from the kids and steely eyes from pencil thin Miss Donald, the teacher. I forgot myself! Miss Donald should've understood? After all, she's our neighbor at the bottom of the yard and was certain to have seen them on the line. But if she had she didn't let on and she told me to "Watch my tongue." Or maybe it's "Wash your tongue" she says because then she told me to "use soap and water" (although she didn't make me do it!).

So I yank and I pull and I get my mother tight and into her corset. The pink fleshy one. I hate helping her with the beige one. It has eyelets and hooks. Lots of them. To get them connected I have to get real close and squeeze them together, Mum breathing in. I don't like getting too close. There I am, virtually with my face upon the fabric, squeezing sideways together, working on the hooks, grabbing the fabric with my hands. After a while I got the hang of the pink fleshy one and lifted my foot up to Mum's back to get a better grip. It worked and although she objected at first we both discovered that it got her tied up better and faster. But that was when I was younger!

> Corsetry was not one monolithic, unchanging experience that all unfortunate women experienced before being liberated by feminism. It was a situated practice that meant different things to different people at different times. Some women did experience the corset as an assault on the body. But the corset also had many positive connotations—of social status, self discipline, artistry, respectability, beauty, youth, and erotic allure . . . Moreover, women wore different kinds of corsets: they laced their corsets more or less tightly and to different ends. In short, their embodied experience of corsetry varied considerably.[5]

Mother's body always looks strong. Especially her legs. When I was about 11 years old, I trained for rugby by cross-country running all round the countryside west of town. Five or so miles at a time. Sometimes more. Invariably my mother wanted to run with me. I always tried to persuade her otherwise. She was physically active all though my school days, playing sports and working (in her foundation and all).

My mother's a good cook and we always have a hot meal at noon—even Dad's mid-day meal is driven to him each day. Baking was her specialty (as it was her mother's—together they'd operated a bakery before the Second World War). We ate well at our place! At some points I was a bit on the heavy side and I think that Mum was too (after her competitive, athletic days). Mum always told Dad not to eat too much butter—and meat fat. And we'd eat fresh cream everyday. So, maybe we were all a bit on the heavy side! Just a little. For a while.

> There is no such thing as a "stylish stout." Stoutness is forever unhealthy, unstylish, and unnecessary. If you allowed yourself to become overweight, get your waistline down again. Flatten it. Strengthen it. Make it your aim in life to keep your muscles so strong and elastic that you can free yourself permanently from the one-piece harness called the corset. Your own muscular corset is the best of all undergarments.[6]

I returned to the motel bed, lying on it till my mother finished her tasks. With the bright lights and the mirror to aid she quickly applied make-up, emerging radiant, subverting the fact that she is in her ninth decade. She smiles at me, well, kind of. It is more of a smirk. She is ready and I am not. "Get cracking," she says, and as I respond she adds, "No time to waste," as if in unison with my conditioned movement. Her plane would depart in four and a half hours and at that point we'd part our ways—me traveling to North America alone and she meeting relatives at Auckland's international airport.

Our visit together is a memorable occasion. Even though I was reminded of how our responsibilities toward each other have changed over the years and were changing moment by moment—even as we readied ourselves in the motel—I marveled at how certain elements of our relationship and our individual identities, roles, and mannerisms remained intact.

> Sometime in the early 1960s, when I was a high school student—maybe I was 14, or maybe 16—my mother stopped asking me to help her in the mornings. I wasn't disappointed, just relieved I think. Not that it'd really been onerous or anything. "Tying her in," as my father used to say, was an experience—and it gave me insight into women's bodies. Wow! I think perhaps I was much more mature than my mates over the sight or thought of a partially dressed woman. But who knows! Anyway, I've this hunch that she stopped wearing them, the corsets I mean. Perhaps it was the women's movement that did it. The freedoms of the 60s. I don't know. She got slimmer, a bit, and heaven knows, without the bulk of those things—especially the beige colored one with the long dingle dangles (which must have worn out by then, I can't remember)—anyone'd look slimmer.
>
> The other possibility was that I'd become too old to do this morning task. Perhaps I'd become a man—well, sort of! Or maybe Dad took a renewed interest in the task. Who knows?

> The transition from the whalebone corset to the muscular corset took the greater part of the twentieth century. Despite a growing emphasis on diet and physical exercise, and notwithstanding the development of more flexible girdles, some type of foundation garment continued to be an integral component of the female wardrobe until well into the 1960s.[7]

A few days earlier, in Auckland, I convinced my mother to allow me to take from her home and possession the seldom-opened, incomplete, family photograph album—a rich rust, marbled covered, khaki paged, expandable book. With it was a yellow rose-decorated, cardboard, chocolate box—Cadbury's Roses—bursting at the corners, containing all manner of photographs that never made it to the khaki pages of the album. I wanted to explore images that had not seen the light of day for years. I had not looked at the album in several decades. A jumble of glossy and matte finished, black and white photographs awaited my rediscovery.

My mother, now dressed and completely ready to face the day and her travel itinerary, sat down in the easy chair near my bed. I retrieved the album from my luggage. I opened it at the beginning page. Flipping through it was like walking into the family home. Faces and places and things, some not even known by me, hinted of my past life. I presume she started the album about the time of her marriage to Dad, just before the outbreak of World War Two, but lost interest in maintaining it just before I was born. The last photograph arranged on the army-colored pages is that of my cousin—her favorite brother's boy, two years older than I.

We sit together, closely, my mother and I, and she tells me about some of the photographs—people and places, roles and experiences. She tells me about the times she has had. But, mostly, now, I am interested in those images which depict her. I want to get a sense of her physique over the years, especially before I came along.

There she is, standing straight, almost to attention, smiling. It is a basketball team photo. The Otago provincial team. My mother looks content yet serious. An athlete. Her waist is small for her size, accentuated by the dark, well-above-the-knee gym frock. The picture is taken sometime in the late 1920s or 1930s, There is no date on the back.

Again, a photo that seems to be connected with a major basketball competition. It is 1939 in Invercargill. She looks directly at the camera. Wearing a knitted woolen dress she covers her shapely knees with her hands. Beside her are two friends. They are all slim. Another shows her with a table full of trophies. Her legs are well developed. Her waist small. She was the club team captain.

The Otago provincial cricket team. Standing in the back row (as in most of the formal team images) she is dressed in cricket creams, the dress of male cricketers. Shirts and long pants, all cream colored. Body shape is difficult to determine apart from the waistline. She looks trim.

Mum and Dad in their bathing togs. They are at a beach—probably Brighton. Both costumes look almost identical, the fashion of the time—at least in New Zealand. A great head of wavy hair! Large breasts slump in the wet, woollen suit. A fine waist and shapely hips.

It is the Gore Races Labour Day (horse racing, that is, and it is spring) in 1946, the year before I was born, and Mum and Dad are walking across a mown field from their car. He looks dashing, in his tweed suit and felt hat, and she is wearing a fine tam-like hat with a great feather, a two-tone suit with birds and flowers embroidered on the lighter colored front. Carrying a dark handbag and matching shoes she looks solemnly radiant. Again, her well-formed breasts are evident. She looks pleasantly shapely.

In these photographs, and many more, I see my mother as a healthy, fit woman, one whose image fits prevailing, early-to-mid-century notions about womanhood and beauty—moderately slim, shapely, hourglass-like. I wonder about her use of the corset in the years of my youth. I have come to understand its purpose in artificially maintaining acceptable body shape but I wonder why my mother wore one. Was it just the fact that it was the acceptable, fashionable thing to wear? I never asked her!

> Worn by women throughout the western world from the late Renaissance into the twentieth century, the corset was an essential element of fashionable dress for about 400 years. Yet, throughout its history, the corset was widely perceived as an "instrument of torture" and a major cause of ill health and even death. Today the corset is almost universally condemned as having been an instrument of women's oppression.[8]

We depart the motel for the airport. There, our parting, as always, is difficult. I wonder when I'll see her again. I worry about her living alone. I am concerned about her well-being. As for her, she's grown accustomed to the great geographical distance that separates us, my absence from her everyday life, and my rootlessness (though she's never understood my decision to leave New Zealand). I acknowledge, though, the power of our respective personal histories in shaping our respective lives and our responses to each other and the world around us. As she passes through the security area and out of sight I remind myself of the many bodily images of my mother that frequently reel through the projector of my memory. She is all of them at once and I celebrate the unique ways in which I came to know her. They are indeed foundational.

Notes

1. V. Steele, *The Corset: A Cultural History*. (New Haven, CT, and London, UK: Yale University Press, 2001) 1.
2. The Plunket Society is a venerable New Zealand Institution. In operation for nearly a century, it is an independent agency which serves the country's mothers and young children. In the 1950s, run by volunteers and paid, full-time staff, Plunket Clinics served the prenatal, neonatal and postnatal needs of mothers and provided monitoring and health and well-being services for infants and young children. Besides the Clinics the Society operated children's health camps and hospitals. Rural areas were served by itinerant Plunket Nurses and the Society's interests in mothers and children are credited with inducing some of the lowest rates of infant mortality in the Western world. In the period of my childhood the Society was one of the most esteemed national institutions.

3. An outdoor, hard court game, now called netball (since the arrival of North American basketball in New Zealand). Netball is similar to basketball, in that there are hoops for players to pass the ball through, but the game is played more like soccer or field hockey in the moves, positions, and rules.
4. Steele, 160.
5. Steele, 1. See also G. Hauser, *Look Younger, Live Longer* (London, UK: Faber & Faber, 1951).
6. Hauser, 171–172.
7. Steele, 143.
8. Steele, 1.

CHAPTER 18

Celeste Snowber

(Wo)man Time and M(other) Sins

I escape
into woman time
one rose craning
candle burning
rain dropping
loud echoes
from boys
    downstairs
two teenagers
two pre-adolescent
three are mine
spoons clanking
fights beginning

Drained, I crawl
into silky robe
sip green tea
and hide
in amberlit room.

No matter
    how hard I try
to parent well—
be centered

firm and free
tender and treelike
I f a l l short
   and fall often.
Nerves frayed,
my voice raises
daily at least, I'm told
the supper isn't liked
by one
another wants something NOW
and it is my fault.

I've been told—
   I cry too much
the fridge smells
I'm not cool
my jeans are up too high
I'm gone too much and
times I'm in the way
the food is too hot, too cold
I forgot the right cereal
and there are
I love you's too.

I was even asked once—
can't you bake cookies
instead of writing books?
or why don't you dress
like the other mothers?
or when will you stop
being premenstrual
or perimenopausal?

Mother Sins

They are endless
I wear thin
and feel fat
with (re)quests.
I am on another quest
and I long for you to quest

to be intimate with
soul—not gel.
Could there be a gel of soul?

The weight of single parenting
is loss of deep touch
in middle of tyranny.
I long for a bodysoul
to put arms around me
drink me in silence
just bear with me.

All I can do
in this moment
is to be intimate
with myself.
Cherish coming home
to deep gentle place
where my breasts
roam free
openings are ripe
eyes soften their gaze.

Return, I must
to moist crescent
moon lush
vulva rose
presence in chaos.

Wo(man) time
where I can bear
the weight
and be born
to light.

PART V

Of Dresses and Weddings

CHAPTER 19   *Claudia Mitchell*

Bridesmaid Dress: Thick Description

Peacock blue peau de soie knee-length scoop neckline
Cinched waist, french taffeta bodice.

Dusty rose chiffon over maroon crushed velvet
Sleeveless with elbow length matching gloves

Cream chantilly, lace and organza, puffed sleeves
Plunging neck, empire waist.

Satin pumps dyed to match
3 shades of green—aquamarine, chartreuse, jade, jaded, envy, jealousy

All phenomenologically and tastefully arranged into discrete standpoints
According to Margot Ely et al, Max Van Manen, and Ann Oakley—not the cowgirl but the other one who interviews women: a contradiction in terms.

Narrative inquiry triangulated with participant-observation laced over mid-calf ethnography

Starting with ourselves . . .

Gaining entry, coming down the aisle, open-ended questions, remember to turn on the tape recorder and get informed consent: "I do."

Of Dresses and Weddings

Exiting (up) the aisle and into confetti and endless transcription

"That's not what I said," she said.

Locating one's self, positionality, maid-of-the-bride: all dressed up and nowhere to go.

"The thesis," she said, "is just like the bridesmaid's dress—you always think you are going to get your wear out of it—a few cocktail parties, a conference or two—but somehow you never do. Nobody takes it out and you can never dress it up."

Notes

For the Insiders: Qualitative Research Methods, McGill University, April, 1997.
Acknowledgments to my mother, who for all those years read aloud from the *Gopher Creek Chronicle* and the *Virden Empire-Advance* thick descriptions of local weddings.

CHAPTER 20 Kathryn Church

Try This One On for Size: Poetic Notes from Wedding Dress Research

Figure 20.1. Close up of bow on bridal gown.

Figure 20.2. Bridal gown with sash.

Resistance

Imagine a bride
who has seen some
Hard Times:
too many cigarettes
too much booze
too many men who don't give
a damn.

The one she is with now isn't much good.
"Why should I marry you?"
she asks.
"Because no one else will have you,"
he replies.
She's so far down that
she believes him.

The wedding dress that she creates is
Vivid
with imagination.

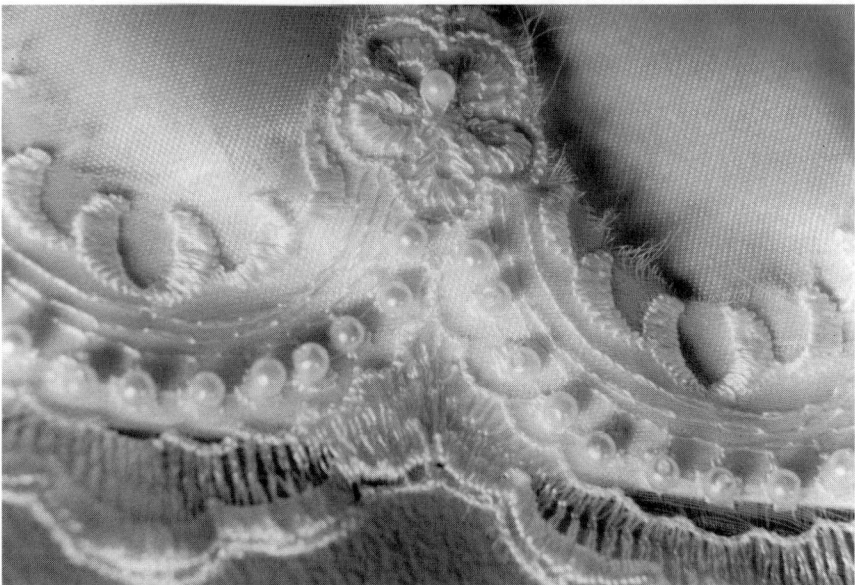

Figure 20.3. Close-up of bead work on bridal gown.

"White is for virgins and I am not"
she declares.
And so the garment is ivory
its lines playful to the point of
Sexy.

It is a clever move using the
Strength and Comfort
of her sexuality to counter the
Weight
of her depression and self-loathing.

This dress is not a dress.
It is a mask.

Revenge

Imagine a bride
who was sexually abused
as a child.
Violation
stirs in the shadows
Restless
as she approaches
her wedding day.

She knows
Precisely
what she is doing with her dress.
Into its voluminous white depths
she sinks
her freakish long legs and the brain that thinks
like a man.

Thus cloaked she becomes
a walking protest(ation)
of her own innocence.
"This is how you are going to see me,"
she insists.
And so for a time she escapes the sense of being
Damaged Goods.
She retrieves her stolen purity.

Redemption

Imagine a bride
who had failed at marriage
her first time out.
She lives that failure as a broken
Love Story
but also a breach in the
Covenant
she made with God before a
Company of Believers.

And then she gets a
Second Chance.

The dress that she creates
turns her life.
It does not eradicate her past
"I would not dare to be married in white,"
she exclaims.
But it does retrieve damaged images
and remake them for her use.

One is the fairy tale princess
not Cinderella
so much as Grace
of Monaco.
Each stitch that draws together the satin fabric
also mends the ragged edges of
Happily Ever After.
Ironically, its Hollywood lines
renew her position in a faith community.

The dress then becomes
not just sacred but
Magic.

CHAPTER 21

Jo Visser

Nailing It: My Wedding Dress

Figure 21.1. "Crucifiction," Jo Visser. Courtesy of the artist.

> "No one has ever asked me to marry them. I won't ever wear that white wedding dress. But I'd love to be that woman for a day. How can that be? How can I be this woman who is such an individual, and yet admit there's a part of me that pines to be a princess?"
> SOPHIA[1]

The Crucifiction: Art vs. Artistic License

For almost ten years, my wedding dress was yellowing, stashed away in a garbage bag at the back of closets in the various Montreal apartments I inhabited during that period. Why on earth I dragged it with me from apartment to apartment, given my negative sentiments about my marriage, I really couldn't say. I just did. It was a lovely dress (better off than on, mind you) but what was I to do with it? You never wear a wedding dress again, although my mother had her short, 1960s, white peau de soie wedding dress dyed what was supposed to be emerald green with the intention that she would wear it again. But it turned out pea green and she never did. Which only serves to reinforce that it's never a very good idea to try on your wedding dress years after your wedding. (Especially if you thought you were fat the first time you wore it.)

Why, then, do so many women, including me, feel compelled to keep their wedding dresses? Should I sell it, I wonder? Or cut it up and make something else out of it?—But what? What on earth should I do with it? Out of respect for the seamstress-artist who had made it for me, I initially felt it would be wrong to cut up her creation, even though it is now my dress. Where does her artistry end and mine begin? What is the right thing to do with another artist's creation? This was part of my initial dilemma as I pondered what to do with my banished and yellowing dress. It seemed such a pity to keep it hanging in a green garbage bag in my closet. That too seemed like an insult to its maker.

Finally, not that long ago, in a fit of artistic inspiration and glee, I knew exactly what I had to do with it. My regard for the seamstress' artistry flew suddenly out the window, and I nailed—crucified—my wedding dress to a wall in the living room of my condominium. I cannot begin to describe the intense diabolical pleasure I derived as I drove large brass nails into the soft ivory linen; once and for all nailing my contempt for the institution of marriage in this rather dramatic, and artistically fruitful, gesture. I saw this as the beginning of an installation on the institution of marriage. Part of the process would eventually be to splatter the dress with red paint (or menstrual blood if only I could collect enough!), although this further act of decoration is not something I have yet had the heart to do.

On the wall, thus far *sans* paint or blood, the dress seems to have a life of its own. It looks as if it's caught in a dance or a free fall—dipping backward into a void. People comment on how beautiful and elegant it looks on my wall. Indeed, I find it far more elegant there than it ever was on me. Looking at it, I wonder what the saleswomen who sell posh dresses in the holy temples of today's couture wedding boutiques would make of this breach of wedding etiquette. But, yet, the dress is mine to do with as I wish. The installation is my own. For me, this piece is a symbolic representation of my resistance to the institution of marriage. I wonder what other once-married-now-single women would say and do with their closeted wedding dresses. What hidden stories would tumble out of the folds of their yellowing gowns?

Finding a way to "preserve" the dress is not only a question of nostalgia, but also an aesthetic one. I've even kept my wedding bouquet—a small, beautiful arrangement wrapped in a wide, white silk bow. My mother made it with flowers from our garden, just shortly before we went off to the church. The faded, dry, fragile flowers rest on an antique wedding nightie that belonged to my nana's sister. Again, my reason for this little "still life vignette" in my room in my parents' home is aesthetic. Because my mother made the bouquet, I cannot deny the sentimental value I also attach to it. My mother might be touched by my need to preserve her floral artistry, but the seamstress may not embrace the artistic license I have taken with her *oeuvre d'art*.

Martha Stewart has written about the aesthetic success of her own wedding.[2] She described the (manic) work involved in the creation of one hat she made for the event:

> . . . a Jackie Kennedy–inspired pillbox covered in the same embroidered Swiss organdie as my dress, which my mother and I made. I used scraps left over from the dress: the interlining of the bodice, a silk peau de soie; a very fine China-silk lining; and of course the organdie itself, embroidered with delicate daisies. I found a snippet of beautiful veiling in one of those fascinating stores somewhere on West 39th Street, and I stitched and snipped and fitted everything as carefully as I could, hoping that no one would know or notice that my head-dress had not been made by Halston, the reigning hat-maker of the day. I still have the hat and the dress, and when I look at the workmanship and the detailing, I am still pleased with my mother's and my handiwork.[3]

The mention of her and her mother's workmanship—their artistry—stands out and reminds me of the dilemma I felt in defacing the artistry and handiwork of the designer who made my wedding gown. I wonder what Martha would say or do if someone were to crucify her handiwork to the wall? What installation might she make of her wedding dress? Has she, too, preserved her wedding dress, not for sentimental reasons, but for aesthetic reasons?

Halloween Bride: Parading in Costume

The first Halloween costume that I recall wearing was a bride's costume. I was determined to have a wedding dress for my disguise. I think someone made the costume for me; perhaps a kindly neighbor or relative. I seem to recall a lot of work involved, the occasional fitting, and negotiations—much like the process involved in the creation of a "real" wedding dress. I also have memories of the fabric: lots of coarse, prickly, synthetic tulle. In primary school where there is the requisite showing-off of costumes on the afternoon of Halloween, I remember parading around the periphery of the school gym with the other students, modeling my bride's costume to an audience of parents, teachers, and peers. People thought I was a fairy princess, but I would have to correct them, saying that I was no fairy princess but a bride. Always the strong desire to be the bride.

Why is it, that from an incredibly early age, little girls dream of being princess brides? Why is it, since ever I can remember, I wanted to be a bride? Chrys Ingraham writes:

> The marketing of everything from weddings to gowns to children's toys to popular wedding films to Disney is laced with messages about fairy tales and princesses . . . it is this romance with the white wedding gown and the fantasy bride that conceals the workings of the heterosexual imaginary throughout the wedding-industrial complex. Moreover, the interdependency of weddings with the historical needs of capitalism become virtually invisible.[4]

Through popular culture and a multibillion dollar wedding industry, the hierarchies of race, class, and sexuality are secured, further benefiting the patriarchal status quo of state, religion, and multinationals. Popular culture and the media play powerful roles in defining, promoting, and maintaining the heterosexual, romantic illusion of the white wedding. From the time we are born into this society, we are bombarded with the imagery—the "heterosexual imaginary"—everywhere we turn, starting with the fairy tales we learn as children.

And indeed, later, when I "grew up," I got my chance to really be "that woman," and "wear that white wedding dress."

Like the Halloween costume of my childhood, the practice-run at design, my real wedding dress was hand-made to my specifications. After all, the dress is everything, and I was looking for the perfect dress. In my opinion, most store-bought dresses were gaudy with all that tulle, lace, flounce, and glitter—an Italian nightmare in chiffon. That said, however, one cold February afternoon I still managed to find myself in one of those upscale wedding boutiques that thrive on bride hysteria. Like Lilith, the first "first" woman—created before Eve—there was a first wedding dress.

The Lilith Wedding Dress

The winter before my wedding, my friend Christine and I wandered into a wedding dress boutique in search of the "Salon du Mariage" that was supposedly taking place in some hotel nearby. Not able to find the event, we decided to stay put and on try on wedding dresses so that I could get some ideas for the wedding gown I would have made. With schoolgirl glee we delighted at the thought of trying on wedding dresses together, each finding a few we liked and parading around in front of the mirrors. Much like trying on jeans, but only better and far more glamorous. Unschooled were we in the etiquette of the wedding boutique. One does not waltz into a bridal shop with one's girlfriend and try on dresses like they were a pair of Levis. As we were the only two customers in sight, an entourage of saleswomen descended upon Christine and I in a flurry of excitement and protocol. How naïve we were, like proverbial lambs being led to the "wedding-industrial complex" slaughter. And all before I even got to the altar.

Only the bride-to-be was allowed to try on dresses. I quickly understood why. We were not to be left to our own devices to browse, pick a garment off the rack, and disappear into a cubicle. A bride-to-be needed the boutique's ladies-in-waiting to help her select and, most importantly, slip into the gown. This was not a shopping spree for the frivolous or the faint of heart—it was a lot of work getting into those damn dresses; you practically needed a crane to hoist them up over your head. Throughout the extravagant process, conversations are had and, oh so subtly, information is elicited: How did you meet your fiancé? What does he do? What do you do? Where is the wedding? Oh, how lovely! A wedding in the country at your family home, you say? Flowers and food provided and catered by your parents and friends? How intimate! Read: that wedding isn't going to cost the girl hardly a penny. We'll get her to spend a fortune on the dress.

Before I knew it, I had it on. A beautiful ivory silk wedding dress. On the rack, it wasn't one I would have ever chosen for myself because it was more ornate than I like, but to see it on was incredible (those gals know their stuff). I looked beautiful in it. All $3000.00 of it. This is how they get you, standing there in all this magnificence staring into a full-length mirror. *Now* how could you possibly imagine your special day without this dress? You only get to do this once in a lifetime, why not splurge! You look so gorgeous! Maybe Mom won't mind forking out $3000.00. After all, we're not hiring a band or DJ!

With bride hysteria kicking in, I inquired about putting the dress aside for a few weeks so that my mother and bridesmaid could see it when they visited me in town. Before I made any final decision, I explained, my mother had to see the dress and OK such an expensive purchase as she was the one paying for it. All smiles and maternal understanding, the boutique ladies assured me there was no problem. All that was involved for a lay-away was a deposit, because, you never know, it might get sold to some other lucky bride who beat you to it. That would be such a shame because it looks so perfect on you. I agreed and innocently offered to purchase the undergarment—the not-so-cheap, strapless uber-brassiere—as a guarantee of my return with my mother. Suddenly, the pleasant faces of the ladies-in-waiting fell and the noses turned upward. A deposit, Mademoiselle, is usually half the cost of the dress. As if we're all walking around with a cool $1500.00 in our pocket. Explaining, yet again, why I could not make that kind of final financial decision until my mother saw it, the wedding boutique saleswomen grudgingly acquiesced. They took my measly deposit of one hundred dollars as I signed the bill.

Sitting at a café after our foray into the shark-infested waters of the bridal shop, Christine said she had a bad feeling about what had transpired. The sickening thought had just crossed her mind that I might be locked into the $3000.00 purchase. Always wisely more skeptical about things, Christine smelled a rat. I figured, at most, I was out one hundred dollars. But, I had signed the bill. My meal was becoming a rock in the pit of my stomach. A quick phone call to her mother (who comes from a family of lawyers) confirmed Christine's suspicions: "Go back to the store immediately and get your money back!" advised her mother. Unable to finish our meal, we returned to the wedding boutique. Ever the "good girl" that I was in my 20s, I politely said that I was having second thoughts about the dress and that I was feeling rather uncomfortable about having it put aside under these conditions. Would they mind putting the gown back on the rack, and I would take my chances on it still being there when I returned in March with my mother and bridesmaid. Oh yes, and could I please have my cheque for one hundred dollars back?

By this point, I had gone beyond breaching wedding boutique etiquette. In a huff of supreme indignation I was told that this would be impossible. The deal had been processed, the cheque registered in the cash, and I had signed the bill; the machine was in motion. I was Dr. Faust. Then they gave me a line that to return my cheque could get the saleswoman fired. Of course I didn't want anyone to lose their job because of me. Christine had noticed one of the saleswomen getting ready to rip up my cheque, and kicked me. Not taking her cue, I explained, for the umpteenth time, that my mother needed to see this dress before any deal was made, and that I was just beginning to look at wedding dresses. Incensed further, eyes bulging, a lady-in-waiting exclaimed, "You think you can have us spend an entire afternoon serving you, and then not buy anything?!" With this remark, I snapped. No longer the nice girl but the haughty customer "who's always right," I snarled back, "Madame, it is my consumer right to go into any store, try on as many garments, spend as much time, have as many salespeople serve me, and not buy a thing. We spent a pleasant afternoon together but now I feel like I've been screwed!" (Gasps of indignation from the saleswomen.) I continued, "Furthermore, I am really no longer interested in the dress. It is now tainted by this experience."

The Eve Wedding Dress

Although the $3000.00 dress was a better fit, the wedding dress I did end up wearing was one I had made by a very talented local seamstress. My dress was a simple, ankle-length, ivory linen dress designed to my specifications. I had originally envisioned something sleeveless and sleek, but after discussion, we decided on off-the-shoulder, short cap sleeves and a fuller, flowing skirt. Now, with the passage of time, I am trying to recall exactly why we didn't go with something sleek. I do know that at the time I hardly felt sleek or sexy. I felt dumpy and conservative; something totally out of character for me. However, I think the ultimate reason I settled for the softer, fuller, and sleeved dress was because of the fabric I chose. Or rather, I think it was the fabric that chose me.

I had gone into Montreal to shop for material for my wedding dress at a store, on Ste. Denis Street, which my seamstress had recommended. I was like a kid in a candy shop. It was almost impossible to choose from all of the overwhelming textures and colours. I eventually decided upon several swatches of gorgeous material: creamy silks, gold brocades, and two types of ivory linen. The linen won out even though it was a fabric that I never would have considered for a wedding gown. I was intent on using both types of linen; one was light and delicate, the other sturdy, more substantial. I loved how the textures contrasted yet blended so beautifully. They were soft and informal. And they looked *comfortable*. What I especially loved was that, to me, they seemed like an unconventional choice, yet there was an informal elegance about them. For practical reasons, it seemed that to go with the linen, given the nature of the fabric, I had to abandon the ideal of a sexy, sleek, sleeveless number. To do justice to the material, I had to go with a style that lent itself to the fabric; a style which was soft and flowing.

The cap sleeves of the dress were my compromise for something sleeveless. They curved out from the top of a low-cut, fitted bodice, producing a shawl-collar effect. The gauzy folds of the soft linen skirt flowed out just above the hips from the bodice, which was made of the heavier linen and reinforced with whalebones for maximum support of an ample breast (thus the "whale" in whalebone). Unfortunately, with all the built-in hardware to keep my boobs high and dry, the bodice never really fit all that well and my breasts looked rather 1950s-pointy. The seamstress was a lace collector and, with my cautious blessing, she included some very interesting and antique pieces. One unconventional piece she used was the gorgeous lace from a Catholic bishop's robe, which she attached to the linen at the bottom third of my dress and then swept up toward the lower back. Into this, she sewed an antique hankie my fiancé had given me, creating a small bustle effect. As with my Halloween bridal costume, I remember negotiations and several fittings over the course of about four months.

I wore no veil, hat, gloves nor any other wedding paraphernalia, except for the powder blue silk and lace garter I borrowed to honour the tradition of "something old, something new, something borrowed, something blue." I refused to wear impossible bras (like the one from the wedding boutique), corsets or other harnesses known to woman—underwear for which you need an engineering degree, or entourage of ladies-in-waiting, to get into. And, in late July all I wanted under that dress was a pair of silk panties. I wanted elegant comfort as much as possible, going so far as to ask the seamstress to put neat side pockets in the skirt. At this, she drew the line. My only accessories were two pairs of shoes: white tennis sneakers with a big white bow on each shoe and a pair of ivory leather sling-backs with a low heel. The sneakers were to get me down the street from the church to the reception at my parents' home. (In retrospect I should have used them to run far, far away!) The delicate sling-backs were the first purchase of my wedding trousseau—months before the dress was ever created. Those shoes are my favorite part of the whole ensemble. In fact, they are the favourite part of my entire marriage. Instead of lingering and then yellowing in the back of a closet, the sling-backs presently hang on a wall in my living room. I still wear them on occasion.

The Marriage: Get Me to the Divorce Lawyer on Time

> For centuries the institution of marriage was the instrument for controlling the rights, persons, and property of women. In the words of the 18th-century English jurist Sir William Blackstone, "By marriage, husband and wife are one person in law." That one person was the husband (Marion Botsford Fraser).[5]

It wasn't until after I married that I realized how much I disliked the institution of marriage (even though I was married in Quebec, Canada, where both the provincial and federal Charters of Rights are more avant-garde than the American constitution). I realized I was more in love with *The Dress* and *A Wedding* than I was with the man and the institution. My short-lived attempt at marriage—13 long, miserable months—is something I'd prefer to forget. Now, looking back through hindsight to childhood, I remember that marriage never *really* figured into my little girl passions: the Greek goddesses who filled my imagination were not married—at least not the goddesses I admired. Nor were my later feminist heroes, until I learned with a twinge of betrayal, that Gloria Steinem decided to marry.

"Married" is an identity that I discard, like poorly fitting clothes. It is not an identity I wear very well. Even my beautifully crafted wedding dress was not a perfect fit, from the pointy boobs to the over abundance of fabric which added more girth to my frame. Those 13 months still feel like such an oddity to me; a distant "blip" on a life line. People who know me—especially post-marriage/divorce—find it as strange as I do. As a teenager, I was voted the least likely to marry before age thirty. I should have listened.

In retrospect, I didn't want to be a wife, I wanted to be a bride. I choose to be single. Curiously (sadly?) none of this changes the fact that I have always loved weddings, with the exception of my own. Mine was an almost-perfect wedding, the groom notwithstanding, of course! Aesthetically it was a great success. It was an at-home wedding in the beautiful house I grew up in. Sumptuous food was prepared by my mother and other family and friends; the flowers were from my parents' garden; the house and grounds looked elegant and impeccable. It was another perfect "Visser party." When I announced my divorce 13 months later, my god-sister confessed to me, "On your wedding day, Jo, you smiled, but your smile didn't reach up into your eyes."

My Kind of Wedding

I'm still a sucker for a wedding but, by no means, necessarily a white wedding. After seeing *Monsoon Wedding*—Mira Nair's gorgeous, colorful film about a Punjabi family and an arranged marriage—traditional white weddings look rather insipid in comparison. It is not the romantic, but the aesthetic aspects of a wedding that hook me every time. Growing up, a friend, who was eventually my bridesmaid, used to tease me and say, "Jo, why don't you just get a cut-out cardboard groom so you can have a wedding? We'll just prop him up somewhere." I probably should have listened to her!

One day, not too long ago, while discussing a friend's wedding plans, I caught myself nonchalantly announcing, "At my next wedding . . ." The words came tumbling out of my mouth as easily as saying, "At my next dinner party . . ." Like Sophia in Marion Botsford Fraser's book, *Solitaire*, I must acknowledge and question my irrational desire for a wedding in order to indulge "that part of me that pines to be a princess." As girls and young women, we fantasize about being *brides* NOT wives. If only we could be one without the other! A wedding without the fuss and muss of marriage and husband! There are women who long to participate in the ritual; to be that bride on that day; to receive gifts; and, most important of all, to wear that white wedding dress. If we were more honest with ourselves, and weren't so willing to settle, would we come to realize that what we really want is a wedding, not a marriage? A wedding to our self, not another—a grand celebration with friends and family to mark a significant passage in our life—a public recognition of our commitment to our self and our community, a celebration of our life as independent, contributing, whole, and fulfilled human beings. Why couldn't women have a day all to themselves to celebrate their full lives with those they love? Why couldn't they marry themselves? Now, THAT would be a good thing. Wouldn't it?

Notes

1. Marion Botsford Fraser, *Solitaire: The Intimate Lives of Single Women.* (Toronto: Macfarlane Walter & Ross, 2001) 96.
2. In "A letter from Martha" in the winter 2002 issue of *Martha Stewart Weddings,* Martha recounts tales of her own wedding and includes a black and white photo of the happy bride on her wedding day—with the groom cropped out, of course.
3. Martha Stewart, "A letter from Martha." *Martha Stewart Weddings* (Winter 2002) 50.
4. C. Ingraham, *White Weddings: Romancing Heterosexuality in Popular Culture.* (New York: Routledge, 1999) 30.
5. Botsford Fraser, 286–7.

PART VI

Dressing Identity

CHAPTER 22

Xiao Lan Curdt-Christiansen

Made in China

> *La toilette devint tout à coup pour elle ce qu'elle est pour toutes les femmes, une manifestation constante de la pensée intime, un langage, un symbole.*[1]
>
> H. DE BALZAC, 1839[2]

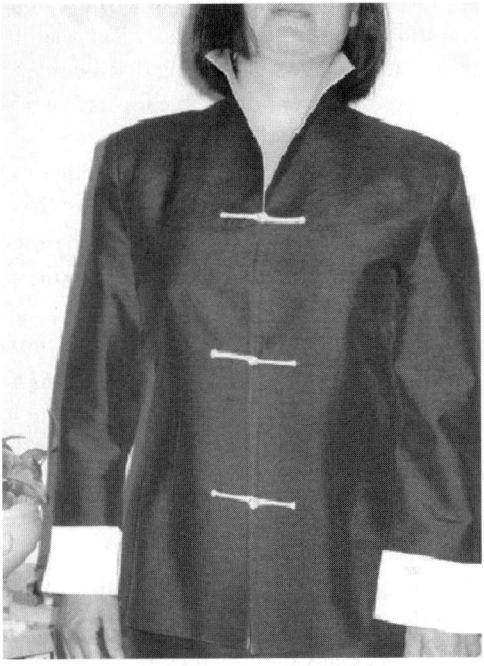

Figure 22.1. The author's adaptation of traditional Chinese dress.

"This must be Shanghai Tan!"

An elderly and well-known professor of literacy approached me at an education conference. I was somewhat puzzled, but I smiled politely, as if in agreement, and continued the conversation:

"I believe that was a famous TV series in China in the 1980s."

"Yes, but it is also very popular now in New York, Paris, and London." I became even more confused.

"Have they translated the show? And why is it so popular?"

"Not the show, your outfit."

I finally understood what he was talking about. He was referring to my Chinese dress, the outfit that I was wearing that evening, and he was comparing it with the famous Chinese fashion brand, "Shanghai Tang's"—a Hong Kong–based fashion house-cum-boutique chain.

A month later, at one of my husband's international medical conferences, a similar incident occurred. This time I was smarter and knew how to reply to the remark.

"Thank you very much! But it is not Shanghai Tang's, it's *my own* design."

✳

The outfit I wore on both occasions is an adaptation of a traditional style of Chinese dress. It is a two-piece suit, which I had a tailor in Beijing make for me two years ago during a vacation at my parents' home. I had made a sketch of some of my ideas which I showed to the tailor, explaining that I needed a dress that was simultaneously Chinese and Western and suitable for formal occasions. He understood me well, and together we chose the materials.

It is made of black Shangdong silk—a silk variety similar to Thai silk, without the shiny effect of satin. Like any other suit worn in the West, it consists of two pieces, a jacket and a skirt. What makes my suit different from the contemporary western style are elements of traditional Chinese design—the collar, the cuffs and the buttons.

Traditional Chinese clothes use very brightly colored fabric with strong contrast in hems and edges. Using this color contrast, the jacket has a three-inch cuff in white satin. The same kind of white silk is also used as lining for the entire front. The front panels of the jacket are cut so that they connect with the collar as a whole. The collar itself is a variation on the traditional Chinese 旗袍—*qi pao* collar with its high, standing-up neck, rounded at the closing, and tightly fitting. But instead of being rounded at the closing, my collar has a straight line. When the jacket is worn, the collar opens up showing the white satin lining. Buttons are placed in the middle of the jacket, using the same white satin. They are hand-made double-buttons called —*pan kou* in Chinese. They are shaped like a pair of straight hairpins facing each other and are placed on the two opposing sides of the jacket. The right half has a plaited ball-like knot and the left half has a loop that takes in the knot. In China, numbers are important, so my jacket has *three* such double-buttons. Four or six buttons are rarely used on clothes.

As the Chinese language has many homonyms (making it particularly suitable for wordplay), many numbers have obtained a special significance as well, based on other meanings of the word and reflecting cultural and aesthetic values and traditions. A good example is the number four, which is pronounced as [si], also the word for "death." Other numbers are significant because of their relation to philosophical theories or historical events. For example, five is a lucky number as it is the number of the senses (sight, taste, smell, hearing, and feeling), there are five primary directions (north, south, east, west, and center), the world consists of five elements (water, fire, wood, metal, and earth), there are five basic colors (green, yellow, red, black, and white), and we have five basic social obligations (to be a responsible father, loving mother, caring older brother, respectful younger brother, and a dutiful child).

Six is a good number, because six [liu] is part of many lucky expressions such as 六六顺 —*liu liu shun* and 六六大顺 —*liu liu da shun* and is often chosen as a wedding date (my own wedding was on the sixth of June—on the sixth day of the sixth month!). In spite of being a popular and beloved number, six can also be a forbidden or unlucky number, at least in certain contexts and in certain places. In Hubai province, a dinner of six courses is associated with a funeral banquet; in Shandong province, six buttons cannot be used on clothes for people to wear; only animals.[3] My family comes from Shandong and I remember that my mother always said "四六不成材"—*si liu bu cheng cai*—a proverb meaning that "four and six never become a useful person." Consequently, I chose three buttons for my jacket.

The skirt is long with high slits on the sides—an adaptation of the *qi pao*. At the end of the slits, two pairs of white *pan kou* buttons are attached.

This suit is one of my favorite dresses; it is my "power suit" which I have worn on many formal occasions.[4] The black color gives it a severe look, which I consider a key to acceptance in the academic world. The Chinese design with white satin is used as a softening element to moderate the severity, making the suit more feminine and more consistent with contemporary fashion discourses. I like it because it makes me feel elegant and different—and Chinese. Elegant because the pure silk and the beauty of the cut place me on a par with other well dressed, modern professional women. Different, because no one else has a dress like it; I designed it myself. And Chinese, because the design elements I have used underline my ethnic and cultural heritage.

So this China Chic outfit of mine, with its striking cut and strong contrast of colours has frequently attracted considerable, and always positive, attention from colleagues and friends at academic meetings and conferences, while emphasizing my Chinese origin and cultural roots.

I have always been very conscious of my "Chineseness." This consciousness grew intensely through living in foreign countries: seven years in Denmark followed by another seven years in Quebec, Canada. My living experience outside China has made me very aware of how I present myself in clothing, language, gesture and posture. When I participate in various social events, questions like "How should I dress?" "What should I wear?" and "Whom am I representing?" come up repeatedly. After having been greeted a few times with "ku ni chi wa" (Japanese for "how are you"), I felt a strong desire to reveal my Chinese ethnicity up front, to promote my Chinese heritage, to advertise for all to see that I am "made in China."

So I decided to dress à la chinoise. As dress is the most direct and visual vehicle to convey the cultural image of an individual, it aids the construction of subjectivity as presentation. "Dress is a coded sensory system of nonverbal communication that aids human interaction in space and time" (Eicher).[5] In China, we have an old proverb, "人配衣服，马配鞍—*ren pei yifu ma pei an*," which can be translated as "clothes make the man as the saddle makes the horse." In the West, a very similar perspective was given a literary form in G. Keller's famous novel *Kleider machen Leute* (1856), whose title has become a proverbial expression in several European languages.[6] In moral terms, there is little truth in the statement that "clothes make the man," but in social terms this is undeniably so. Clothes, thus, are a non-verbal language that reveals or emphasizes an individual's gender, ethnicity, social status, attitude towards life, and often also social-political orientation.

As the 旗袍 *qi pao*, the traditional Chinese gown, for more than a century has been considered the unofficial national dress and symbol of femininity for Chinese women, I chose it as my initial attire for social events. Scarlet red, hot pink or more modest blue, I have several *qi paos* all made of brightly colored silk. They fit snugly to the body with a high, stand-up collar, and thigh-high split slits on the sides. The front of the *qi pao* is normally embroidered with traditional mascots such as a phoenix, butterflies or peonies, lotus flowers, or some lucky Chinese characters or iconography (particularly popular are the characters for longevity, double happiness, and good fortune). All the embroideries contain some sort of folklore. Contrasting colors and eye-catching hems also characterize the *qi pao*.

As clothes can be seen as cultural resources that empower us and make us suitable for certain social positions—make us "look the part," I view the suit I have designed and the *qi paos* in my wardrobe not only as symbols of my cultural and ethnic background, but also as symbols of my social identity and my belonging to a certain "class."[7] My wardrobe indicates my affiliations and perhaps even my accomplishments; it allows me to present my social image and construct my identity as a member of a certain group (doctoral candidates at a university). Moreover, dressing well—as speaking well—facilitates professional contacts and helps me obtain an advantageous position in the social power game.

"A dress is not only a cultural symbol, facilitating the *Erlebnis* ('lived experience') of a given (or chosen) identity, but is also a display, a statement of that identity, and has an important political significance" (Brown).⁸ Sometimes clothes reflect political changes and historical events.

I grew up in a military compound in Beijing during the Cultural Revolution (1966–1976). It was a revolution that opposed feudalism and bourgeois culture. Feudalism was defined by the communist party not only as a social and political system that structured the individual's position in the society, but also as a series of sociocultural practices that Chinese people had inherited from former generations. At that time, anything old and traditional was considered "feudalism" and referred to as "四旧—the four olds" (old ideas, old customs, old culture, old habits). Thousands of classical literary works were burned; hundreds of cultural heritages were destroyed. Religious practices were forbidden, classical music was no longer played, theatres were closed down, and traditional dresses were banned. Especially the latter may seem strange, but major importance was attached to the way people dressed. Not only were traditional dresses old-fashioned and therefore "wrong," they were also used by both politicians and ordinary people to show individualism and cultural or political orientation or preference. A traditional dress was seen to demonstrate sympathy for bourgeois culture and the values of the past; a western style dress was considered opposition against the communist party.

The ten years of the Cultural Revolution were not only a disaster for traditional culture and the maintenance of the national heritage, but also a disaster for Chinese fashion.

I remember very vividly an incident from the beginning of the Cultural Revolution. A documentary film was shown in the military compound where I lived with my family. It showed chairman Liu Shaoqi, a colleague of Mao's, being criticized as antirevolutionary. His crime was driven home by showing that his wife, Madam Wang Guangmei, possessed more than twenty *qi paos*, which she wore when accompanying him on formal occasions such as state visits. The film showed her in several of those very elegant dresses. I hardly noticed anything else in the film but her beauty and those elegant dresses.

My childhood was spent in a sea of military green. Mao's doctrine for women in the new China—that women should "不爱红装爱武装"—*bu ai hong zhuang, ai wu zhuang* (i.e. "love military clothing, but not feminine clothing")—underpinned all choices of clothes for our generation. Our wardrobe was filled with green military uniforms and grey and blue Mao suits. A traditional *qi pao* was never seen in my childhood, neither in my home nor anywhere else. During my school years, I remember military uniforms as being the most fashionable clothes.

Because my whole family was in the military, I—the youngest of the family—often had the opportunity to inherit one or two sets of military uniforms from my older brothers and sisters.

I was popular at school in those years as I had access to authentic military uniforms and hats, which I sometimes loaned to my friends so that they could go and have their picture taken. A portrait in a genuine military uniform was seen as very desirable. Dressing up in various clothes—always a fun thing for children to do—was for our generation an activity heavily marked with political implications. How we dressed was a reflection of the prevailing political thinking and the particular sociocultural attitude of that particular period.

No matter how fashionable the military uniform was, the simple elegance of the *qi pao* that Madam Wang Guangmei wore never disappeared entirely from my memory. I always hoped that one day I could be wrapped in such a beautiful, elegant dress.

The *qi pao* is not only the dress of *my* dreams; women all over the world wear it, from barmaids, pop singers, and film stars at the Grammy Awards to ladies attending high-society dinners and state banquets. In the middle of the 1990s, the world-famous Chinese actress, Gong Li, appeared in a white silk *qi pao* at the international film award ceremony in Cannes, catching everybody's attention and receiving much praise in the fashion press. As celebrities traditionally have had a strong influence on how "ordinary people" dress, the Chinese regime triggered an *hausse* in Chinese fashion by presenting visiting political leaders with traditional Chinese jackets. At the closing ceremony at the Shanghai APEC meeting in 2001, all participants including several world leaders were seen dressed in Chinese jackets based on the traditional Chinese fashion styles. Underlying this was a political motive: an aim to call attention to the presence of China on the international political stage, to promote China in the global era by including China into the WTO and other international political and economic organizations.

Political and economic developments have provided resources for a revitalized Chinese fashion movement, which has emerged in an atmosphere of intense nationalism. Last summer, I went back to Beijing and experienced a cultural shock. I saw traditional style dresses all over the place, in the streets, in shopping centers, in restaurants. Young and old, men and women, all seemed to be wearing clothes with one or more traditional design feature. Some had traditional embroideries on the bottom of their trousers, some had Chinese characters on the front of their jacket and others used plain material with Mandarin collars. This growing interest in and understanding of the values of the national heritage signals nothing less than a cultural awakening and a desire for cultural recognition in the era of globalization. The success of Chinese films like *Crouching Tiger, Hidden Dragon* and *In the Mood for Love* revealed both the rich culture and the beauty of traditional clothes for the entire world to see, contributing to China's influence on modern

Western fashion. More and more Chinese elements are integrated into the Western style, setting new fashion trends, usually referred to as "China Chic." The almost extreme interest in this "new" Chinese fashion is an indication of a cultural renaissance in China, and "a genuine expression of broadening cultural horizons around the world."[9]

Dressing is a form of social action. We dress to make a certain impression and convey a particular message, we dress to stand out or not to stand out, as the case may be, as well as to align ourselves with a particular cultural, political, and social group.

To me, an embroidered dragon on the front of a jacket or a lotus flower patched on the bottom of a pair of pants are cultural emblems, revealing not only a cultural heritage, but also implicitly delivering the cultural knowledge of "Chinese," as they represent in symbolic form either a folkloristic or historical event. I view these Chinese elements as nonverbal linguistic forms (like lexical choice, intonation, phonological units, etc.) that reflect deeply rooted cultural practices, ideologies, and beliefs of the Chinese.[10] These Chinese elements, signaling cultural associations, illustrate a kind of nonverbal communication that utilizes dress "as a socially and culturally constructed symbol system in ways that reflect macro-level social meanings."[11]

Just as the *qi pao* becomes a two-piece suit, Chinese traditional clothes become more and more westernized; however, the nonverbal "linguistic forms"—the Chinese elements—remain, as ethnic markers and cultural signifiers. These non-verbal "linguistic forms" provide pivotal cultural resources that an individual can draw upon to establish his/her alignment. In Bourdieu's words, such cultural resources are "cultural capital," which enables individuals to draw upon to construct their cultural identity.[12] At the same time, Chinese elements or nonverbal linguistic forms also provide contextual information for others (on-lookers, interlocutors, conversational partners) to draw upon to construct meaningful interaction. By relating these contextualized cues to their background knowledge, individuals are enabled to make situated inferences about the cultural heritage of others. Thus, nonverbal linguistic forms create both groups and boundaries. Identity is achieved through clothes to position self and other in culturally meaningful ways.

As a Chinese woman living in the West, I am very aware of my multiple identities. Dress has been a pivotal mediator for me to achieve my identity. How to dress every morning is both an artistic choice and an identity combat, but I still enjoy looking at my clothes. I have a variety of choices from very traditional styles to modern "China Chic," from very western to purely oriental. My favorite clothes are still the ones with Chinese elements that can both show my ethnic background and my cultural heritage and, at the same time, boost my confidence in the persona I am today.

For a banquet, I choose a silk *qi pao* in traditional red; for a less formal cocktail party, I put on a *qi pao*-inspired jacket or top in fluorescent purple with a black ankle-length skirt; to go to a conference, I wear my black-and-white two piece suit; for everyday activities, I go out with a *kung fu* jacket in white silk with ideographic pattern; for a chilly autumn day, I would put on my black wool jacket with a round red Chinese character "福" (good fortune) patched in the middle of the front.

Nowadays, I go everywhere dressed à la chinoise.

Notes

1. A woman's dress suddenly became for her, as for all women, a permanent revelation of her most secret thoughts, a language, and a symbol.
2. H. de Balzac, *Une fille d'Eve*, 1839.
3. Wang, & Meng, *Numbers in the Eyes of the Chinese* (Beijing, China: Tuanjie Publication, 2000).
4. For interesting insight into dress and power in academia, see S. Kaiser, J. Chandler, & T. Hammidi,"Minding Appearances in Female Academic Culture," In A. Guy; E. Green & M. Banim (Eds.), *Through the Wardrobe: Woman's Relationships with Their Clothes* (New York: Peter Long Publishing, 2001) 119–136.
5. J. B. Eicher, "Introduction: Dress as an Expression of Ethnic Identity," In J. B. Eicher (Ed.), *Dress and Ethnicity* (Oxford, UK: Berg, 1995) 1–5.
6. G. Keller, *Kleider machen Leute*, 1856.
7. P. Bourdieu, "Language and Symbolic Power." In J. Thompson (Ed.). (Cambridge: Polity Press,1991); J. F. Keenan (Ed.), *Dress to Impress: Looking the Part.* (Oxford, UK: Berg, 2001).
8. M. D. Brown (2001). Multiple Meanings of the Hijab in Contemporary France. In J. F. Keenan (Ed.), *Dress to Impress.* Oxford, UK: Berg, 2001) 105–122.
9. V. Steele, *Shoes: A Lexicon of Style.* (New York: Rizzoli, 1999).
10. J. Gumperz (Ed.). *Language and Social Identity.* (Cambridge: Cambridge University Press, 1982); D. Schiffrin, *Approaches to Discourse* (Cambridge: Cambridge University Press, 1996).
11. Schiffrin, 315.
12. Bourdieu.

CHAPTER 23   *Roksana Bahramitash*

Revealing Veiling and Unveiling

Cairo, 2002, Eid Fitr[1]

Reveiled in Cairo

I started writing this chapter while seated comfortably in a café in Cairo overlooking the Nile, far away from my current home in Montreal. I had anticipated that visiting Cairo would in many ways be like going back home to Iran, yet once I arrived, the city overwhelmed me. I felt terribly lost and shy and timid. And so I decided to wear a hijab (veil)[2] while visiting the city, not because I have to, and not that I have suddenly become religious, but because I wanted to. Wearing the veil enables me to blend into the local scene and gives me a sense of belonging. I do not particularly like standing out as a tourist. Veiling myself to look as non-Western as possible is one way of dealing with this unwanted feeling of being a stranger here.

With all this longing for belonging, this trip has made me realize that I may not belong to the Middle East as much as I had assumed I do. I may have become more North American than I thought. For example, I have more problems, now, than I used to with sexual segregation and gender boundaries. It bothers me to see a lot more men in the streets than women—far more. It seems a very male space, and what is worse, so many men seem to feel free to look at you or stare at you, all of which makes me very uncomfortable.

Many years ago, back in Tehran where I was born and lived most of my life, I had no problem with men in the streets looking at me. It didn't bother me the way it does now. I could stare back at them with a very stern no-nonsense look, or say something to put them in their place if necessary. But I discovered upon arriving in Cairo that that old strength and confidence seems to have left me. And so wearing a hijab was an effort to make up for the confidence I no longer always feel.

The funny thing, though, is that all this fear evaporates into thin air as soon as I start to communicate with men here. It only takes a few words in Arabic from me and they immediately become like brothers, wanting to help me in any way they can. Not a day has passed without me hearing "welcome to Cairo" from men with big smiles on their faces, warm, welcoming smiles. If I smile back, they continue and say, "I hope you like being here." If I linger a little, I am asked to sit down and have tea or coffee or I am offered chocolate and fruits in a very friendly way. I no longer feel like a stranger, but part of the extended family of Egypt. What role does my being veiled play in all this? I cannot be sure.

My hijab here consists of a tiny black scarf over what is otherwise a completely Western outfit (though still very much covered and modest), a pair of dark trousers and a loosely fitted jean jacket. In a Muslim country like Egypt, where the hijab is not compulsory, what would they think of me if they knew that I am a highly educated woman, a Canadian citizen wearing a hijab? I have no doubt that my attire would be very puzzling to some. All of this may be confusing for the reader of this chapter but is, in fact, a perfect way to start writing about something so complicated by layers upon layers of meaning.

The fact of the matter is that veiling is a phenomenon whose meanings change depending on who is wearing the veil, in what context, for what reasons, and where. The wearing of a hijab can assume multiple meanings that are shaped and reshaped through symbolic actions and interactions between people, collectively as well as individually. The veil can symbolize something very personal or it can represent a highly political act, or it can refer to both at the same time, or to neither. Sometimes it is just more a matter of "that's what people wear," something taken for granted without any special personal or political significance. Moreover, the meaning and intentions behind the veil can be very different for the woman who wears it as opposed to those who see her in it.

To explore the veil (and more specifically, the hijab) further as I write this chapter in Cairo, I will describe my own experience that has thus far included many different encounters with veils. Indeed, I have veiled and de-veiled myself at different times during my life and in different parts of the world. My story is that of a woman originally from the Middle East but now residing in North America where I guess I am "the other" who has become part of "the self."[3] As an insider/outsider, my story travels between two seemingly different worlds, the Middle East/North Africa and North America.

First Encounters with the Veil: Tehran Childhood Memories
De-veiling Policy and the Public Baths

As I wander through streets of Cairo, trying to understand the nature of the Islamist movement, so many memories come alive. I grew up with the veil. My grandmother on my father's side, madar (the mother), and my great-grandmother on my mother's side, khanom bozorg (the great lady), were both veiled until the day they died. My grandmother and great-grandmother raised me in Iran, where I was born. The many bedtime stories they told me were the memories of their youth. One of these memories was about Reza Shah's de-veiling policy, a policy which had not been very successful among my grandmothers' generation of women.

Reza Shah, who was brought to power by the British after the WWI, exerted a great deal of effort to Westernize Iran, and de-veiling was part of this grand project. The police were ordered to pull women's veils from their heads in the streets. Women could not leave their homes without being stopped by the city police for wearing the veil. As a result, going to the popular public steam baths, along with any other ventures outside the home, was an increasingly daunting experience. Veiled women were harassed so frequently that many of them stopped going to the baths altogether. Instead they had to take their baths at home, often with a great deal of difficulty, particularly during cold winters. Not going to the public baths was all the more keenly felt as a loss because the public baths were the traditional meeting places for women.

A bath could take up an entire day. I remember, for example, that there used to be a feast for the first public bath that a new mother took, where everyone would be invited to eat, drink, dance, and celebrate her initiation into motherhood. The feast would occur after the birth of each child, but it was the first birth that received the biggest attention. I still remember a few of those occasions when I was taken to the baths as a young child: A group of women would gather and play music (using big copper bowls as drums) to which the youngest and prettiest among them would dance. Our voices echoed in the bathhouse—and what with the music and the dancing in that warm and misty scene, all observed and heard while crunching chilled pomegranate seeds—well it was easy to feel oneself in paradise.

Everyone would be naked expect for a thin towel wrapped around the waist. The women who worked in these public baths offered us skin exfoliations which involved a lovely back rub. The exfoliation would be followed with the washing of our hair and body with soap after which one had a choice of mint or lemon tea, or one could drink a huge metal cup of iced buttermilk sprinkled with dried rose petals as an aperitif. Saffron-flowered rice with barbecued lamb would follow, and then, dessert. Feasting in these steam baths, listening to women singing and dancing, used to make me feel like a Persian Princess.

By the time I became a new mother myself, however, there were no more public baths: that tradition was gone and I felt very sad about it. All through my childhood I had been looking forward to having a new-mother feast of my own at the public bath. Instead, my mother performed a very poor version of it at home, not nearly as interesting. The public bath had vanished from major cities such as Tehran and taking a day off for a bath was too traditional for a Westernized middle-class family like mine.

Public baths had also been traditionally the place where older women took a good look at the younger ones to find a possible future wife for their brothers and sons. Older women would keep their eyes on a beautiful girl from a good family and often competed with each other to make her part of their own clan. A healthy, beautiful daughter-in-law was a great way of improving the gene pool of the family and keeping one's son happy and securely in the mother's orbit. The de-veiling policy that put an end to all of this activity of the public bath thus posed a significant, if unintentional, threat to the important social role that older women played in forging family ties. Worse, it cut them off from each other, because, unwilling to conform to the new policy and give up the veil, many of them were too scared to leave their homes and had to rely on the second-hand and possibly selective information brought to them through their male kin and children. They could not exchange news, not just about their neighborhood, but also ideas about politics and business deals. This was not what Reza Shah had in mind, of course. He wanted to make women more public, not less influential, but he wanted to do it his way, the European way.

Dilemmas of Etiquette: How to Veil without Looking Veiled

The de-veiling policy posed a problem for men, too, especially those who were in the army or who were higher government officials. They would often be invited to official parties given by Reza Shah, a dictator who few dared to challenge. The problem with these invitations was that guests, who included many from foreign embassies, were expected to come accompanied by their unveiled wives. There was no question of showing up in a hijab. This was not a problem for those couples who were comfortable with the de-veiling policy, but there were many cases where at least one spouse could not bear the idea of the wife going to a party without a veil. To many pious Muslims, being unveiled was the equivalent of going to a party naked.

My grandmothers both had stories about the huge panic that such situations created and the many unconventional solutions people tried. Some women, for example, wore very large hats with long skirts and deep dark stockings. Others just refused to attend these parties altogether, necessitating a search for a suitable substitute escort for their husbands. Often the task fell to the lady in the neighbourhood who went from door to door threading women's legs and faces (threading is a way of getting ride of unwanted bodily and facial hair). Wearing a big hat, dark glasses and gloves, it was hoped that no one would recognize her. If the "threading lady" was not available, there were other options.

I was told that in some cases, male escorts would be brought along, disguised as unveiled women. They had to make sure their voices did not give them away! Dressing up as a woman was considered to be a degrading act, so these male "females" were often members of lower social classes who were pressed into service. But occasionally, friends or members of the kin of the elite men and women invited to these parties were persuaded to sacrifice themselves for the sake of the family! Some men could empathize with the women's dilemma and were moved to extend their sympathy in a real way by volunteering to dress as a woman and attend an official party. There is no way of knowing whether this cross-dressing gave any of these men any pleasure but I like to think that maybe it did, at least to some of them. And some men received money for their help.

De-veiling in Iran came to an end with the outbreak of the WWII. The British who had brought Reza Shah to power in the first place invaded Iran because Iran refused to take sides and wanted to remain a neutral zone. The allied forces invaded Iran and in the course of one day, the army that Reza Shah took such a pride in putting together was dismantled. So much for his much-admired European ways! Tehran became an occupied city, and soon anarchy prevailed. With the fall of the regime, the police were ineffective and veiled women could leave their homes again. But Tehran's occupation made the city very unsafe for women. Suddenly, those women who, unlike my grandmothers, had de-veiled voluntarily during Reza Shah's rule, had to veil themselves for their own safety. Young, beautiful women would be spotted and harassed by thugs or foreign soldiers. Rapes and sexual assaults became common. Both my grandmother and my great-grandmother had sad memories of how their preoccupation with de-veiling was replaced with their endless battle to keep their families fed without being harassed on the streets.

My Grandmother, the Chignon, and Me

I was very close to my grandmother and she used to tell me lots of details about de-veiling and the war. I loved to spend time with her and to play, especially when she let me act the role of "uptown hairdresser." My grandmother acted as my model, the one on whose hair I would practice making a chignon like the ones I had seen in French magazines. Her henna-colored long thin hair was ideal for my chignon as I could roll it over and over and over and put lots of pins in it. The chignon would be followed by a bridal make-up session for which I sneaked into my mother's make-up bag. If we had the time and she could bear it, I would then go on to dress her as the bride with lots of things hanging over her head. Thinking about this now, I am surprised that all those ornaments that I used to hang over her head never gave her a headache. . . . But maybe they did and she just kept quiet. She was crippled and half-blind so she never cared about what a clown I made out of her as long as I could clean off the mess I had put on her face before my mother arrived for a visit. My grandmother would quickly undo my hideous chignons and hide all the pins underneath her pillows until the next day after my mother left the house. These wonderful, warm and close times were not without some tension. There was a constant low-intensity war being waged between my grandmother and my mother over just about everything, but especially about how I should be brought up. I was a battleground of sorts between the two of them, much to my dismay.

The sweet memories of my grandmother have stayed with me, and, looking around Cairo, now I think of home. There is much here to remind me of Tehran before the revolution. There are many shops that specialize in wedding clothes with great chignons just like the ones I used to practice on my grandmother's hair. No doubt these chignons are inspired by the numerous European and American fashion magazines that I see displayed on every major street corner. You can't avoid them, and I think about how all these magazine pictures might be giving Egyptian women a very distorted impression of Western women, portraying images that are totally different from the actual experiences of the lives of most women in the West. For example, there are hardly any images in magazines from Canada that represent the lives of the many immigrant, native, and other women of color or women from low-income households. If the magazines are to be believed, we are all stylish and rich and happy.

Growing Up Unveiled: Miniskirts, Bottom-loose Trousers and High-heeled Shoes

Somehow the fashion in the wealthier parts of Cairo reminds me of my teenage years in Tehran. Just like the old days in Tehran, there are veiled women as well as un-veiled women on the streets. Like many other girls of middle-class background, I was very fashion conscious. I was among the minority of girls in the country who were *not* veiled. To my eyes, the veil was not fashionable. My mother used to take me to our local shop where we would buy locally produced fabrics to have dresses made for me that looked like the latest fashion in London and Paris. I started with bottom loose trousers. The problem was that local cotton was not suitable for this style and after the first wash my fashion trousers would look like a pair of pajamas. My dressmaker and I soon discovered that it was not the way she sewed but the material that was wrong for that fashion. My mother finally bought me a pair of the new fashion trousers from a friend who had brought some extra pairs from Europe. Wearing them, I then set out to learn to dance the twist in front of the mirror, just as I saw people doing on Iran's newly established television. My father adored me and would take quick peeks at my dancing practice, which always embarrassed me. I would tell him off, saying that this way of dancing was a new generation's thing and he should keep out of it. But he loved it. He loved it when I told him off and he teased me constantly, asking me about what exactly the new generation thing meant.

At that same time, the most popular English model was Twiggy, a stick-thin girl who became the center of world attention in the late 1960s. She reportedly weighed 42 kilos, which, come to think of it, could only be the weight of an anorexic woman given her height. She was pale, tall, and blonde. I wanted desperately to look like her. Twiggy. Unfortunately, I had olive-colored skin, ordinary height and dark hair. But what I could do was wear the same clothes that she was wearing with the help of our local dressmaker. And so I wore my first miniskirt when it became the latest fashion in Europe. It must be hard for the reader to imagine Tehran in the 1960s with lots of miniskirts. My dear father pretended he did not have a clue. That is how he handled everything that I did which he did not approve of. He played stupid but I knew what I was doing was outrageous and so did he.

Looking like Twiggy was really difficult because I had dark eyes. I had a complex about the color of my eyes until I heard that with certain lenses it was possible to change one's eye color. As for blonde hair, well it was possible to dye my hair as many Iranian women did in those days. There were many casualties of the desire to be blonde. Many women completely ruined their hair with constant bleaching. In those cases that involved poor hairdressing skills or cheap materials, the victims of heavy bleaching would never have healthy looking hair again. Looking back now, how I wish there had been a model who celebrated thick, lush, dark brown or black hair. So many women would have been saved. In Cairo, today, I come across the same type of blonde hair from time to time. It is rare but it reminds me of the old days back in Tehran. Cairo is full of large posters of Lady Mubarak with blonde hair and heavy make-up.

I was never allowed to dye my hair. I consoled myself by promising myself that when I was old enough not to need my parents' permission, I would dye my hair blonde. I used chamomile compresses, which brought bright red natural highlights rather than blonde hair. Thankfully, by the time I was indeed old enough to dye my hair, I had developed enough sense to appreciate that my lush and shiny brown hair was very pretty and I was grateful not to have subjected it to heavy bleaching.

To wear a miniskirt was considered quite daring, even outrageous, in some parts of Tehran. But my father was a General in the army and that meant that I could get away with wearing anything I wanted, no matter how revealing it was. A young girl with lots of miniskirts and a bit of make-up in Tehran was something of a sight. My father had no problem with me wearing a miniskirt and pretended he did not notice my make-up. He would come with me wherever I went, making sure that I could comfortably wear miniskirts and pale lipstick. He was there to protect me.

The increasing popularity of the hijab in Egypt these days reminds me how my own taste for Western looks began to change in the early part of my teens. This was the time my mother divorced my father and took custody of my brother and me. Slowly I was pulled out of the orbit of my father and his politics. My father had an unquestioned love for the Shah. He had gone to the same military school as the Shah. But my mother was against the CIA-engineered coup that had brought the Shah back to power. My mother, like many Iranian nationalists, never forgot the toppling of popular Prime Minster Mossadeq in 1953.[4]

After the divorce she became active in Tehran nightlife in which I took part as well. I became aquainted with her close friends who all had different politics; one was a member of Iran's communist party married to a Kurdish separatist, the other was a nationalist, and the third one was a social democrat. Late-night gatherings with these vibrant, exhilarating women and their circles were the beginning of my political consciousness. It was during the 1960s that my sense of commitment toward social justice became politicized. I started to read clandestine literature on the Russian and Chinese revolutions, the Hiroshima bombing, the Spanish Civil War, the American civil rights movement and the Vietnam war, as well as the liberating pedagogy of Paulo Freire.

Before my eyes Tehran had become more and more affluent in the North while the impoverished South of Tehran also grew in size. It was dangerous to join any clandestine organization; people were abducted and imprisoned just for possessing what I was reading. My profound politicization was a turning point in my life after which wearing fashionable clothes was no longer the most important thing to me. I started to realize that the fashion world was shallow and I needed to look more like most girls around me and be a little more modest in my attire. I wanted to be an Iranian, or at least to search for what it meant to be an Iranian. I was tired of being a failed copy of a model or some Hollywood star I could never be like.

As an ironic side note, I remember the first time I traveled to London in the early 1970s how startled I was to see that English girls were less obsessed with fashion than we were in Iran. They were frumpy in comparison. It was hard to imagine that all those fashion clothes I had admired came from a city like London. (Paris was a different story.) London in the 1970s was not a place where one would come across many elegantly dressed women, yet Tehran was. In the London of the 1970s, dressing up was not very fashionable, dressing up was out, dressing down was in, left over from the 1960s I suppose. This was a real eye opener for me because all those fashion magazines that poured into Iran left so many Iranian girls with such a great desire to be English. It was all about making money, selling fashions and movies to Iranians and the rest of the Third World. I no longer wanted to be a victim of the profit-making fashion industry. Each time I pass by a magazine shop in Cairo and I look at the front pages of *Cosmopolitan, Burda, Vogue* and such, I recall how I suddenly lost my taste for these magazines. It is no longer surprising to me that women veil themselves.

My Own Veiling

The political climate in Iran started to change in the 1970s: the defeat of the communist party and the fall of nationalist leader had left the Islamist movement as the only option. The Islamists slowly gained support and gradually many women started to adopt the veil. But it was not the type of veil that my grandmothers wore: it was a new type. Before the early 1970s only the elderly, working class, and peasant women wore the veil along with the members of the old merchant class. Their veil was a black head-to-toe cover in the case of the elderly and the old merchant class. As for most of the working class and the urban peasants, light colorful cotton was the usual veil. Women in the countryside never wore head-to-toe veils. Only women who live in the cities can wear these head-to-toes. Women in the countryside who work all the time need to wear much more practical outfits. They usually wear folk dresses that are far more colorful and interesting in style and appearance.

The new veil that became popular in the 1970s was a revolution in itself, not so much in its appearance but in the message it was carrying. It consisted of a scarf, a long coat or a baggy male shirt and trousers, always in simple colors usually in dark plain shades. Those who wore it were also a different type of woman: they were young, educated and many of them from secular families like my own. The new veil heralded a new political movement. Young Iranian women who had come to reject Western political and economic domination and were protesting against the Shah took up this new veil as a sign of protest. Initially, most of those who wore the new veil did it because they had developed a new commitment to their religion, but as more and more women put on the veil, the new veil became a political symbol too. As public discontent against the Shah increased, many women from the leftist and feminist movements adopted the veil too. Wearing it was like a walking "no" referendum to the regime. Wearing the veil meant that women were no longer willing to buy fashions that came from Hollywood and the Western media. The veil meant a rejection of Westernized consumerism. Or at least, that's what it meant for me and many others.

Anyone old enough to have seen pictures of the revolution in Iran can remember the huge number of women who took part in street demonstrations, usually placed strategically in the front. For major demonstrations, women would be carrying flowers to put in soldiers' gun barrels to stop them from shooting. Most of the women in the front line facing armed police and the army wore the traditional hijab to show their commitment to Ayatollah Khomeini. They were extremely religious. But the head-to-toe veil also became a demonstration uniform for others like myself who were not necessarily wearing it for religious reasons. The leftists, feminists, as well as the Islamists became united in appearance to convey one solid message.

The regime fell and Khomeini came to power. Women like me no longer felt the need to wear either the new or the old veil. The battle was won and many of us fell back to a simple modest form of dress. But Ayatollah Khomeini's new power signaled a return to traditionalism for women. Slowly signs were put up in the shops asking unveiled women not to enter. Many women had a perfect strategy: they carried a scarf in their bags and put on their scarf to go into the shops and took it off as they left. But the veil policy was soon adopted by major government institutions, and wearing a hijab became compulsory, with police patrols on the street to impose it. History was repeating itself, only the focus on whether the veil was to be on or off had changed.

The Ayatollah promised free education, food subsidies, free health care, housing, as well as self-sufficiency and economic justice. For me forced veiling and legal changes against women's rights in areas such as divorce laws became the price of social justice. I remained with the Islamist movement, a decision that was frowned upon by many of my friends and family members. I decided to stay with Ayatollah Khomeini for two reasons. One was for the sake of Iranian national sovereignty and the second was Khomeini's support for free education, public health, public housing, economic self-sufficiency, and justice for the poor. When Ayatollah Khomeini announced a jihad against illiteracy I was determined that my place was within the Islamist movement because it had always pained me greatly to realize how many women were illiterate, women who could never go to the Shah's adult schools because the lower classes were always excluded from the dominant politics of the country. They never felt welcome to take part in what was meant to benefit them. Moreover, the lower classes were often religious and they were not supportive of the notion of a secular education for women.

When Khomeini announced the Jihad, I wore the top-to-toe black veil and headed to the local mosque along with janitors' and construction workers' wives and maids. I was the only woman from the middle class of our fairly affluent area who attended the Mosque. To my mind the opportunity to volunteer for a literacy campaign was golden. It was my life-long wish to be able to give what I had to those millions of women who were deprived. My work at the local mosque was very successful. As the days went by, I gained confidence in my teaching, which was a new activity for me. Those were extremely exciting times in my life. I would often wonder about the future effects of this mass-based literacy campaign, which would undoubtedly have major implications for women and their female children. Now that our women had become so politicized and were getting an education, what could possibly stop them?

De-veiling Myself

Towards the mid-1980s I grew disenchanted with the Islamist movement. With the end of the war and Khomeini's death, the regime moved away from its welfare programs and I could see no room for me as a new president (Rafsanjani) took over. This was the end of my support for the Islamists. The new regime dropped its welfare commitment and privatization became the buzzword. Disillusioned and disappointed, I felt it was time to leave. I left Iran with great sadness, not knowing if I would ever be able to go back. The decision to leave one's country of birth to a world unknown is a huge shock.

As I watch the Islamist movement growing in Egypt, I wonder to what extent, if at all, the reasons for women's support for the Islamist movement for Egyptian women resembles mine of many years ago. A walk through the street of Mohammed Ali, where musical instruments are sold, exposed me to a familiar face of the Islamist movement. Apparently, the street used to be a place where belly dancers made frequent visits and at one point in the early part of the century it was a place for prostitutes. On the wall of this street I came across posters of veiled women and underneath the poster was written "Wearing Hijab is a religious duty" in Arabic. It did not quote the Qur'an directly, as the compulsory nature of hijab is an issue of debate among different Muslim scholars. Verses that are about the hijab are by no means uncontested. As more women become experts on religious texts, the trend towards challenging a long history of male interpretation of the Qur'an and Hadith is becoming popular throughout much of the Muslim world and this is true of Egypt as well.

September 11 and Re-veiling in North America

After spending so many years in North America unveiled, I have taken to re-veiling myself on some occasions for reasons that are myriad and complex. In the aftermath of September 11th, people like me, from the Middle East, North Africa, and Muslim countries, slowly became the representatives of evil in the public eye when President Bush named Iran, my birthplace, as one of the Axes of Evil. Prior to September 11th, the occasional harassment of veiled women on the streets of North America was mainly verbal. Since then, however, some of these attacks have become physical. A friend of mine working as a social worker in Montreal told me that as a result of their growing fear, some women have started to wear hats instead of the hijab to avoid street harassment. But this same fear that causes some women to de-veil provokes a different reaction in many of us who have started to re-veil. It was partly the increase in attacks on the Muslim community that motivated me to start veiling again in solidarity with Afghan women who have suffered so much and with the veiled women who are attacked in North America. I re-veil myself, too, because I want to understand and publicize the harassment and discrimination that veiled women experience. Moreover, wearing a veil in public places gives me a chance to show that women who wear the veil include women like me, women like you.

And so ironically, despite the harassment, the number of veiled women I see on the streets in my city has grown. Many of the veiled women I see out and about are young and educated; some of them second-generation immigrants. I cannot help but be reminded of the processes that I myself went through at their age. There are likely a lot of differences in their experience compared to mine, but there may be some similarities as well. Perhaps they too are rejecting consumerism and searching for role models inspired by their own cultural background rather than accepting as role models those whom one can never be like. Or veiling could also be for them an expression of a sense of belonging to a larger community, a way of dealing with alienation, estrangement, and marginalization in the place where one lives.

Back to the Café in Cairo

As I continued to work on this chapter in Cairo, I became convinced that as President Bush's foreign policy continues to alienate Muslims and the military build-up in the region increases, more people will move away from the West. There are some women I see here who cover their faces with black fabric as well as the ordinary hijab, and they wear gloves. When I see them, I wonder if some of them belong to Jamat Islamia'a.[5] But then I think, how do I know? There were times that I too have felt like covering my face to create a private space in the otherwise extremely communal spaces of a big city with more than 19 million inhabitants. I too have wanted to cover my face with something, even if it's only wearing dark glasses to cover my sadness and madness about the craziness of war, while trying to find my way though the busy streets of Cairo. How do I know why another woman veils?

Writing as an insider/outsider on my first trip to Egypt has been very interesting. As an Iranian I am an Aryan, not an Arab, who are Semites. Iranians are also Shi'a Muslims which is a small minority, far smaller in total percentage than the Protestants are among Christians. Egyptians have certainly treated me as an outsider, albeit a welcomed guest, invited to luncheons and dinners. The food and the reception I have received have made me feel very welcome. I always knew that as a guest what I am offered is more than what they have; this is how Egyptians welcome you. If there is not enough food they borrow from friends, neighbors, and family members to treat me the way they think I should be treated. I have had to learn to deal with their great sense of generosity and my lack of ability to reciprocate.

Old Cairo

At the end of an exhausting day I decided to take a walk through Old Cairo, a place I had always dreamt of visiting. With thousand of years of history to enchant you, this part of the city can posses you and make you forget everything. It bothered me that the streets were full of men and they seemed to be looking at me. But, maybe on that particular day I was just tired and being paranoid and hypersensitive. Maybe they just wanted to say "welcome to Cairo." My hijab was all proper and I was confident that my clothes made me look like an Egyptian . . . I guess it was the copy of the Lonely Planet Guide map that gave me away!

Feeling suddenly brave, I decided to challenge sexual segregation and upset the system a little bit. I stopped at one of the small street cafés which are, by and large, male-exclusive places. I sat down and asked the old waiter dressed in Bedouin clothes to bring me a mint tea. It took him a long time, but finally he came back with an ordinary tea with lots of mint in it. I realized that he had gone to a great deal of trouble for me and took out a big bill to pay him, but he refused and sat next to me pointing to a man sitting at the next table who was the owner and told me that I did not have to pay. The owner politely smiled and I gracefully accepted, though I was a little nervous about his intentions. I had not quite got into the habit of accepting Egyptians' generosity without questioning the motive behind it. I brought my hijab up a little higher to make it clear that there was no flirting involved, and, thus protected, entered a serious conversation with him.

What could be more serious than asking him and the waiter how they felt about the war with Iraq? When I asked him how he felt about the war he lifted his hands towards God and said, "Allah only knows." He took the lead in the conversation and continued to say "hard time for Muslims." Then he gazed at the street and mosque in front of the café and with a very wise expression on his face told me,

"People will die when the time comes, everything is in the hands of God." This must have been exactly how people felt in Iraq, powerless to change their fate. But that was not how I felt. Each night when I listened to the news my heart sank. I thought of Iraqi women and wonder how they would they raise their children in a country about to undergo a military assault. Hearing how calmly this man, like many of the people most affected, talked about the war made me notice my obsession with it. I became too engrossed in thought to worry about the state of my hijab. It had slid down on my shoulder. I felt the air was too thick to breathe and it was time to end the conversation. I finished my tea and politely said farewell making my way back to my hotel. The sound of "allah o akhbar" calling Muslims for the evening prayer broke the deep silence of the night. There were many women veiled in black with their children eating dinner outside Mosques. I smiled and they smiled back. As I walked towards the Metro, Old Cairo was flooded with glittering lights coming together from the Amr Ibn Al-As mosque, St. George's Church, and the Ben Ezra synagogue. The blending lights emanating from these monuments are a reminder of a long history of harmonious coexistence of the three Abrahamian religions in one of the most ancient parts of the world. I admired the beauty of the quarter, hoping somehow that the impending war on Iraq would not happen.

Some Final Veil Questions on the Cairo Subway

Since that walk through the old city, my initial impression of the streets of Cairo being a male space has been somewhat confounded by a view from Cairo university where I discovered that more than 70% of its students are female. An increasing number of them have been taking up the hijab of late. Remembering my own support for the Islamist movement in Iran in an earlier time of my life as support for an agenda that promotes social justice, I wonder how much I can use my own experience in trying to understand the increased popularity of veiling as a movement in Egypt. I look at the veiled women traveling beside me on the Cairo Metro and wonder if this particular woman is wearing the hijab to resist a social structure based on class inequality?[6] Or is she using it as a form of bargaining power with male members of her kin or male values of her immediate or larger community?[7] Or is this hijab a sign of deep faith?[8] All or none of these reasons could apply to any particular woman that I see.[9] Some of their reasons for wearing the hijab could even be different again from any that I have brought up in this chapter.[10] What does a veil mean? Who can reveal or unveil it?

Notes

1. This is the most important Muslim Holiday, celebrating the end of the holy month of Ramada.
2. For more on the hijab, see Fadwa El Guindi, "Veiling Resistance," *Fashion Theory*, Volume 3, Issue 1 (March 1999) 51–80; and Alvi Sajida, Homa Hoodfar and Sheila McDonough, Eds. *The Muslim Veil in North America: Issues and Debates* (Toronto: Women's Press, 2003).
3. Edward Said, *Orientalism* (New York: Vintage, 1979).
4. Mossadqu had nationalized the oil industry previously owned by Anglo American interests and fought for Iranian sovereignty. He was overthrown through efforts by the CIA.
5. The Islamist movement is not a homogenous movement at all. There is a whole range of factions, from progressive and more political to conservative and non political. Just as in international politics there was the Taliban and Saudi Arabia on the on hand, while there was Indonesia under Wahid, Iran under Khatami on the other. Within each country, there are different groups of Islamists, those who support a social welfare agenda and others who are pro-free market. Last but certainly not least, there is the fact that there is an increasing number of Islamist women's groups who challenge dominant male-perspective Islamism.
6. Sheriffa Zuhur, *Revealing, Reveiling: Islamist Gender Ideology in Contemporary Egypt*. (New York: State University of New York Press, 1992).
7. Deniz Kandioyti, "Bargaining with Patriarchy" in Visivanthan, Nialini, Lynn Duggan (Eds). *The Women, Gender and Development Reader* (Halifax: Fernwood Publishing company, 1997).
8. Katherine Bullock, *Rethinking Muslim Women and the Veil*. (Herdon: International Institute of Islamic Thought, 2002).
9. Yvonne Haddad, "Islam, Women and Revolution in Twentieth-Century Arab Thought," The Muslim World 74 (1984).
10. This chapter was written while I was doing my field work for a project on Islamisation and women's employment funded by the Canadian Social Science and Research Council of Canada. A comparative study of Iran, Egypt, and Turkey, it is a continuation of my earlier work on the same topic in Indonesia. The results of some of this work have been published as: "Islamic Fundamentalism and Women's Employment in Iran," *International Journal of Politics, Culture, and Society* (Winter 2003); "Revolution, Islamisation and Women's Employment in Iran," *The Brown Journal of World Affairs*, Volume IX, Issue 2 (Winter/Spring 2003); and "Islamic Fundamentalism and Women's Employment in Indonesia," *International Journal of Politics, Culture, and Society*. Volume 16, Issue 2 (Winter 2002).

CHAPTER 24

Joan Reider

Scarf Signatures

Figure 24.1. Photo of author, 1966.

The upper right-hand drawer is the most treasured one in my dresser. It always receives loving attention from me—its contents will never be "dumped." Inside that drawer, soft piles of scented scarves snuggle in soft waves of recollection. . . .

My first memory of a scarf, other than the never-ending, long, red woolen thing that was part of many a Canadian 5 year-old's Red River Winter Coat outfit in the early 1930s, was a pink chiffon rectangle that lay alongside a white pair of kidskin gloves inside my mother's lingerie drawer. I loved to hold it. The attraction then was the perfume that lingered among the folds, floating up to greet me as I carefully held it to my cheek.

A close relationship with scarves of my own began in the early days of my adolescence when I received one as a birthday gift from a great aunt. It was a reversible silk oblong, pink on one side and blue on the other. Wearing it tucked into the collar of a suit, I felt like a fashion model, very sophisticated. I used it to create a "New Look" of my own in the late forties. Actually I alternated it with a round white dickey which was then the fad of the high school crowd.

In the 1940 and early fifties, my attachment to scarves was more a matter of neck protection, something to keep me warm on cold winter days. Scarves that ranged from hand-knitted lengths of wool to flannel and then, finally, to soft luxurious cashmere became a part of my everyday wardrobe. But warmth was not the only reason I needed scarves.

I did not fully appreciate hats, even though my mother wore the most beautiful creations daily, and so I gradually fell into the practice of wearing a scarf as a head covering. For many years, as women's hairdos grew more bouffant, and convertible automobiles provided little shelter from the wind, it was natural to wear a chiffon scarf around one's head and then casually draped twice around your neck. Oh the glamour of it all! One had only to add a pair of sun glasses to feel, "Hollywood, here I come!"

Time marched on. I became a "gay divorcee," and suddenly found that a handful of beautifully tinted and embroidered sheer scarves could be used in many interesting ways, some of them erotic. Once, for example, I created a filmy garment that I used as a prop for my version of the dance of seven veils, pretending to be a temptress, a femme fatale. I felt alluring and daring. A heady feeling indeed. And, ever since those childhood pleasures of caressing my mother's scented scarves, I always remembered that scarves and perfume should be bosom buddies. By that point in my life, scarves had become an essential part of my wardrobe and, more than that, an expression of sensuality, creativity, and style. I always wore them, and took the time to learn techniques of folding and tying them in many different ways.

Occasionally, I wore scarves to hide or emphasize certain body parts. Often, I wore a scarf to protect my neck from air conditioning drafts. But even then, the feel of scarves and the way they looked was important. I chose colors which enhanced my natural skin tone or "season," a popular fashion fad in the 1980's for classifying Caucasian people's skin in order to determine what color groupings best suited them. I was classified as a "Winter," and assigned brilliant colors. Accordingly, jewel-toned silks and polyesters joined the family in my drawer. By then, they whispered of affluence, designed by Dior, Oscar de la Renta, Gucci, and others.

Beautiful and conveniently packable, scarves are also a very crucial part of my wardrobe when traveling. A different flowing scarf gives new life to repeated wearings of the same outfit. I always have one or two tucked into my purse in case of Who-knows-What. The scarf has thus become my signature. I have no idea what people think about my little quirk, but it matters not. All through my life I have felt very confident, comfortable, and brilliant. Can that feeling be ascribed to the wearing of a scarf? Or is it what inspires me to wear one?

CHAPTER 25 *Liz Ralfe*

Love Affair with My Isishweshwe

Figure 25.1. Photo of isishweshwe, 2003.

I like walking down the street wearing my *isishweshwe*. I enjoy wearing it to the university where I lecture, but I particularly like to wear it out in public. I feel that it communicates something about me that I cannot easily verbalize, but want people to know. This is a new feeling for me because I have never worn clothing that draws attention as this does—my style has usually been more Marks and Spencer's than anything else—sensible, durable, economical, not the kind of clothing to attract attention. So what is an *isishweshwe,* you are probably asking, and why does it make me feel this way? And how did I come to discover that a piece of fabric could have this effect in the first place? Where to start? Do I begin with telling you that I am writing as a white South African woman in 2003, or do I start with telling you about this distinctive, and what might be described by some as "traditional" print that is typically worn by black women in South Africa? And how do I get to the point of this chapter, which is about how the simple act of wearing a skirt made out of this print can make me feel differently about who I am? Let's start with how I came to buy and make my *isishweshwe,* an event that was not so much deliberate as incidental in its origins.

"Just Bring National Costume or Traditional Dress"

I had never given much thought to "traditional dress" or "national costume" until very recently when my daughter was leaving to travel to the USA on a student exchange program. The college she was going to be attending sent her a package of information including a list of what she needed to pack in the way of clothing. At the bottom of this list were the words: *National costume or traditional dress.* What on earth do they mean by that? Do all nations have a "national dress?" What is the "national dress" of the USA, the host country? And what do they mean by traditional? Garments people actually wear or historical clothes from the past? And what today would be considered "national" or "traditional" in South Africa almost ten years after the first democratic elections? What terminology does one even use to talk about "tradition" and "culture" especially in a society as multiracial, multi-ethnic and multicultural as South Africa? In addition to the many different indigenous cultures of South Africa (some of them endangered or battered by colonialization, past intertribal strife, and the implacable forces of Westernization) there are other cultures which have migrated or been brought here, each of which has its own distinctive language and customs. For example many people were brought to South Africa from India as indentured laborers to work in the sugar fields of Kwazulu-Natal where they eventually settled, flourished, and prospered. Durban, where I live, on the East Coast, in the province of Kwazulu-Natal, boasts the largest population of Indian people outside of India today. The population of South Africa also includes Malaysians who were brought to the Cape by the Dutch; the

French Huguenots who left France because of religious persecution and settled in the Cape; and the British who came here to farm or set up the colonial bureaucracy. People from all over the world were drawn to the country in the 19th and 20th centuries to work in the diamond and gold mines, as well as others whose forefathers just immigrated here looking for adventure and new opportunities. So whose costume is a "national" costume? This thinking about a national costume or traditional dress for my daughter forced me to consider my roots as a white South African. I now needed to ask questions such as: How do I define myself? Where do I really belong? Whom do I identify with in this country of varied colors, diverse cultures and blurred racial lines?

White South Africans are often associated with the Afrikaner nation, who imposed apartheid and ruled this country for over 40 years. Their forebears were the Dutch people who settled at the southern tip of Africa in 1652 and who moved north in order to escape British rule when they moved in and colonized the Cape. Afrikaner symbols became national symbols. My roots are not with that group. I have never been able to identify with the traditional "Voortrekker"[1] women's costume, a long dress in the early 19th century European style, made of a drab, grey serge material with a white apron or pinafore and topped by a white "kappie" or bonnet. In the early days of the Miss World beauty competition, before the boycotts prevented our sending an entrant, Miss South Africa usually wore an outfit like this in the costume section called "traditional."

But if my roots are not with the white Afrikaans group, my identity is not really with the British either. Kwazulu-Natal is sometimes known as "The Last Outpost of the British Empire" because most of the white population have British roots and speak English. Despite our British heritage, however, neither my husband nor I identify with the British or anyone else who grew up in the United Kingdom.[2] What we mostly have in common with British people is the language we speak.

But all of what I say about this must surely look simplistic to those from the outside looking in. Is it no wonder that we now find terms like "traditional" and "culture" minefields! How can I just *state* what I have just said? And what does dress have to do with it?

Shopping for Identity

The "problem" of finding a "national" or "traditional" dress led my daughter and me into a part of Durban not normally frequented by white, middle-class women. We made our way to the Victoria Street market, a colorful, vibrant, noisy place where bustling Indian traders sell everything from traditional beadwork, crafts, and basket work, to fish, meat, and herbal medicines. It smells of spices, exotic foods, and incense. I was sure we would find something there among the seamstresses who plied their trade on the upper floor—but it was not to be. While there are upmarket designers who make garments "influenced" by traditional clothing, these seemed to be making conventional modern clothing.³ We then started exploring the narrow, crowded streets surrounding the market, looking for fabric that could be run up into something that would be distinctly South African.

It was in a narrow, dark Indian shop that I saw it—the *isishweshwe*—a thick, indigo blue cotton print. It is very distinctive. Many black women wore or still wear it for everyday work tasks in rural communities. I had long admired it from afar. I pounced on the fabric. I simply had to have it in order to sew myself a skirt like the ones I had seen, complete with colorful rickrack and bias binding decoration. I asked the shopkeeper what it was called and it was he who told me it was "isishweshwe" fabric, something I had never known before. I have since learned that German missionaries and traders who came to the Eastern Cape region in the second half of the 19th century first brought it into the country.⁴ The prints are German peasant designs, which have long gone out of vogue in Germany and are now produced locally in the Eastern Cape. Because it was cheap to buy, thick, and durable, the Xhosa women who lived in the region slowly abandoned animal skins and

Figure 25.2. Photo of Isishweshwe, 2003.

Figure 25.3. Photo of isishweshwe, 2003.

used it to make their clothing—circular and crossover skirts, pinafores, and simple dresses. Because the print was white on a single color (red, indigo blue, or brown) background, the women decorated their clothing with brightly colored binding, tape and rickrack. Gradually garments in the fabric became part of what has come to be associated with "traditional culture" although even there, the definition of traditional is fluid. In some areas, for example, clothing in isishweshwe is worn by women who are in mourning, in others areas it signifies that a woman is newly married, while in others they are used as ceremonial dress.

The cloth is stiff and heavily starched although it does soften up slowly as it gets washed. It is so thick and stiff that the print doesn't penetrate through to the inside of the fabric, which is plain. I have been told that this stiffness is important and that regular wearers of the fabric will test this by tasting and smelling the fabric in order to check that it is the real traditional thing. However, what makes isishweshwe really distinctive are the patterns, which are made up of a series of small white dots or stipples and delicate, fine lines. Sometimes the lines can be used as guides to sew on decoration or to make small tucks. Sometimes the fabric has an allover print, but often it is printed with a border. There are a number of different patterns available, but they all have a similar, distinctive look. When purchasing isishweshwe fabric, one can buy by length, or by the panel.

So, I purchased the heavy cotton calico-like material. The particular one I chose is printed in shaped panels so all I had to do was cut down the lines and then sew the panels together on my sewing machine to have, as you can see in the photograph, a gently flared skirt. I chose a dark indigo blue, delicately printed in white with a heavier white printed border. Light broken lines are printed onto the fabric to provide a guide to where to sew the rickrack, binding, or colored tape used to decorate it. I chose white binding and white rickrack to decorate my skirt (see photographs 2 and 3, above).

All in the Wearing

When I bought the fabric and as I ran the skirt up on my sewing machine, I never thought about what it might symbolize to those who saw me wearing it or what it would really symbolize to me either. It was just another item of clothing that would be cool to wear in the heat and humidity of the Durban summer. I certainly had no idea of the response it would evoke and how it would in some ways change me or my perception of myself. *It was just fabric made into a skirt.* Or was it?

As I said at the beginning, I work at a university, and the first time I wore the skirt there I was aware that it was creating something of a stir among certain members of the staff. There were no students on campus that day, but as I walked from my car to my office I met a group of Zulu support staff. Their eyes lit up when they saw it and they all complimented my isishweshwe. They asked me where I had got it, and when I told them I had *made* it, they acted impressed, but most of all they seemed to be pleased that a white woman should be wearing such a garment. Throughout the day my skirt was a talking point—the Zulu lecturers, the library assistants, in fact every Zulu person I met—noticed the skirt and passed a favorable comment. Other staff didn't seem to notice it, or if they did, they made no comment.

However, none of this prepared me for the reaction of my students when I wore the skirt. As I walked into a large lecture venue I was greeted by loud ululating and whistling from the students, many of whom are Zulu. I was overwhelmed, but at the same time concerned. I am a white woman living in a country where racial and cultural sensibilities are understandably still raw, and where issues of race and privilege are ones that continued to be contested. While their response seemed very positive, might some of them have been offended? Did I have the right to wear a garment that is not part of my "culture"? But then, as I've said before, what is my culture? I don't seem to have a ready answer.

I decided to speak to one of the Zulu lecturers and ask her whether I might have offended any of the students by wearing the skirt. As tricky as this might sound, asking and not just assuming is something that we are learning in this country.

"Nonsense," she said. "They are pleased to see you wearing it. They like it. After all, they all wear western clothes. It is a compliment to them that you are wearing a skirt traditionally worn by women in their culture." I realize that the issue is *more* complicated than this. My colleague's use of the term "western" for example opens up yet another issue of how South Africa is positioned more generally. When is our country "western" and when is it "African"? And where do either of these questions fit now within issues of globalization?

And then there is my colleague's reference to that term "traditional"! The very next time I wore it on campus I was giving a small group tutorial to a group of students who would be described as multicultural. Again the skirt caused a stir among the Black students who are often described as African. A young Zulu male student in the group shyly said, "I like your skirt, Mrs. Ralfe."

"Why?" I asked.

"Because it's what African women wear."

"And that's exactly what I am!" I heard myself answering.

For that moment at least, I had a sense of what it means to say "I know where I belong."

And, what about my daughter's traditional outfit, I am sure you are asking. What did she finally take with her to the United States? Well, she did take an *isishweshwe*, but not as her "traditional outfit." She wanted to wear the *isishweshwe* on a daily basis. As to the rest of what she packed, well, that's another story.

Notes

1. The voortrekkers were the Afrikaner people who left the Cape Colony in 1836 and moved into the hinterland of South Africa to escape British rule.
2. Both my husband and I have our roots in England. My husband's family were Byrne settlers (so called after Joseph Byrne, the man who brought them and many others to Natal), who emigrated here in 1850. His great, great-grandfather left England with his wife and six children. They endured over three months at sea in a tiny sailing boat before being shipwrecked off the small settlement of Port Natal (later renamed Durban). Much of what they had brought with them to start their new life was lost, but they were not daunted. They traveled by wagon to the inland settlement of Byrne where they stayed for about two years. Unable to make a living farming there, they moved on into the uninhabited interior of the colony. They finally settled in the midlands of this province and have farmed there peacefully ever since. They hold the original title deeds of the property they still occupy. My parents immigrated to Durban after the Second World War. My father came here as a serviceman to train during the war and liked what he saw. After the war was over he gathered up his young wife and returned to start a new life. I was born here, and still live in the same house I grew up in.
3. For a similar discussion of this European influence of textiles and women's clothing in East Africa, see Elizabeth Linneburgh's "Kanga: popular cloths and messages" In K. Barber (Ed.) *African Popular Culture*. (Bloomington and Indianapolis: Indiana University Press; and Oxford: James Currey, 1997).

CHAPTER 26 — *Charlotte Hussey*

Fashion Statement

> *I dedicate my mirror to Aphrodite:*
> *For I will not see myself as I am now,*
> *And can not see myself as once I was.*
> — PLATO

Figure 26.1. Photo of author, 1995.

Legs spread, hip out,
I have been centred between lines of tape
on this off-white island of laminated paper.

The photographer is closing in,
probing the airy lilt of my thousand dollar
evening skirt, rippled by a wind machine
against my cooling ankles.

"You're the star," the hair-stylist whispers.
Crawling towards me on a piece of cardboard,
he flicks back a lock shadowing my eye.

"You've eaten away your lip-line again,"
the make-up woman chides, a risky accomplice
who inches closer, waving a sharpened pencil.

Seating me, she leans my body back over a chair,
a pipe cleaner or a crash dummy
who politely complains that its hands
are being tied behind its back.

And now two giant wafers of light promise
to soften everything, even the photographer
who comes like a creeping prince
and kneels by my silvery, sandaled feet:
"Please, your hands, if they lie
like that, will be too large!"

Thirty-six shots per roll of film. Flash
after fading flash,
I purse my bee-stung lips,
blindly licking at the gloss.

Note

Originally published in *The Gazette,* Montreal (March 21, 1995) F6.

PART VII
Bodies, Dress, and Mortality

CHAPTER 27

Lorri Neilson Glenn

At the Ugly Ducklings Anonymous Meeting

My turn? Uh, okay, my name is Annie, and I think it began when my boyfriend's sister laughed at me, a hippy hippie she thought I was and I guess I was wider than her, well, a bit, with more hair, and in different places, but at least my toenails didn't scream in Fisher Price colours and I never blew two weeks' wages on make-up—you can buy six books for the price of a beauty system; they call them systems now, you know—or treated myself to lunch and eyelash dyeing with my mother. C'mon, some women keep their lips so slick you'd think they owned their own Zamboni, their hair treated, permed and frosted—I mean they pay someone 100 dollars to put tin foil in it—and speaking of hair, I never, ever owned a hairdryer, I mean why: air is free?

So I have a problem, I know it, and I understand some women need to pull out a mirror for each new face they're going to greet, but I don't, well, sometimes, when I have to drive to the Save-Easy for bread I'll grab the same lipstick tube I've kept in the bathroom drawer for years, but that's all. And maybe, maybe just a little eyeliner, just a dab, if I can find it. You can let these things get out of hand, and before you know it, there you are, well into your pension years, yellow hair and blue eyelids, trying to close the fake gold clasp on the white shorts, looking for chips in the purple polish on your toes, which by the way, look like leather, and you're reaching for your wallet with claws for hands you know you can get sparkles now on your fingernails? looking for all the world like a Disney lizard, and what have you got? Well, not your dignity, that's for sure.

                                                             And so what,
and so what if men look right through me like I'm a hedge or a
lamppost—and when they do look they probably think Birkenstock Bertha or
something. Well fine. The ones that do make eye contact always look like the
kind who'd spend time browsing through a bookstore or working on a
crossword or sitting by the water talking which is my style, really, not sitting
by the poolside in Florida waiting for the free pink drinks and a bus trip to
the casino, and it all smells like chlorine and Estee Lauder. Phew.
                                                              So, okay,
so that's how I feel. I'm not, like, proud of it, you know. But you won't see
me ordering those ceramic dolls with teardrops in women's magazines, and I
don't think rat-sized dogs should wear doll clothes and I can't say Mary Kay
without wanting to burp—or is that Tupperware?—and I just don't get this
thing about collagen and silicone. Who wants lips like a llama, or tits that
don't roll over when you do? I'm tired of baby boomer Barbies whose bodies
have been tested on animals, who advertise large corporations on their
backsides and still seek the perfect little black dress. I mean, really. Okay,
I'll stop.

No, wait. Maybe it's personal. Maybe it all started in the bathroom in grade
nine when Cherie Libbrecht stood squinting at the mirror, she had a
contraption your big toe would fit inside, and I stood there, flatchested with
my ponytail, braces and all, my chunky mouth wide open, as she pointed
this, this Thing at her face. Isn't that a toenail clipper? I ventured and
suddenly the walls are echoing

in guffaws, red mouths are open and squawking, teenage crows with lipstick,
they were, and even my friend Sandra is hooting from the stall, and I am
standing, alone, confused, the scent of Noxzema on my skin, a too-tight
elastic tweaking my hair.

It was, I learned later, an eyelash curler. You knew that, I bet. Okay, I'm
done.   Your turn.

                                                                     Note

This poem was published in another form in *All the Perfect Disguises* (Broken Jaw Press, 2003).

CHAPTER 28   *Celeste Snowber*

Writing Bare-breasted

Berry breath
blue expanse
eucalyptus scent
rushing water
(under)girding
(over)riding
meditation house

Body sheds
clothes as soul
sheds layers
of extraneous
fibers

What could be
more beautiful
naked flesh
against Pacific
blue sky
dipping into
mineral baths

I must
dip into
this place daily
finding my internal
mineral bath.
Live naked
while clothed

I sit
perched
on wooden chair
propped against
leaning fence
steep invitation
to rugged coast

I cannot
bear my
purple straps
of cotton
This too I shed
writing bare-breasted
on edge of Pacific
only for seagulls
to see
I've been told
it is only the pool
area and hot baths that
are clothing-optional
but once my breasts
have been outside
they seem to pop out
for breaths
in-between.

I wonder if the
man riding the lawn-mower
will say anything as I sip
my licorice-peppermint
tea, semi-clothed.
Truly we need to see

bare-flesh
against the natural world.

Sensuous curves
of torsos against
undulating shapes
of wind bent trees
Buttocks with ocean
worn rocks
arms extending palms
against bamboo
navels in hills of grass
and chests
open to sky.

Nipples need a break
from the rapture
of garments
let the air in and restore
all they've given
down the years.
Feeding three children
and various lovers
along the way
They are mine
after all
2 round pomegrantes
the texture of tangerines
Shouldn't I decide what
I want to do with them.
Expose them to the
wind of mother earth
let the salt lick aerola.

They did say Esalen
was a pagan monastery.
I return to the
monastery of my own body
even in its state of
voluptuous line, no washboard
stomach at this stage or

> twig formation.
> I sing from the
> inside out—
> home at last,
> with cellular knowing
> of caves of innocent waves.
> Naked, I return
> Naked, I go
> to cherish
> the fruit of
> my own
> flesh.

CHAPTER 29   *Ilana Abramovitch*

Not Just Any Little Black Dress

Figure 29.1. Black dress with flowers. Courtesy of the author.

The small-minded admonition to wear immaculate undergarments, in case one is in an accident, works for me today, not that I expect anything out of the ordinary to happen. But I am wearing a long clingy black dress, and while dressing for work this morning, I unearthed, to my great delight, a forgotten full-length black slip with lacy bodice. If an accident was to happen and some one finds me, they will know what great lingerie I wear. If I am found and recognizable.

The shoes—platform slides, they are called. Like mules. They go "thwack" against the heel with each step. Not meant for lengthy walks. Meant to set off the foot as they disable it mildly. Women's shoes offer a quivering range of straps, teetering heels, square, pointed, snub-nosed, arrowheads pointing at the world.

What do I wear to work at the museum? The look of a professional. Dark, down to business. Clean crisp minimalist, fresh shirts and suits. No monkey business neutral unrevealing except when calculated. Calculation motivation competition.

Liberated from graduate school shabby genteel poverty, I have for 5 years earned enough to go beyond the thrift shop, go beyond the cheesy $10 store. Cheesy, but where I found my unlikely wonders. Wonders to transmute by my own touch. What the world sees of me: race, class, gender, aesthetics.

Now I can go to those stores where professionals go, people not easily intimidated by the sales clerks, people who know what they want and expect to get it. Demand it. Impossibly svelte know-their-accessories women. Well put-together, well pulled-together. Women trained by their mothers by their girlfriends to purchase profoundly. Who will starve themselves for a look. I join their ranks—not svelte, never rail thin, but muscular sweaty, endlessly female.

But every once in a while, instead of the shops for the sleek and the trim, I am drawn back to the Salvation Army Thrift Shop with their impossibly good deals and the sense of the hunt. The excitement of discovery. I have become expert in critical shopping. How to find a $100 skirt, in almost perfect condition selling for $6.95. My friend EJ taught me all. I once was lost, overwhelmed, in thrift shops when I first discovered them. All I could see were the amazing deals, but not how to choose wisely. EJ, still the queen of thrift shops, taught me to move swiftly through the racks, to be discriminating, as discriminating as in a regular retail store. To know from the start which contours would never work. Not to be a patsy for the glittery and the glitz, as the theater queen in me urged. Yet always to be open to the find, even if out of season, out of synch with expectations.

Whisking through the hanging gardens of the clothes rails. The horizontal files of the almost-worthy, the copies, the coffee stained, the cacophonous prints, bejeweled sweatshirts, skirts your mama told you not to wear.

Not much here today. As usual I feel a little soiled touching all these clothes that have lived other lives. Are they washed, cleaned, purged of their past lives? But no. The past lives still inhabit the clothes, calmly awaiting the new occupant. Whose arms did these black silk sleeves encase? What was the occasion of this dress's glory? Or demise? Was it for the cocktail party that ended in disenchantment, a feeling so deep that the whole garment was impregnated with frustration? Did it then hang in the closet, always passed over, finally to be yanked out and given away in a fit of purging?

What's this? . . . hmm . . . Shows definite potential, yes . . . a long, form-fitting dress, black rayon with small white sinuous flowers.

OK, they are not exactly sinuous; they are more like sprouts, buds, tender shoots. Young supple life, lithesome and lissom.

Is it an office dress? Marginal . . . but the weather has been summery and a long black slip makes it cling less. So it's much more respectable in this sultry weather, when everything sticks.

A normal day. Early fall, brightly lit Indian summer.

I get into the office and pursue my minor rituals: poke my nose through the hallways on the way to the kitchen, see who is in, get my large mug of milky tea.

I am feeling svelte today. The long straight skirt of my new black dress makes me feel elongated even, a rare delight for me at five foot two.

Warm glowing Indian summer day. Ensconced at my desk. Radiant views of New York harbor. Where river meets river meets ocean. Light shimmering from the water, bouncing off wave peaks and meeting my eyes. Calming sparkling waters. Day of dancing sparkles. Ice cream sparkle day.

Down the hall is my friend Sharma. Devout Hindu from the West Indies. Makes a great pliant roti everyday, waking up at 5:30 to prepare fresh lunches for the kids. Her shiny long dark hair and easy smile adorn her flowing Indian outfits.

Suddenly, a flurry in the hallway. Sharma: "A plane crashed into the World Trade Center."

"What, a plane?! How could that be?"

Running down the corridor.

"A small plane must have lost its way . . ."

"Must have gone off course."

"Must have been avoiding another plane."

All kinds of crazy stunts have been attempted recently: a parachutist landed on the Statue of Liberty just a week ago. What is this? A gag? How could a plane be flying so close?

We all run to the picture window in Amber's corner offices facing north. Run goggle-eyed giggling, jaws drop as we stare.

A great billowing crest of smoke . . . and tons of paper scattering slowly through the air, catching the sunlight, sparkling and spiraling in the air.

Alarmed but puzzled. How could this happen? Luz: "Planes are not allowed to fly over Manhattan. They have to fly along the Hudson River."

I think of the blimps that fly low and seem to take up so much sky.

Like watching a TV special with the sound off. We spot a small rim of flames still raging. Fire still burning up high in one of the towers. I want to see police and fire helicopters putting out the fire, but I see none. We do not think of the people in the towers. We cannot conceive that anyone is on those floors. Because it seems so quiet.

Gazing at the twin monoliths. One has a hole in it, a dark wound tracing the skewed shape of a large plane, mimicking wide wings. The flames shoot out scarlet against the gray tower. I ache watching the stark, frightening beauty. Thousands of pieces of paper slowly twist in the air, dancing in the sky.

Without the sounds, the smells, the shrieks, it is a sleight of hand, a mindless ticker tape parade through the canyons of Manhattan. (Who first thought of dumping ticker tape, of throwing paper ribbons into the air in a spasm of celebration? The joy of throwing garbage together? Must be an ancient expulsive ritual. In Naples they throw garbage into the street on New Year's.)

I do not often wear my glasses—call it vanity—so I do not see what others later report—that people are jumping out the windows, way up high. People choose air to fire. Air to smoke. Hoping against hope to land safely. I see it only later, in the replay videos. And the white curtains waving from a window, a plea for rescue and refuge.

We stand there gazing from the 25th floor of our building just eight blocks away. It's eerily calm. The accident appears contained. The buildings stand as before; the only difference: one has a hole in it.

Most of my office mates drift back to their cubicles, ready to get back to work. Still wondering how this could be, but after a few minutes, accident shock is over. This is New York, after all. A shock a minute. There are always crazies out there, keeping us amused and frightened. Keeping the tabloids full and frothy.

Back to daily routines. A few of us stay and are still looking out the window, wondering. Musing. But what if . . . and HOW did . . . ? and, I WONDER whether . . .

Suddenly, from the left periphery, an over-large shape zooms in. Much too close to be real. Then a picture, slow slow yet fast.

And it's so big and flying way too low. It turns smartly and swerves left on a sharp diagonal. As the plane is heading straight—no—not—yes—for the tower, the horror hits me: no, this is not an accident!—not a Coney Island ride that veers away at the last minute. No, straight to the heart. The dagger went into my core. It smacks in. Explosion! The world is on fire.

The other one must have been done on purpose too. I cannot imagine that world. But I have seen it with my own eyes. Suddenly, a voice says: "I'm out of here." No, it's not my voice, but it could be. We do not wait for instruction.

We are all thinking, what will be next? Our building, just blocks from the WTC? Our Museum of Jewish Heritage—A Living Memorial to the Holocaust?

People are running, and I hear Delia begin to cry. No one knows what to do.

I am with the people who evacuate. As soon as possible.

Get me out of here. Get out. Out away. Going.

What happened to those people sitting at their desks in the tower, chatting and drinking a cup of coffee when a plane's nose penetrated their tower? A murderous nose meant to explode and kill. Only now as we run do I begin to imagine the people in the towers, how they ran, how they faced a building on fire, filled with smoke.

Outside the building we stand jittery, babbling. Where should to go? Where is Ann? Where did Peter go? How did this happen? Are we waiting for Jonathan? This is not real! Who has seen Florence? Why is Jennifer going back in? What is happening to the world? I forgot my medicine inside. Where will we go? Stop! Let's wait for Clara. No, she is staying inside.

Finally, we agree, we must run to the park, get away from the building. Park is near water. Water is safe. Maybe. Water is open vista. We could jump into water to escape fire.

Phone calls. Call families. Cell phones not working. Horror film. A line has formed at the pay phone, one lonely pay phone in the park. A line snakes around. A hundred in the line. We need hope. Something still works. The pay phone.

Sit stand move. Rumors freshen; tears are falling, sage advice offered, leaders and followers. As we stand: joking, crying, biting lips, jockeying.

We stand in line. It's hot in the park. Now I notice. No water fountains. A radio booms from the snack bar, newly animated. As we stand and wait, the radio announces: a plane attacked the Pentagon. I do not love the Pentagon. But this, this is carnage, this is killing.

Suddenly. Glitter glitter crash, the ultimate celebrity event—for an insane minute destruction looks creative. The top of the tower sparkles, tinkling in the fierce deranged sun and as it sparkles and explodes, it suddenly faints, swoops down, collapsing, sending out glints of itself, lustrous shards hurled with terrifying force through the air.

What was it? A bomb? The building is gone! Vanished! What more? Where is safe?

Run.

As I run, I am suddenly in a war movie. I am guided by dim memories of Holocaust survivors persevering in terrifying conditions. That's been part of my job, these past years, reading fragment after fragment from the diaries of Jewish survivors of World War II. Now they come whispering at me, unbidden. I must escape. A bomb has exploded in the camp, and I have a few seconds before the Nazi guards recover and chase me with ferocious dogs, guns raging to kill.

My platform mules are not meant for running, much less walking. No, they are for posing, for parading along the avenue. Not for a slalom path through a frightened incandescent crowd. Not for a fast track to safety. As I run, I lift the bottom of the skirt like a Victorian lady.

Escape at all costs. With fierce determination, the lady leaps over fallen poles and squeezes through the edge of a construction fence. And as I run, I look around: I can no longer see my companions. Are they hiding? What do they know that I don't? I run in a wide arc trying to find them, calling their names. Where did they disappear to?

As I run in my movie, I am halfway towards twisting my ankle. "No, you cannot twist your ankle," instructs a powerful voice of survival. Quickly, I flick my ankle back into line. I must look after myself. More scenes from the Holocaust. Snap decisions that keep survivors going. A young daughter suddenly attacks the hulking guard threatening to kill her mother. A sister seizes a moment when the guards are lighting their cigarettes to throw a pellet of dry bread across the fence to her starving brother.

Alone, yet relieved to be alone. Moving more swiftly. Less encumbered. Feeling guilty—what about my companions—but relieved. Yet my long narrow dress turns me into a caricature. A woman running but she cannot run. Bound by her own sartorial choices.

Around me screaming surging swelling crowds pushing to get onto the Staten Island Ferry. For a second, I feel the pull of their panic-stricken mood. I want to scream and run in circles and sob. But no, I pull back. I do not want to be squashed in the swarm. I run on, on my own. Ahead of me: a decision. Where to go? Away. Get a destination. Away where? Across the bridge. Yes? Away. If I can. If not, to brother Lavy's. Bridges could be a target.

Move far east, along the East River. People are running. It's hot. Smoke everywhere. People are running with handkerchiefs to their noses. Some move arm in arm. Some alone. I think: should I be looking after some one? Is there anyone who needs help? Looking around, I see no one needing help. I keep forging forward, relieved that I do not have to be put to the test.

Dammit, it's exciting. Call me stupid or call me perverse, but at this point I am almost loving the extra-ordinariness of it. The difference of it—not only the abnormality of it, but the friggin' unpredictability, the scary-exciting big fast mess of it. I have seen no one hurt and am not hurt myself. But at this point, I know nothing of anyone's fate. No palm pilot, no portable radio; no Walkman to guide me. Just my running shadow, adrenaline pumping.

As far as I can see, no immediate danger. But who knows what is around the corner? It is extraordinary to be consumed with survival—but then, my daily work has prepared me. My mind occupied daily with atrocity, escape, survival. Reading stories, editing stories, talking stories, listening to stories about running, hiding, split-second decisions, on the edge or even in the middle of atrocities. Intuitions proved wrong. Or right. Murderers in control.

I could tear up my dress to make bandages. Or tourniquets. I could save lives.

If I don't take the bridge, I am stuck on Manhattan this island bull's eye.

Walking briskly along the edge of the water, I remember I know how to tread water for a long spell. Had to pass the Red Cross test in summer camp in the Laurentians. Allow yourself to sink, then bob, you can go on forever. If I need to leave the ash and the smoke—who knows what's next?—fire, hail, bolts of lightning from hell?—if I need to leave the dry land, I can bob forever in the dark greasy waters off Manhattan. My office mates had pleaded: don't take the bridge! Bridges are next! And it may be so. But . . . where to go?

I want to go somewhere safe—Home! Home is across the bridge. Home is where I have the illusion of control. I could shrivel up there, if we are all to die today. I could shrivel up there, next to my books and pictures of loved ones. Home is the cool dark closet where the black dress lives.

As I head steadily north, closer and closer to the crossroads of the Towers, I curse myself for not knowing which street I need to get up onto the ramp to the Brooklyn Bridge.

Whatever it is, I don't know how to find the approach. Some people are walking on the elevated FDR Drive. I see them as angels, high above the streets, but I am below. How do I rise?

A crossroads. As I reach it, a great billowing snarl of cloud and dust explodes. People are scattering, running away from the direction I am heading. Oh-oh, this does not look good. A burning smell inflames my nostrils.

I see a group of Hasidim heading together around and below the bridge as if they know a special route. I ask one for directions. I don't understand his answer. Do his customs change in this mayhem? Was there divine guidance? For some? For any? I don't follow his vague directions and keep heading up the bridge ramp.

People are streaming off in my direction. I think: why am I going up when all these people are going down? Common sense calls this foolish.

The bridges may be next.

Suspended over the shimmering water, a feeling of dread: we minuscule humans are relying on the bridge's dangling platform, so thin over the deep river. Is this the day that Martin Amis describes? "The world has been to so many parties, been in so many fights, lost its keys, and had its handbag stolen, drunk too much. It all adds up. A tab is presented."

The thought does not stop me. I find a stray *Wall Street Journal* and covering my mouth and nose as best I can, swing forward. Everyone is covering their snouts.

Every day I carry wads of tissues, today I have none. The *WSJ* is not the best mask, but it feels like I am covering something, somehow.

Circling up the ramp, I have started to notice objects, personal items that have been abandoned on the road. Losing their personal attachment, they are transformed into artifacts in the public domain—a bag of groceries abandoned, a pair of stiletto heels—useless today . . . symbols of what is not essential. A hoarding impulse seizes me—grab the shoes! Free food!—but I let it go. Even food is less important than escape. If it ties you down, if it impedes progress, dump it. It takes a disaster of this kind to get people to suddenly stop identifying with their commodities.

By mid-bridge, the air is miraculously cleaner, the sky is blue—what a beautiful day! Start to see groups of people walking together, many having escaped together, some having bonded en route. A sense of camaraderie. This is one day you can talk to strangers. Some are marching arm in arm. I think of a pilgrimage: this one is away from, rather than towards. I join two guys with cell phones. One lets me call my brother.

Long live the Brooklyn Bridge! So many people, so many artists, have loved this bridge, it is a wonder of the world. We are grateful to it and are loving it too, but its flowing skeleton structure does not keep us from being covered in dust and ash; we are layered in it, disheveled with it; impregnated with it. Its puce ash fine as silt.

But who cares?

To keep it in perspective, we are walking, rather than crawling—we are still in human form—and we are ambling away from the apparent disaster. We are alive, unhurt and we have hope, though we wonder if this day will be our last.

We have been pushing forward, but now we dare to turn, like Lot's wife. Looking back, we can see the pillar of smoke from the disaster. It has become more compact, a diagonal pillar, swiveling towards Brooklyn, blown by a southward wind north. Brooklyn is our destination, but it is also where the smoke is aimed.

Rumors abound. *They got New York Hospital now!* I am anguished: how could they bomb a hospital? This seems the lowest of the low, and I truly want to cry out: Enough!

My mind is torn between the beauty of the day, the feeling of being on a pilgrimage with fellow urbanites, and the emergency which has drawn us together. Ahead we see a vision of daily Brooklyn; behind us a disaster site, burning and smudged.

What is covering me?

The day is so hot, so bright. My skin is getting burnt as I walk across the reflecting waters. Yes, I did inhale the smoke and ashes, despite the *Wall Street Journal*, and I begin to have visions. What is in the powder that covers me? Poison gas? Biological weapons?

A memory of a voice in the Museum's exhibition, a voice too sad too full of dread. The videotaped voice of a woman remembering the camps. And I looked at the ash falling from the chimney and asked myself whose ashes are those? Are they the ashes of my mother, of my father?

My sleek long dress is a barrier. It protects but also restrains. Its skirt is narrow; I can't walk quickly. I am burning in this heat and this sun. To my puzzlement, I am feeling sexually aroused amidst the terror. I am burning in this heat. Let me take off my dress. Let me take off my dress, I am wearing the long black slip underneath. I can take off my dress. Today is a day outside of the rules. Today the world is turned upside down. And after I take off my dress, by the time I reach the other end of the bridge, I will be making love passionately with a stranger. It does not matter if I make it home. We will be making love forever. The billowing smoke and mounds of ashes, the disaster will be out of our mind; we will be consumed with heat; driven with incomparable ardor, almost detonating, as we block out tragedy and pain. We will laugh a laugh of victory over death. A laugh that includes those in pain. We will laugh for you; we will continue to play like squirrels and monkeys, leaping dizzyingly from branch to branch, although you can no longer join us. We will be playful for you.

Black and white dress continues to cross the bridge. Little white flowers burning in the hot sun. This passageway across the water is our birth canal, as we escape the death and destruction behind our backs.

Stepping off the bridge. Brooklyn never looked so beautiful. In 1917, Christopher Morley saw it in black and white: "New York is Babylon; Brooklyn is the true Holy City. New York is the city of envy, office work and hustle; Brooklyn is the region of homes and happiness . . ."

Thick yellow tape has closed off the subway entrances, hundreds waiting at bus stops.

Another call to my brother: I am on the other shore! I have crossed over to the other side. I am free!

Feet swollen, covered in blisters, walking slowly now all the way to the old neighborhood. Friendly, funky, fully gentrified by now, Park Slope. I wander into the food coop, the oldest coop in the country. Our coop of people who eat organic, care about the environment, cooperate. It's infuriating, rule-bound, but it's our community.

Wandering in a daze through the organic fruit and vegetables. Breathing more slowly now. Gazing at a miracle of the ordinary: People shopping for food, food lovingly grown without poisons. I love the normality am mesmerized by it but I am outraged. How can they keep looking at the celery and the arugula when the world is burning?

Out of the blue, like a vision, Lena appears. Handing out flyers about donating blood. I am thrilled to see her. A dear friend. What joy!

She has already swung into action. We can do something, not just run away. Give blood. That's what I can do! Give blood. We amble toward a bakery for tea and comfort. How will she get to teach her class in New Jersey? Or can she tell her students in time that it is canceled? The two of us have no idea that all travel will be disrupted for weeks, months. Later she tells me, I was covered in ashes and smelling strongly of smoke.

Wander through my old neighborhood, loving it, heading home.

Finally arrive to my flat. I want to be alone, upstairs.

I take off my dusty dress and ashen shoes, gingerly. I look in the mirror, ash-dipped, trembling.

What to do with my dress and shoes? Shoes go straight into Ziplock, from which they have never emerged.

As for the dress: Throw out? Wash? Shred? Cover in plastic? "Air" out? The pillar of smoke blew towards Brooklyn. We are in its cloud. What is in the air? Who is in it?

The dress, I have decided, must be buried, given a decent funeral. In the meantime, it is thrown over the banister in my hallway.

I spend the next three days undressed watching television, talking and talking on the phone, trying to reach family and friends, seeing if my flight to Montreal is canceled.

After ten days, we return to work. Every weekday, I rush out of the apartment and before lunging down the steps, confront the dress, lying limp on the banister. I wonder what it is radiating. Is it contaminated? Am I contaminated? Why do I keep it here?

I avoid it. But it does not let me avoid it. It is right there. I pass by its silhouette at least twice a day. I wonder whether its contact with the dead of the World Trade Center renders it holy or tainted. The chemicals in the air and now in its weave are industrial and polluting. But the bodies never found exist as molecules in its texture.

A metallic smell lingers for months in the air near work in down town Manhattan. Anthrax fears are in the air.

But as the weeks go by, the barriers on the streets shift, the National Guard outposts shrink, and the sense of wartime alert lessens. The dress begins to reassert itself. No, it need not be buried. It needs to be cleaned and worn again. It would stand up again and sway and continue. The dress is my woven fragment of that day and that time, my flag. Now is the time to face the transformed world.

Uncertain how to do this, I sheepishly bring the dress to the dry cleaners. Can it really be cleansed in this way? I explain to the Asian proprietor where this dress has been. I think of Hiroshima and the contamination that stuck around. Will he refuse, be angry? No, he seems accepting. He nods silently, with what seems like due respect, and accepts the dress.

Two days later. I have the clean beautiful dress back. White flowers resplendent against the crisp black background.

CHAPTER 30　　　　　　　　　　　　　　　*Claudia Mitchell*

Dressing Death:
Elsie Never Wore a Prom Dress

What they [clothing and photographs] have in common is that they are simultaneously presence and absence. They are both an object and a souvenir of subject, exactly as cadaver is both an object and a souvenir of subject.
CHRISTIAN BOLTANSKI[1]

It was cold—close to 40° below they said, *but no wind though*—not a small point in an environment when the weather reports regularly include the detail of "wind chill factor." Basically, on such a day as Elsie's funeral there was no wind chill factor at all because there was no wind. Prairie cold-dry and no wind.

It was funny when you thought about what the body should be laid out in for the burial. The undertaker insisted that we bring in a full outfit of underwear, slip, panties, pantyhose. Did they want a bra too? No shoes, though, he specified. We, the family, just complied although the idea of Elsie without shoes (or at least slippers) didn't seem quite right. Elsie was not big on people going around barefoot on cold floors, certainly not in January. She always linked going barefoot in winter to catching a cold but there was something more than that since she didn't abide bare feet in the summer either. Probably more of a type of lolling around that bare feet suggest. Her grandchildren, the worst offenders, talk about the collection of knitted slippers in all sizes and colors that she kept in her closet for when someone came along in snowboots, or just left their shoes at the door even when it wasn't necessary to take off shoes at all.

The dress, though, was a bit more contentious. What did Elsie want to be buried in? Aunt Rachel, the type of woman who planned for these things, had made it well known that she wanted to be buried in her navy blue, the one she had had for her 85th birthday. That was usually the way people identified dresses—the one I bought for Kenny's wedding, or the one that I got in Winnipeg for Marg and Al's golden anniversary. A dress—getting dressed up. Elsie often spoke about people who seemed to be "over-dressed" as being "dressed to kill." But did people also dress to die? People didn't go out and buy something new in anticipation of the burial, did they? Rather, it was a case of targeting "a good dress."

It should not have been an issue when the undertaker called for them to bring in Elsie's things. Elsie's last new dress had been the one for her 80th birthday, purchased almost two years ago at the Fashion Shoppe. Navy and white polyester, short sleeves. She wasn't actually big on buying dresses, hadn't been since the advent of the pant suit. Church sales only complicated things because she often picked up a sweater or skirt or even dress there but not something you would wear "for good." What she did have were hangers of polyester pants; every color in every subtlety you could possibly imagine—the Crayola box writ large: ivory, marine blue, dusty rose, primrose, terracotta, and so on. So her good dress probably was that birthday one. The only problem was that her birthday was in August and everyone knows that it is almost always a scorcher around there in the middle of August. Not that this dictated buying something too summery. It wasn't as though Elsie would have put out money for a good dress that was too summery. You'd want to get your wear out of something, "serviceable" being the operative word here. She would never, for example, have bought something sleeveless and white or off-white for such an occasion. But in this case, even what was serviceable as a summer "good dress" somehow didn't seem appropriate for a January funeral. Like wearing white shoes after Labour Day or before the Queen's birthday. It seems a bit silly, of course. It wasn't as though Elsie were going to feel the cold in her summer dress. It wasn't even that many people were going to see her—beyond the most immediate family who were to view her the night before or first thing in the morning of the funeral. It was going to be a closed coffin. It was just that Elsie wouldn't have necessarily totally approved. Or if she had approved, it would have been something she had to have come around to.

She couldn't have known the birthday before that it would be her last. There was no sign at that point that the cancer would be back. By the end of October, though, she must have known things were going downhill. And by late November, even if she had realized all of that, it was too late to start thinking about dresses for burial. *"Poor dear,"* the nurses might have said, *"she's past it."* And what could be more a case of being "past it" for Elsie who always cared to do the right thing, than to be past caring what she was going to be buried in, summer or winter?

Serviceable, something you could get your wear out of: those were pretty key elements of an outfit. Even her wedding dress had been just that and it had been purchased when Elsie was only 20. Wine-colored or perhaps it was called burgundy—full-length sleeves since it had been a winter wedding. Not dowdy, though, and made of sort of rather elegant *ruched* taffeta, nothing of the *peau de soie* or *chantilly* lace or any of the other French terms that Elsie regularly read out from the wedding announcements in the newspaper. Her command of French was totally wrapped up in fabric and color: *turquoise, chartreuse, beige*. Then there was her New Year's Eve Frolic dress from about 1954, the one she'd have worn to the dance at the armory. Kind of a gray green—although she probably used a much more exotic term than that. Sleeveless with a loosely pleated skirt. Hard to imagine wearing such a dress at that time of the year, just a few days before she would die some 45 years later when it was so cold—though no wind—and we would be worried about the summer quality of the burial dress. But maybe Elsie really, would have had no concern about the burial dress. Or maybe in her late thirties issues of warmth and serviceability weren't quite so important. There was a bit of romance there, after all.

Elsie never had a prom dress, though, that we know. Partly because she never graduated from anything and partly because of the era and location. Elsie declared herself never much one for school although she did write her school leaving exams for Grade Eight. Did she pass them? Did anyone who finished up school in the early 1930s in the rural areas of Manitoba have a prom dress, or a formal gown for a graduation? But if she had graduated, and if she had had a prom dress, what would it have looked like? Did she have had mad fantasies at age sixteen or seventeen in which she imagined herself seventy or so years later preparing for burial in her prom dress,

Of course most women outgrow their prom dresses anyway, so even if Elsie had had one, she wouldn't necessarily be buried in it. All that childbearing and nursing of babies and working on the farm and the various natural stages of body "adjustment." Elsie too. A size 5 and then a size 7 and then lordy, right up to size 11 and 13 and for a time even the 13 was tight, but then she started working back down the scales again—13 tight then 13 loose, then 12 and so on. Something that she and her four sisters—often did when they got together for some family occasion like Christmas or Thanksgiving was to haul out the weigh scale. Right after all the dishes had been finished and the children all playing down in the basement and the men engaged in a game of euchre or crib, they first went through the photo box ooh-ing and ahh-ing and wondering whatever happened to this one or that one. Then as a natural extension of looking back at themselves and others, out came the weigh scale and they would see where they fit. It was all declared good for a laugh but of course it was more than that. Younger sisters could keep track of what was happening to the bodies of the older ones, and all of them were lighter in weight than their mother whom they could rarely coax on to the scale, and when they could, she was usually heard to say, *"The hand is just coming around; it's not quite on anything."* And no one could get quite the angle to see what she actually weighed. By the time Elsie died—all frail and wizened and, as they always say of someone in her condition, "riddled with cancer"—she probably was closer to the size she was when she was seventeen. She could have worn the prom dress after all. Too bad she couldn't have gathered together her sisters for a weigh-in.

She wasn't as skinny as Bill her husband who predeceased her—as the newspaper always put it—fifteen years earlier and who was also riddled with cancer. When, after courting her, marrying her, impregnating her three times and then predeceasing her, Bill "went" (that's what happened to people—always some version of "to go": *"When did Bill go?"* someone would say if they had been away off to Arizona for the winter, only to discover in the spring when they returned that Bill had gone in late November) he was just skin and bone, and probably weighed no more than 50 pounds. People either "went" usually "just like that" or, as in the case of Bill and Elsie, they began to fail (Elsie faster than Bill) and then went, although they could also "pass away"—most often safe into the arms of Jesus, as one of the most popular funeral hymns went. In these cases it was never anyone's fault. Like it wasn't that Jesus was taking you. You just went but at least you had some place to go. And mode of travel was important. How you got there—what kind of burial, what kind of ceremony, what you wore, open or closed casket (never a coffin), the type of casket, the cemetery plot—those were all the important issues.

Even Elsie, who hadn't designated a dress for burial, had at least, over the years, made it known to one family member the kind of casket she wanted. That's what the family member said, and no one had any reason to contest it. As a grieving nephew, he seemed to have nothing to gain by fabricating the information so he must have been telling the truth. What he said was that she had observed that she wanted a casket like Bill's. In fact, since Bill had made no requests known before his death—after all, he hadn't even got around to disposing of the family farm, let alone choose a casket—it is natural to assume that what she chose for Bill she would want for herself. Fortunately with only one undertaker in town and a good system of record keeping—all computerized—there was no need to rely on memory. The computer screen showed some code indicating blue metal casket with metal lining. What was Elsie afraid of with all that metal? The only problem was, when she said she wanted something like Bill's, was it the color blue that was important, or was it the metal, or both? In the end, it was easier to have a casket sent for from the next large town—actually from another province—that was exactly the same, rather than try to figure out Elsie's thinking.

Of course it wasn't exactly the same. In fifteen years you might expect a change in the undertaking business just as with anything else. New models of cars and dishwashers and stereos. Caskets too. But close enough. It was a little more expensive than a lot of the other caskets, but at least the family could feel that it was "honoring her wishes" as the undertaker put it. Would she have been annoyed, though, to think of spending all that money on a casket for herself—metal and all—when it was just that she wanted a blue casket? Or was the matching-quality the point? Or was this a way of claiming a space for herself in death, never as she had it in life? Parity and equality, after years of serving her husband and children, deferring to the doctors, ministers, lawyers, and what have you, all of whom were male. Eating dinner, along with the other women who were helping out with the threshing gang, after the men had returned to the field. Years of carrying food out to the men in the field. Having to listen to her husband's mother talk about her sons and her homeland in the Old Country. Having to sit up late waiting for Bill to come home from the many service organizations he belonged to when be could just as easily have been home with her. Having to sell the family farm—his family's farm.

This was now her time. The undertaker seemed to think so, and could easily convey the importance of matching caskets. She and Bill were now going to be sharing a grave, and they had already been sharing a headstone for years. All that had to be done by the monument company was to just engrave the date of Elsie's death. Her birth date and her full name had been there for years.

So with attention to this kind of detail, and notwithstanding the fact that nothing had been said explicitly about the nature of the burial dress, would Elsie's prom dress be a prom dress based on looking back? *"If had my life to live over again— here's the life I've led and it's not as though I never bad a chance to wear a long formal evening gown, I mean once they were all the rage in the seventies, they were just what we wore to a-frolic."* Or would it be based on looking ahead? *"If I am going to be buried in my prom dress, I'd better choose wisely. This is as good as it gets so let me be buried in something formal?"* Would it be from the mail-order catalogue? Probably. I mean you could get formals from the Eaton's catalogue in 1933. You could get fur coats and actually order a whole house if you wanted to. And there were wedding dresses in the catalogue, at least up to the Sixties.

Elsie would talk about how, when a dance was coming on, Blanche Davidson used to send to the catalogue for a dress, wear it for the night and then send it back, complaining to Eaton's that it didn't fit properly. She might have wondered how Blanche managed to avoid sweating whilst doing a polka at the dance, or spilling parts of an egg salad sandwich served at the lunch at midnight. Or making sure that it wasn't smelling of smoke, although maybe people paid a lot less attention to smoke in those days. And what if Earl Metcalfe or some one like him got her outside by the cars and made a pass at her. Would she say, *"Okay Earl, let's do it, but I'm not doing it with this dress on. So unzip me."* And then would she proceed to lay the dress out carefully on the front seat, while Earl was waiting patiently for her to get ready? Earl probably kept his pants on though and his shirt and jacket. While he was waiting he would just take another swig from his flask—a bit surprised that Blanche had agreed so readily, or maybe just in need of a bit of fortitude. It would be just Blanche then who was stripped down, although she would keep her slip and bra on, and underpants too. She wasn't like that, you know. Took off the silk stockings though. It really wasn't worth it to have Earl rip her stockings when, as far as he was concerned, the stockings were just a nicety for the outside. There was really only one thing Earl was interested in once he managed to get her underpants off. All of this in the confines of Earl's Buick was a little tricky—first because it wasn't easy to navigate from laying out the dress in front seat and settling into the back seat. And second, because it wasn't as though they wanted to be discovered making out in the back seat of a car. Lots of other men might have slipped out for a drink, and more than themselves as a couple who might have the same idea. Blanche hadn't actually come with Earl, and she didn't intend to go home with Earl either.

It made sense, then, to order a prom dress from the catalogue—for one night only. You only graduate once, or you only need a prom dress once. Like ordering a wedding dress for one day. Elsie knew someone who had died and been "laid out" in a cowboy suit—complete with shirt, western tie, belt and boots—all retired for the occasion. It probably made sense for a cremation, but for any other kind of burial it added a layer of ceremony. Once the casket is removed from the church, the minister could announce to those gathered that there would be a 30-minute "preparation time" before proceeding to the graveside. "Preparation time"—maybe that wasn't the right term. It had to be something suitably euphemistic, something that would go with "passed away" and "bereavement" and "loved one." *"Was Mum a smoker?"* asks the undertaker in that overly familiar, empathetic voice. Not, *"Was your mother a smoker? Or what about Mum's hair? How would you like that?"* No point in trying to fix it as she had just had it. After all, she had been lying in a hospital bed for close to eight weeks.

Getting back to the ordering of the dress from the catalogue, though—the undertaker could hardly say, *"Ladies and gentleman, we will now have a 30 minute recess whilst we strip the body of the dress, available, if you are interested at Sears, or the cowboy-V suit at Jewitt's Western Wear. Removal will also include watches, rings, gold fillings. Processional to graveside to reconvene afterward."* Of course they would have to act fast. And what were the mourners supposed to do in the meantime? At a wedding, when the bridal pair was out signing the register, a soloist could favor the congregation with a selection chosen by the couple; however, half an hour would be too long for the distraught to sit waiting to have the rented clothes, or the catalogue number removed. And a bit nerve-wracking for the undertaker to not spill embalming fluid all over the garment. Never mind Blanche's underarm sweat on the blue silk number. *"What's that strange smell?"* the next unsuspecting Earl might say. *"Yeez, Laverne, where did you get this cologne?"*

If Elsie never had a prom dress, does it really matter? Or does it matter more that we aren't quite sure now what she would have wanted? Or is that just the case, that she *deserves* a prom dress? I mean, how is it possible to go about caring about other people's prom dresses, or one's own prom dress, or the significance of prom dresses in the lives of girls and women and not care that Elsie never had one? What's the point of making sure that she has a proper burial, wearing something appropriate, only to turn away from some other ceremony that she also would have enjoyed? If she were graduating earlier this year, it would be a princess dress. And last year it would have been a slinky black number. Don't we need to look at a magazine or catalogue from 1933? Too early for *Seventeen*. By the time *Seventeen* came along in 1944, she had given birth to one child, and Bill was off to Winnipeg as part of the dragoons—no overseas service though. Would she have regarded it as extravagant to have a prom dress? The dirty thirties and all that. She talked almost up to her death about the time that she tried to make bread when she was still living at home, and how it had failed. Her father yelled at her for using up all that flour and yeast and she never ever attempted for the rest of her 81 and a half years to make bread again.

So, can we agree that the prom dress has to be, at the very least, serviceable? Something you can get your wear out of? Not strapless, not white or off white, not too hard to dance in, not dated, something, really, that you could wear for a special occasion including a funeral regardless of the season? After all, she was buried in January on a cold day-no wind though—in short-sleeved navy polyester, full set of underwear. And can we make sure that she gets shoes?

Note

1. Cited in C. Mavor, "Collecting Loss," In *Becoming: The Photographs of Clementia, Viscountess Hawarden.* (Durham and London: Duke University Press, 1999).

CHAPTER 31

Kathy Sands

Fashion for the Soul

Not for me the garish, grieving garb of black. I prefer to wrap my body in a quieter, more sombre shade of grey. I am told it suits me, sets things off. Like what? The blue of my eyes? The golden glow of my sun-tanned skin? The red-hot needle of pain in my neck—like a precious jewel in a showcase, displayed on a bed of crushed grey velvet?

My mother remarks on the "eldedy" length of my slate grey dress. "Why not add some colour? Dress it up with a red belt!" "How gauche!" I think to myself, while continuing to humour her. "Don't you remember? I'm above it all! Untouched by your madness, pills and screams. Besides, who would have cared anyway, much less suspected—after all, mine was only internal bleeding."

One may count oneself fortunate, a Spanish saying goes, if "el muerto" (death) has sat
down by one's side. Well, I certainly have been blessed. Now, if only I were Spanish, I could bleed in public—on the black lacquer tabletops in a Flamenco cafe, or on the dry sandy floor of a bull ring. Instead, I am a Northerner who dwells in a cold,
grid-like city, dressed in a matching shade of grey—the colour of near-death.

PART VIII

Interpretive Dress

CHAPTER 32

Sandra Weber
Claudia Mitchell

Theorizing Dress Stories

> *If I were able to choose one book from among the many that will be published during the 100 years after my death, do you know which one I would choose? No, I would not select a novel from this library of the future, nor a history book (when a history book is of interest, it is also a novel). No, my friend, I would select a fashion magazine to see how women will dress a century after my demise. And those bits of fabric will tell me more about the future of humanity than all the philosophers, novelists, commentators, scientists, and scholars.*
>
> ANATOLE FRANCE

> *Clothes, as despicable as we think them, are so unspeakably significant.*
> T. CARLYLE, SARTOR RESARTUS[1]

Dress Matters

In this final chapter, we focus not on theorizing dress itself (an area of scholarly investigation which is already rich in theory and practice[2]), but rather on theorizing the idea of the "dress story" as both a mode of inquiry and a mode of representation within social science research. It was in the course of conducting research for a previous book, *That's Funny, You Don't Look Like a Teacher* that we first became aware of the significance of dress stories to the investigation of broader questions such as professional identity and the influence of popular culture.[3] In speaking with people about their emerging or changing professional identities, we were struck by just how preoccupied pre-service and beginning teachers often are with their clothes and appearance. Deciding how to "dress to teach" was no small matter to many of them. Some of the stories they told us, for example, revealed how torn they felt between the desire to express themselves personally, to be true to who they felt they really were inside, and the desire to comply with perceived notions of how teachers should look. Their concerns call to mind questions raised by anthropologist Fred Davis regarding choosing what to wear:

> Whom do I wish to please, and in so doing whom am I likely to offend? What are the consequences of appearing as this kind of person as against that kind? Does the image I think I convey of my self reflect my true innermost self or some specious version thereof? Do I wish to conceal or reveal? . . . and so forth. We are all too familiar with the oscillations and dis-ease these identity uncertainties evoke in one's self.[4]

Thus, as Madeleine Grumet points out, an absorbing problematic in modern pedagogy (albeit one of the least discussed) is *what to wear*. This statement applies even to those who say they don't care about their appearance, people who just throw on "any old thing." They too must get dressed.[5]

Several of the female student teachers we interviewed were particularly conscious about dress, especially when asked to draw a teacher or to draw themselves as teachers:

> My idea of the perfect teacher has pretty much remained the same over the years. The idea is that of a person (male or female) who was always well-dressed, prim and proper with no visible faults. Hair and makeup was always perfect and well applied in women, and men would be in neatly pressed suits, matching ties and always smelling good . . . and were all-knowing . . . I suppose this rubbed off on me to some degree because when I did my first practice teaching, I found myself always going in well-dressed and made up. (Tina, elementary teacher)[6]

> Another thing that is important in my drawing is my clothes. I drew myself in my favorite "first day" outfit. Dress is important as it helps demand respect. I am very nervous about having a grade 5 class. It is important that they respect me as a teacher, and not a babysitter, or older sister. I find that being short, and not looking harmful are two things that work against me, so I must dress and act in a way that demands respect. (Roberta, student teacher)[7]

The above comments suggest that to many, clothing is not only a means of identifying oneself as teacher, but is also a pedagogical strategy in itself, a means of commanding respect and order, of establishing a serious working atmosphere, and of exerting control. For Roberta, for instance, dressing "well" is perceived as a means of gaining students' respect and attention. She seeks a business-like seriousness or severity in attire to compensate for her short stature and nervousness. For Tina, a teacher has to be impeccably dressed and perfectly groomed in order to project distance, superior knowledge, and status. It is not overstretching matters to begin to talk of a pedagogy of clothes.

In *Reinventing Ourselves as Teachers: Beyond Nostalgia*, we describe another school-based project wherein we asked beginning teachers to bring in their own old class photographs to a workshop on memory work.[8] These images from their childhood days as well as from their more recent school-based lives were used as memory prompts to help them critically examine their past experiences. We also participated ourselves by interrogating our own school photographs and memories. Once again, we were struck by how frequently dress stories were central to the narratives people construct around their photographs. People would talk, for example, about how much they minded wearing a certain item of clothing that their mother had "made them wear" for the picture or lament about how what the teacher was wearing in the photograph spoiled the image for them. Others, as we see from the account below, spoke of the way that picture-day was a special "dressing up" day:

> My mother and I would pick up my best dress the night before, and I would model it for her to make sure it was the perfect outfit for my big day. I would wake up extra early to get dressed and make myself look very special . . . One year I was really sick on picture day, but I made my mother dress me up, make me look healthy (with a little make-up) and take me to the school especially for the picture.[9]

These lasting impressions of schooling are thus often dominated by lasting impressions of clothing, demonstrating the importance of *dress as a phenomenon and a form of self-knowledge in and of itself.* But equally striking was the power of *dress as a method of inquiry* into other phenomena and issues. In talking about the clothing people wore in the photographs, people incidentally but tellingly revealed a lot about their attitudes, thoughts, and views on questions of body, identity, relationships, teaching strategies, and orientation to the world. Not that answers to such basic questions are clear or simple. Interpreting dress stories is neither an exact nor an easy enterprise.

Dress-meanings

> In sorting out the messages of clothing, the idea of a "language of clothes," though currently a popular notion (such as, perhaps, the business suit) communicate a fairly direct message. But many clothing messages are more like music: they are expressive in an indirect and allusive way. There is rarely a single meaning attached to each article of clothing. Instead, its meanings depend on the context—Who wears it? When? Along with what other clothes? What was the history of the garment? Although we speak of a language of clothes, there are no true equivalents of nouns, verbs, and sentences.
> (STEELE)[10]

In wearing our clothes, or in writing about them, we may not always know what we convey to others—the communicative power of our appearance may far surpass our communicative intent.[11] Some of the information that is transmitted silently from person to person by dress is not easily translatable into words, or would be time-consuming or socially clumsy to communicate orally. Dress can play a similar role in the telling of what we have labelled "dress stories," narratives that—through their concrete descriptions, photographs, and literary or poetic qualities—conjure up and interrogate the materiality as well as the meaning potentials of dresses themselves.

Can dresses be easily "read?" Do they "speak"—acting, for example, as cultural *signs* to point to a person's gender, job, status, economic circumstances, religion, ethnicity, cultural identity, group membership, political values, social aspirations, and so forth? When used as signs, specific garments convey conventional meanings that have evolved and become more or less tacitly agreed upon in a given social group. The meanings indicated by these clothing signs on the surface may seem relatively clear. Thus, for example, a nurse's, soldier's, pilot's, letter carrier's, or taxi driver's uniform, a business suit, a Chanel jacket, a punk rock outfit, an evening gown, a biker's jacket, and a choirboy's surplice are usually read as straightforward indicators or signs of a person's activity or occupation or group membership.[12] But, of course, it would be simplistic to stop there.

Depending on the context in which it is worn or in which it was made, the uniform could be a disguise worn to a masquerade or part of a sting operation, the business suit could be a mere habit and not a job requirement, the Chanel jacket a statement of irony or parody, the punk rock outfit an object of ridicule to a group of youth for whom it is passé, the evening gown the only clean and wearable garment left in the second hand bin, the biker's jacket a wistful gesture of nostalgia and so on. In other words, a more complete reading or construction of meaning around clothes would require access to the details of situation and context, to the *wearer's perspectives* (some of which may be contradictory, partial, fleeting), and to *the symbolic meanings* that clothes can take on for individuals and groups. All of these help improve our readings of these garments on any given person at any given time, which is not to say that there is any one meaning that is *the* "truth."

Steele rather boldly asserts that "an article of clothing has no inherent meaning. Trousers, for example, do not have the idea of masculinity built into them, nor does a skirt automatically signify that the wearer is either female or feminine" except insofar as our culture has come to define or use them that way.[13] It is more the history of clothes and the specific context in which they are worn that determines their meaning. We tend to agree, but nonetheless do not entirely dismiss Heidegger's stance that manufactured objects such as clothes themselves have meaning as to their purpose "built in," reflecting the design intent that informs form and function.[14] One could argue, along these lines, that the very design of a jacket with two sleeves conveys at least some meaning as to its purpose that could travel unaided across cultures, a meaning embodied in or inherent to the garment itself. But then, of course, a film like *The Gods Must Be Crazy*[15] in which a coke bottle fallen out of the sky from a passing small plane assumes a myriad of functions in the life of a Kalahari Bush community, none of them related to Coca Cola, reminds us that what seems obvious in one design or cultural context is less obvious in another. As Roland Barthes so beautifully demonstrates, there is a taken-for-grantedness about the meaning of everyday objects such as clothes that requires challenging. The dress stories in this volume are particularly useful in both confirming and confounding these assertions by offering unique insights into the potential and *multiple meanings clothes can assume*.

A wide range of meanings are constructed and co-exist around and through our clothes—some of them fleeting and unstable, some of them contradictory. There are, for example, the *denotative historical and cultural meanings* that relate to the context in which the clothes are worn, how and why they were made and worn, where they are worn, and how they are inscribed by advertising and dictates of fashion cycles, social class, and specific local contexts and subcultures.[16] Attention should also be paid to the *connotative personal meanings* that dresses assume for the wearer, including expressions of identity, personality, aspirations, and sense of place and community, which may reinterpret, ignore, contest, or confirm the more general meanings associated with certain garments.[17] It is to this connotative meaning of dress that, Lou Taylor asserts, not enough attention is paid, especially insofar as how museums and exhibitions usually treat dress.[18] A wonderful exception and an example of how to showcase the wearer's perspectives can be found in a traveling museum exhibition of wedding dresses, *Fabrications,* that was organized by Canadian sociologist Kathryn Church in collaboration with her mother, the dressmaker of all the gowns on display in the exhibit. The wedding dresses were made over a period of time from the early 1950s to the early 1980s by Lorraine Church who was the local dressmaker and/or friend and/or cousin and/or aunt to the various brides of her small relatively culturally homogeneous home town, Lacombe, in rural Alberta.[19] These individually designed gowns were worn, saved, and have now been loaned back to the dressmaker and her daughter for the purpose of the exhibit, along with wedding photographs and letters detailing stories about each dress and its wearer. This exhibit is a good example of how connotative personal and private meanings of a specific wedding dress can be juxtaposed with public denotative meanings.[20]

And always, interacting with and reflecting back to the wearer or dress maker are *the socially mediated* but also personal multiple readings or reactions of those who see the dresses on display or being worn; *the viewers' gazes*.[21] Adding still further to dress meanings are the more contemplative or interpretive *reader/writer's gaze* of dress scholars, novelists, and anyone else who systematically and thoughtfully considers the possible symbolic meanings of dress. The intermingling of makers', wearers', historians', philosophers', writers', and viewers' interpretations evolves and changes through interaction with the garment itself; constructing and deconstructing meaning through clothes.

Dress and Narrative

Memory Work and Dress Stories

What we call dress stories—autobiographical narratives in which an item of clothing becomes a key organizing feature for a detailed account of life events—are not just "any stories." They are examples of what some scholars call critical or reflective memoir, work that could be located more generally within feminist autobiography.[22] As we have elaborated elsewhere, the object of critical memory work is to make the past usable—a remembering in the service of future action.[23] Moreover, critical memory work *does not assume* that memories are accurate, asking instead such questions as: Why do we remember things one way and not another? What emotional investment is implied? What might be left out? Where are the blanks and silences? How might others implicated in the memories recount them if given the opportunity? What and how we remember things provides clues to how we think *now*, windows of sorts into our emotional and cognitive restructuring of experience and testimony to how the past shapes us. Memories of clothing and the body provide useful scaffolding for structuring a person's life history or memoir, and actual clothing items (as well as photographs of clothes) serve as excellent memory prompts. Some people seem to remember events in greater detail when they begin with sartorial details, and tell more compelling stories when they stop to attend to clothes. Detailing the mundane can unmask the significance of the seemingly insignificant.

In studying the role of memory work and the "afterlife" of popular culture in researching contemporary popular culture of childhood, Mitchell and Reid-Walsh found, for example, that women's memories of playing cowgirl during 1950s North American girlhood often included attention to details of "dressing the part."[24] They cite bell hooks' account of feelings of loss of self now that she no longer has the photograph of herself dressed in her cowgirl suit. In the quotation from hooks' story below, it is both the image of the dress in memory and the absence of the photograph now that is significant. As hooks writes:

> My favorite childhood snapshot then and now shows me in costume, masquerading. And long after it disappeared I continued to long for it and to grieve. I loved this snapshot of myself because it was the only image available to me that gave me a sense

of presence, of girlhood beauty and capacity for pleasure. It was an image of myself that I could genuinely like. At that stage of my life I was crazy about Westerns, about cowboys and Indians. The camera captures me in my cowgirl outfit, white ruffled blouse, vest, fringed skirt, my own gun and my boots. In this image I became all that I wanted to be in my imagination.[25]

It may be worth noting here that hooks' childhood was that of an African-American girl growing up in the Southern United States, which makes her cowgirl play all the more intriguing.

A cowgirl suit also figures prominently in an account by Jacqueline Reid-Walsh who uses her dressing up as a cowgirl story to talk about the ways in which her own childhood play challenged particular notions of "boys' play" and "girls' play," and as well to describe her relationship to her father:

> ... (M)y father took a delight in boys' toys as well as girls' toys and bought me many others ... All I remember is the fringe on the vest, the holsters with guns, and the hat. But apparently, I had boots, and a skirt, as well. My parents related to me how we went to Frontier Land, and my father told me how one of the lead actors of the television series—he played Bat Masterson I think—came out and enacted a shoot-out on the streets ... We explored every area of the "land" with my mother patiently coming along ... What happened to the picture (and indeed the little girl) in her pale blue cowgirl suit? Apart from a frivolous early establishment of fashion tastes (I know I have always liked pale blue denim and jeans skirts), what does my nostalgic image signify?[26]

What is interesting about these two "dressing the part" stories is that they show the potential for the same clothing memory prompt (in this case, a cowgirl dress) to shed light on different but related thematic areas of life. Further reflection on these garment memories, as Reid-Walsh points out in a "second draft" critical rewriting of her memory, point to the taken-for-grantedness of colonial stances that are embedded in children's normally uncritical adoption of popular culture, stances that may be worn unthinkingly along with a garment, but that, like the clothes of childhood themselves, may be outgrown when the children grow up and begin to see the world more critically.[27]

The capacity of clothes to conjure up memories is at least partially rooted in sensory and emotional associations that are automatically and unconsciously established as we go about living our lives in clothes. Almost as a matter of course, wearing, or seeing someone wear an item of clothing establishes connections and association between a particular garment and a particular person, event, experience or moment in time. Thus for example, an Australian artist, Elizabeth Lamont, told us that although she hated wearing dresses as a young girl (she says she was a tomboy), she nonetheless hung on to, and now even draws breathtaking, detailed, larger-than-life size charcoal drawings of the childhood dresses that her mother had bought for her and urged her to wear. Lamont's mother had saved them, lovingly wrapped; hoping that one day a granddaughter might wear them. When Lamont stumbled across the dresses in a drawer many years later, memories of her childhood and her mother came flooding back; the garments acting as a conduit for a mother's love and desires, and a daughter's love and wry recollections of asserting her own dressing preferences. Certain clothes can provoke a series of recollections of "I remember when." As Elizabeth Wilson puts it, "garments, once they have been worn, take on a residue; they become associated with or symbolically represent the person who wore them."[28]

Dress Display as Dress Story

Dresses can be viewed as clothing texts that carry within them their own narration, something that artists and museum curators often capitalize on to great effect. The well established body of feminist scholarship on installation[29] is particularly useful in providing a framework for thinking about the ways that dresses themselves tell stories.[30] It is the very "everydayness" and domesticity of the material culture (and fabric) featured in many dress installations that gives them their power to tell convincing stories that speak to many women. Weber's *"Prom Dress #1: I am a woman now"* is a good example of this.[31]

Made out of almost two hundred unwrapped but not unrolled condoms sewn together to form a lacy strapless short formal gown, the condom dress serves as an example of how the material of the dress (latex condoms), the occasion (the prom), the ritual (association in the heteronormativity of popular culture with the loss of virginity), the design (a conventional low-cut "no longer a little girl" short evening dress) all symbolically work together to interrogate the cultural context of the prom and the transition of identities often associated with adolescence. The fact that the latex of this installation dress has, over several years, begun to deteriorate, adds yet another dimension to the work, and offers in and of itself a further statement about the event of the prom and the various ritualistic associations with heterosexual sex. How, for example, does the latex disintegrate much like the actual memories women have of their prom?[32] Does it evoke, perhaps blatantly, the perils of HIV/AIDS and the preaching about safe sex? To what extent does the very use of latex speak to the *man-madeness* of the event as represented in many of the conventional images of the prom in popular culture where a date of the opposite sex is the norm? Weber's inclusion in the installation of a corsage that features a baby's pacifier at the center speaks to the ambivalence of the adolescent girl at the threshold of adulthood, but also to such danger-images as teen pregnancy (and children having children), the symbol of the pacifier in the early 1990s as an anti-abortion message, along with its association with rave culture. Displayed in this way, dresses tell multi-

Figure 32.1. Prom Dress #1: I am a Woman now. Art Installation by Sandra Weber and Sophie Cloutier. Photograph by Stephanie Anne Weber Biron.

ple stories. So too do the more mundane yet more common displays of dresses in store windows and catalogues, where the arrangement of dresses, the poses, shapes and expressions of the mannequins, and the accessories all interact, encouraging viewers, often passers-by, to imagine certain stories of desire, success, or pleasure.

Dress Performance as Dress Story

Of special significance to appreciating dress stories is the performative nature of *dresses worn*. The significance of performing dress (or dressing performance) as both a mode of inquiry and a mode of representation and dissemination within social science research[33] became clearer to us when we set out to interrogate our own embodiment as professors through writing dress stories: Claudia, by creating short memory work pieces around the role that different items of clothing such as the little black turtleneck or suits have played at different points in her teaching career; Sandra, by writing a monologue about her academic gown;[34] using the garment as a way to unpack some of the theoretical knots that we get ourselves into in teacher education. The more we researched our individual narratives about body and dress, the more we saw a need to perform them. It seemed so evasive, even perverse to write at length about how we ignore our bodies in teaching without finding a more embodied way of testing out and re-presenting the ideas. After all, we are always performing our bodies as Judith Butler points out, and teaching is a special kind of performance.[35] To even begin to embody what we were theorizing, we realized we had to use our bodies (and our clothing) more concretely. And so the written monologues gradually evolved into performance pieces featuring garments for audiences of colleagues at various academic conferences.[36] As we performed these dress stories, physically and mentally up there on stage in our clothes, we gained further theoretical insights into what they were about. It's as if the clothes and our bodies made us listen to and consider them in new ways. This led us to revise and re-write our dress stories, incorporating the insights gleaned from performing them. Moreover, after the performances, audience members would often tell us their own dress stories, demonstrating how one dress story evokes others.

Often, the physical act of performing sparked an insight that was simultaneously emotional and intellectual. For example, it was only when holding a shoe in her hand while playing Claudia's mother Elsie onstage as part of a performance of *Elsie Never Had a Prom Dress* that Sandra began to see the symbolic role that shoes have played, not only in her relationship with her father, Avi, but also in shaping her professional work.[37] This resulted in the writing and performance of *When the Shoe Doesn't Fit: Death of a Salesmen*.[38] But one does not need to write or perform a play to understand how dress stories can be performances. As we explore in the next section, performing dress for an audience is something we do not only in a theater, but also as part of our daily lives.

Dress-body, Identities, and Presentation of Self

Whether or not we know the local codes, and whether or not we wish to fit in or dress "against the grain" or whether we simply don't give a hoot about clothes, dressing is something we can seldom avoid. We agree with Steele that our clothed appearance—the persona we present to the world—is as complex as our selves.[39] Moreover, whether we're looking in the mirror or are getting looks and comments from others about our appearance, the images we see or receive when we are dressed in our clothes provide us with meanings about ourselves that might in turn play a role in the dialectics of identity.[40] How we see ourselves clothed and how we feel when dressed in turn becomes part of who we are, in turn influencing how we dress. A never-ending cycle of dressing today in terms of how we felt or thought we looked yesterday. In short, how we dress can be read as an expression or even an extension of multiple aspects of our identities, or as a way to narrate aspects of self.

Because clothes convey so much about who we might be or who we think we are, dressing can be a very useful way to try on and experiment with multiple identities. Ultimately, "what we wear is and is not who we really are . . . Dress tells us only so much and thereafter keeps us guessing."[41] Dressing, according to Goffman, Tseelon, and many other scholars, is part of our everyday presentation of self, a statement we make consciously or unconsciously as we go about living our lives.[42] Further confirmation of sorts can be found in a series of interviews conducted by Banim, Green, and Guy to explore aspects of women's identity through their day-to-day use of clothes.[43] In analyzing the meanings women attached to their clothing, the authors outlined three interdependent views of self that were evident from their participants' relationships with their clothes: *The woman I want to be, The woman I fear I could be* and *The woman I am most of the time.* These views of self, they claim, reflect women's assessments of the ways they use clothes to integrate various aspects of their identities and bodies in order to create images they feel are appropriate to the perceived demands of any given situation.

Clothes thus mediate the personal and idiosyncratic ways we construct and express and live, in relation to community, as individuals. How we dress provides clues to detailed aspects of ourselves that can be read by people who know us in our particular context—things like personality traits, how we may be feeling that day, how much of a hurry we were in when we got dressed, how much weight we are trying to conceal, what concerns we might have about fitting in or standing out, whether we have an important meeting, who we are trying to impress, and so forth. And always, whatever else they represent, dresses express extensions and connections to the body, and are, we contend, themselves a mode of embodiment.

Women wear their bodies through their clothes, declares Craik.[44] We concur, and go so far as to add that *clothes wear bodies.* Dresses express extensions and connections to the body and are themselves a mode of embodiment. Lurie states that the image our clothed bodies project precedes us, introduces us, and inserts us into the communication we have with others.[45] It is difficult to separate a consideration of posture, gestures, and facial expressions from the clothes and accessories that accompany, hide, or support them. Clothes walk that invisible and ambiguous line between body and not body, mediating our sense of embodiment, and helping us enact or perform our embodied identities, both to our own eyes and to others. And, perhaps more than anything else, *clothes evoke the body*. The very shape of a hanging garment (large or small, two sleeves or shaped waist) brings forth images of possible bodies, known and unknown, of people who might wear or might have worn them. Clothes can be viewed as extensions of the body/self (think high heels, top hats), or as ways to modify, hide, or display the body (think girdles, loose fitting tops, push-up bras, tight fitting skirts). Wearing clothes, fitting into them, moving in them, the sensuality of cloth against skin—all these call us back to our bodies and force us to acknowledge and deal with them.

Another dress activity that forces us to pay our bodies heed and to objectify ourselves is shopping. It is hard to be passive about clothes shopping, the act of which requires not only time and money but which also compels us to gaze at our reflected bodies through our own eyes—and far worse—through the imagined eyes of others. It is this *imagined gaze of others* that is often fraught with an anxiety mediated by popular images and internalized societal expectations of what we are "supposed to look like." In the process of this sort of attending to dress, acknowledgement of body and consideration of how we wish to present ourselves and to whom becomes necessary. The choosing, trying on, and purchasing of clothing pushes us to take dress and the body seriously, if only for a short while. All this of course assumes that one has the opportunity and ability to choose one's garments, a point driven home, for example, in Cole's chapter in this volume about how her mother's Alzheimer's disease impacted her experience of clothes and how, as a young child, Cole herself was dressed meticulously by her mother. Other narratives of clothing dealing with hand-me-downs in relation to issues of class and poverty, along with narratives of catalogue shopping and rural life, re-position the place of body within desire and imagination.[46]

Wardrobe Moments: Conduit to Wearers' and Readers' Perspectives

Marcel Mauss and Pierre Bourdieu have each argued that clothing the body is an active process—a means of constructing and presenting the bodily self.[47] Nowhere is this more evident, perhaps, than during what Banim, Green and Guy label the "wardrobe moment,"[48] when a person ponders that impossibly silly, impossibly significant question of what to wear, a question that, as we saw earlier, shopping attempts to answer by filling the closet with options.

> Most of us daily confront a reality of fragments, in the act of opening a wardrobe to select an outfit: this act, however trivial, may be seen as a metonym for the undoubtedly much more momentous task we undertake when we attempt to grasp our historical identities. At all times, we are expected to make sense of residues of distorted pasts and shred of possible futures, displayed before our gaze not by the agents of a rational plan, but by random events of assemblage, discovery, even destruction. Dress thus becomes the vehicle for the expression of concurrently psychological and historical ambiguities, marked by the fluctuation between a rationalistic quest for integrity and a transgressive infatuation with disunity.[49]

The idea of getting up in the morning, putting something on (or being dressed by some one else), and going out "into the world" is an act that is sometimes taken for granted as a casual given, a routine or everyday experience. At other times (and for some of us, every time) the process of deciding what to wear and getting dressed and confronting one's mirror image is an anxiety-laden affair loaded with meaning. Our perception of our dressed selves is filtered through the multiple lenses of our own past experiences, humiliations, compliments, as well our exposure to media, and to friends', families', and strangers' real or imagined comments and gazes, all of which influence what we see and what we don't see when we look in that mirror.

Banim, Green and Guy describe the "wardrobe moment" from the wearer's perspective, showing how public performance and social structures pervade even this private moment:

> A woman stands in front of the wardrobe, looks through the clothes stored within and wonders what to wear. It's an experience we go through at least once if not twice or three times a day. We ask ourselves a whole series of questions at this wardrobe moment. "Where am I going and what am I doing today/tonight?" "Who's going to be there?" "Does it matter what I look like when I get there?" The problem is, though, even when we assemble our outfits for the day or evening, we take a risk on whether that outfit will "click," go horribly wrong or just be OK. Until we actually take our clothed bodies into the public realm, into the physical and social space we chose the outfit for, we are guessing.[50]

Literary sources provide some of the richest and multilayered analyses of wardrobe moments—what Anne Buck calls "dress in action."[51] Consider, for example, the following scene which occurs in Ian McEwen's novel *Atonement:* Cecilia, just back from Oxford and in anticipation of a dinner party that includes her brother's male school friend, chooses and discards dress after dress because it isn't "quite right":

> On two occasions within half an hour, Cecilia stepped out of her bedroom, caught sight of herself in the gilt-frame mirror at the top of the stairs and, immediately dissatisfied, returned to her wardrobe to reconsider. Her first resort was a black crepe de Chine dress which, according to the dressing-table mirror, bestowed by means of

clever cutting a certain severity of form. Its air of invulnerability was heightened by the darkness of her eyes. Rather than offset the effect with a string of pearls, she reached in a moment's inspiration for a necklace of pure jet. The lipstick's bow had been perfect at first application. Various tilts of the head to catch perspectives in triptych reassured her that her face was not too long, or not this evening . . .

But the public gaze of the stairway mirror as she hurried towards it revealed a woman on her way to a funeral, an austere, joyless woman moreover, whose black carapace had affinities with some form of matchbox-dwelling insect. A stag beetle! It was her future self, at eighty-five in widow's weeds. She did not linger—she turned on her heel, which was also black, and returned to her room. . . . She stepped out of the black crepe dress where it fell to the floor, and stood in her heels and underwear, surveying the possibilities on the wardrobe racks, mindful of the passing minutes. She hated the thought of appearing austere. Relaxed was how she wanted to feel, and, at the same time, self-contained. Above all, she wanted to look as though she had not given the matter a moment's thought, and that would take time.[52]

After running her hand along "a few feet of personal history" of her closet clothes rack, Cecilia settles on a muted pink silk dress with a pleated bodice and scalloped hem, changes her shoes and exchanges the jet beads for pearls, But McEwen is unwilling to end the wardrobe moment there. The pink dress too, once Cecilia is out in the full light, also gets discarded:

Even as she approached the mirror from a distance of forty feet, she saw that it was not going to let her pass; the pink was in fact innocently pale, the waistline was too high, the dress flared like an eight year-old's party frock. All it needed was rabbit buttons. As she drew nearer, an irregularity in the surface of the ancient glass foreshortened her image and she confronted the child of fifteen years before. She stopped and experimentally raised her hands to the side of her head and gripped her hair in bunches. This same mirror must have seen her descend the stairs like this on dozens of occasions, on her way to one more friend's afternoon birthday bash. It would not help her state of mind, to go down looking like, or believing she looked like, Shirley Temple.

More in resignation than irritation or panic, she returned to her room. There was no confusion in her mind: these too-vivid, untrustworthy impressions, her self-doubt, the intrusive visual clarity and eerie differences that had wrapped themselves around the familiar were no more than continuations, variations of how she had been seeing and feeling all day. Feeling, but preferring not to think. Besides, she knew what she had to do and she had known it all along. She owned only one outfit that she genuinely liked, and that was the one she should wear. She let the pink dress fall on top of the black and, stepping contemptuously through the pile, reached for the gown, her green backless post-final gown. As she pulled it on she approved of the firm caress of the bias-cut through the silk of her petticoat, and she felt sleekly impregnable, slippery and secure; it was a mermaid who rose to meet her in her own full-length mirror. She left the pearls in place, changed back into the black high-heel shoes, once more retouched her hair and make-up, forwent another dab of scent.[53]

The above excerpts illuminate certain aspects of the wearer's perspective, evoking the range of emotions, thought processes and "coded meanings" that accompany particular dress choices. But at the same time, by putting readers in the viewer's perspective, it allows us to both empathize with and critique the dress story. The fact that Cecelia owns so many dresses (denoting elite status and wealth) serves to highlight and emphasize what choosing an outfit entails and permits the author to lay bare elements of the wardrobe moment that apply to those of us with far less sumptuous choices. Finely crafted dress stories deepen our understanding of the significance of dresses and dressing in our daily lives even when, or indeed, especially when, the experience depicted in the account is different from our own (and yet, when we think about it, maybe also the same as our own in significant ways).

Although at home we may create private safe spaces where image and identity are free from public scrutiny and not depicted in the pages of anyone's novel, the private wardrobe moment that Banim, Green, and Guy describe still manages to bring the public right into our bedroom or dressing room. We can rebel against the mirror's tyranny, not glancing at our reflections as we don comfortable dressing gowns or jogging pants to relax in, but we know our reflection is there, waiting.

What we do about it varies. Cultural dictates or messages about what "normal" womanhood is supposed to look like exert an enormous pressure to conform, resulting in much frustration for the majority who either can't or don't want to measure up to these often unrealistic expectations.[54] But normative images can be contested individually and collectively though dress; sometimes we create and transform ourselves by dressing against expectations, as early feminists did by donning trousers, or by playfully calling our attention to fashion excesses by flaunting them, wearing ridiculous high heels and a short skirt in the boardroom or by defying intolerant bans on religious attire and wearing it anyway. Playing with the images on display in our society may be dangerous, but it nonetheless remains a powerful if under-utilized tool. Women can and do re-appropriate and subvert the meanings imbued in clothes, although that does not mean others will read them the way the wearer would like. Similarly, readers of dress stories may interpret them in ways their authors did not intend, adding to the multiplicity of meanings that can be constructed through or around dress.

The Politics of Dress-stories

The dress stories in this volume might be dismissed (unthinkingly, too easily) by some as mere stories told by women of privilege. Or, like so many things that women deem important, dresses may be inaccurately labelled as frivolous "chick fluff." After all, if women wear them and write about them, how important can they be?! And some might wonder why responsible social scientists write about something like dresses or encourage others to narrate personal dress stories when the vast majority of people in the world are too poor to be concerned about a wardrobe of ensembles and where there are still children who never attend school (let alone wear a school uniform)? But it is the very ability that clothes have to evoke important social issues, including issues of economic disparity, commodification, gender, race, class, culture and difference that makes dresses, even in their absence, so important to study.

Dress—like the body it evokes, covers, and reveals—is a contested site, and as we see, for example, in Bahramitash's story about the hijab in this volume, personal stories are also always political. This raises many challenges and questions: How to problematize dress within personal dress-stories based on emerging issues of globalization and cultural appropriation? What does it mean, for example, to "dress ethnic," or to try on the sartorial identity of the Other? What to make, for example, of the popularity of tribal prints on golf tee shirts, "peasant shirts" on top fashion models and so forth. Who should wear (and tell stories about) items of clothing and fabric that have been associated with traditional cultures? How can dress story tellers, including academics, acknowledge or interrogate their positions of power and privilege? How do we begin to realize how what we wear may colonize us or contribute to the colonization of others? Few, if any, dress stories can assume the burden of answering these questions, but they do evoke these questions in powerful yet subtle ways that facilitate a critical distancing and that caution us against knee jerk "one size fits all" kinds of answers. Dress stories remind us of the complexities and perils of interpreting any one garment in any one way, arguing against a singularity of meaning.

Dress stories, limited and singular as they may be individually, can collectively point to silences, gaps, and issues of social import. One area where dress stories have been helpful, for example, is in deepening our awareness and understanding of women's bodies in the workplace. Ellen Green, in speaking of the ways women in the work force "manage" the professional body, writes:

> ... Senior women are acutely aware of the need to guard their embodied appearance, lest they invite sanctions or unwanted attention as sexualized bodies within the academy. Most avoided what they perceived as embodied "sexual display."[55]

She goes on to cite the case of Jane, who observes

> ... it's wanting not to have any hint of sexual display so I wouldn't ... Wear anything that was low-cut ... I don't want to feel that X across the table is trying to peer down my cleavage ... I just don't want to be on display in that kind of way.[56]

Similarly Kate Gillen who also writes of women's dress in the workplace lays out the map of "not too" much: "Avoid appearing to be sexually available—'since this will cost them respect,' but at the same time look attractive or 'suffer loss of respect."[57] A further example can be found in *Reinventing Ourselves as Teachers*, where we cite the case of Ellen, a teacher who, in taking off her jacket when the classroom becomes too hot, receives wolf-whistles.[58] Her male counterparts, she observes, would just "naturally" take off their jackets in the middle of class without inviting comment or reaction.[59]

The kinds of questions raised in these dress narratives in Western contexts are also central to work within gender and development. In Zambia, for example, women teachers talk about the fact that they are sometimes afraid to accept a promotion in a school or district because they fear that they will be accused by their families or communities of having had sex with the supervisor in order to get the promotion. Their dress, they say, is just one "indicator."[60] Not unlike the North American context, there is almost no acceptable language for sexuality and desire. As the literature on girls' education within the work of UNICEF, UNESCO, and various donor organizations documents thoroughly, the female body is problematic: menstruating girls require toilets facilities separate from those for boys at school; the skirt or tunic school uniform of girls makes them sexually vulnerable; female students get pregnant, and are prevented from continuing their education; female teachers get pregnant and "disrupt" the school year, and so on. Moreover, as is highlighted in the writing of the South African journalist, Charlene Smith, the politics of heterosexual encounter (and "she was asking for it") becomes even more complicated for women, especially in South Africa and other parts of sub-Saharan Africa, in the age of AIDS.[61]

As the poetic and narrative pieces in this book attest, dress stories are seldom, if ever, *just* narratives about clothing. Even when set in contexts of privilege, they are also narratives of resistance, submission, intergenerational conflict, weakness, pain, loss, power and empowerment.

Future Directions, Areas of Potential, and Cautions

In *Not Just Any Dress,* we have included selections that speak to a variety of different themes including childhood, rites of passage, mortality, mother-child relationships, teaching, the workplace, and so on. But of course, there are many other features and types of dress stories that remain to be explored. Similar collections, for example, could focus on other themes, contexts, and dresses, for example children's dresses, dress in retirement homes, dressing on the picket line, dressing fat, dressing thin, body-based harassment, dressing on welfare, circus dress, dressing illness, dressing to fight, dressing for emancipation. We can imagine many other dress story projects, and indeed have begun working on some ourselves.

Dress, for example, is central to the study of subcultures,[62] and can also be used to study a variety of institutional contexts, such as health care. As an example, we have begun to look at the ways in which focusing on a particular item of clothing (e.g. school uniforms, hospital gowns) might serve as an organizing feature for studying institutional life and policy making. Nurses working in a palliative care unit with terminally ill people, for example, might reflect on how important it is that they are seen just as someone who is there in *civvies* rather than dressing officially as nurses as a reminder of the medical institution itself. How might narratives like these inform other health-policy issues? Of similar interest would be what a practitioner in London, writing about the fatigue suffered by AIDS workers, has to say about the significance of the t-shirts he wears to go out into the community to talk to youth, comparing this *apparent* casual dress with his "real" and off-duty casual dress which also includes t-shirts, but not the same ones.[63] What can we learn from these symbolic uses of clothing in the everyday that deepen our understanding of the long-term effects of this kind of intense community work?

Because there are so many dress stories that remain untold (some of them unspeakable), it is our hope that narratives and poetic pieces like the ones that are contained in *Not Just Any Dress* might do a number of things simultaneously. First, we see them as springboards to further work on narrative and dress. Not only do stories beget stories, we anticipate that the particularized context of wedding dress stories serves to beget further wedding dress stories; burial dress stories beget others and so on. In short, any one of the selections might suggest the possibilities for mapping out a much larger and more focused dress-body project.

Secondly, we see them as entry points to the kinds of *transnational conversations* which can include local, national, and global contexts. Although, we have noted above that the dress narratives on sexual harassment may appear to have some sort of universality about them, in actuality, it is the local and national contexts that are particularly important. What is useful, though, is to see how notions of transactional feminism can provide a space for seeing the potential for working across cultural contexts. Not only do feminists have a great deal to learn through studying wearers' perspectives within a variety of contexts, but we also have interesting possibilities for strategic alliance, as Julia Okely's *Own and Other Cultures* suggests. Indeed, the longstanding ethnographic traditions of studying Other through fabric, textiles, and dress bode well for methodological frameworks that include "making the familiar unfamiliar"[64] or "starting with ourselves."[65]

Finally, we hope that these dress-stories will inspire those working in many different areas of research methodology and policy to provide space for the telling of the perspectives of wearers within a context that takes dress stories seriously. Writing about dress within academic research (and outside Dress Studies) may bring with it a particular set of vulnerabilities. For the contributors to this volume, for example, the very writing of these pieces—and putting into the public arena very personal experiences of clothing—is in itself an act of courage. Contributors may be revealing their frailties and obsessions, evoking in the reader perhaps a sense of impatience: "How self indulgent to worry about the fabric of a wedding dress!" Equally a reader may find a particular piece politically suspect: "why is this author writing about *that*?" Sometimes, there may even be a tweaking of self-recognition that makes the reader want to distance herself from the author: what is written is too close to home (we simultaneously wear and want to cover over a particular dress-story). In one sense, these are of course no different from the vulnerabilities of projects of autobiographic inquiry more generally as many of our colleagues in autobiography, life history, reflective practice, memory work, and self-study have already noted.[66] In another sense, though, they do carry with them another trace of the author/wearer that is harder to dismiss. It is for this reason that we hope that *Not Just Any Dress* will inspire those working on dress and body projects within narrative and poetic inquiry to see the potential for interdisciplinary inquiry, and for drawing on and combining methodologies from a number of areas including feminist visual culture, dress studies, historical studies, and ethnography. The dress, far from being hidden from view then, can serve as a phenomenon in its own, as a mode of inquiry and a mode of representation.

After all, these dress stories are about *not just any dress*.

Notes

1. As quoted in W. J. F. Keenan, "Introduction: 'Sartor Resartus' Restored: Dress Studies in Carlylean Perspective," in W. J. F. Keenan, Ed. *Dressed to Impress: Looking the Part* (Oxford and New York: Berg, 2001) 1.
2. To do justice to the vast body of work within Dress Studies, Costume, Material Culture, and Cultural Studies that focuses on dress is beyond the scope of this book. The success of Berg as a publishing enterprise dedicated to scholarship on dress and body suggests that this is clearly a burgeoning interdisciplinary area of study. See, for example, the journal *Fashion Theory* and the work of scholars such as Elizabeth Wilson, Valerie Steele, Lou Taylor, Amy de la Haye, Joanne Entwistle, and Joanne B. Eicher.
3. Sandra Weber & Claudia Mitchell, *That's Funny, You Don't Look Like a Teacher* (London: The Falmer Press, 1995).
4. Fred Davis, *Fashion, Culture and Identity* (Chicago: University of Chicago Press, 1992) 24.
5. Madeleine Grumet, "Scholae Personae: Masks for Meaning," in J. Gallop, Ed., *Pedagogy: The question of impersonation* (Bloomington, IN: Indiana University Press, 1995) 36–45.
6. Weber & Mitchell (1995) 63.
7. Weber & Mitchell (1995) 63–64.
8. Claudia Mitchell & Sandra Weber, *Reinventing Ourselves as Teachers: Beyond Nostalgia* (London: The Falmer Press, 1999).

9. Mitchell & Weber (1999) 88–89.
10. Valerie Steele, "Dressing for Work," in C. G. Kidwell & V. Steele, Eds., *Men and Women: Dressing the Part* (Washington, D.C.: Smithsonian Institute, 1989) 6–7.
11. Justus Buchler, *Nature and Judgement* (New York: Columbia University, 1955).
12. See, for example, Goodrum, "Land of Hip and Glory: Fashioning the 'Classic' National Body," in W. J. F. Keenan (Ed.) *Dressed to Impress: Looking the Part* (Oxford and New York: Berg, 2001) 87.
13. Steele (1989) 6.
14. We are thinking, for example, of Martin Heidegger's discussion of the "shoeness" of shoes in "The Origin of the Work of Art," in Albert Hofstadter and Richard Kuhns, Eds., *Philosophies of Art and Beauty: Selected Readings in Aesthetics from Plato to Heidegger* (Chicago: University of Chicago Press, 1976) 647–708.
15. J. Uys (Director), *The Gods Must Be Crazy*. (Botswana: Fox, 1984).
16. The work of Stephen Riggins provides a useful framework for "going deep" into the exploration and interpretation of the personal and social meaning of objects and spaces. Riggins, in his autoethnographic work on his parents' living room, outlines the use of the terms *denotative* and *connotative* in relation to material culture and space. See particularly Stephen Riggins, *The Socialness of Things: Essays on the Socio-Semiotics of Objects* (New York: Mouton de Gruyter, 1994). By "denotative," he is referring to the factual and social history of an object: where it comes from, why it was invented, and so on. Applied to dress, we could look to the vast body of literature that looks at, say, the history of military uniforms (Paul Fussell, *Uniforms: Why We Are What We Wear,* New York: Houghton-Mifflin, 2002), wedding dresses (*Wedding in White*), corsetry (Valerie Steele, *The Corset: A Cultural History,* Yale University Press, 2000) and so on, to look at some of the denotative meanings of particular dress texts.
17. By "connotative meaning," Riggins (1994) extends the reading of texts into the personal meanings attached to particular objects. Applied to his parents' living room, it is not just that a particular model of television set that occupies a space in the room dates back to a certain time and so on—the denotative meaning—is important, but equally that its physical position in the left corner of the room, or its role in offering a space of display for family photographs, or its social position as text of controversy in the household serve as features of connotative meaning.
18. Lou Taylor, *The Study of Dress History*. (London: Manchester University Press, 2002).
19. Church, K. & Church, L. (2003). Needle and pins: Dialogue on a mother/daughter journey. *Journal of the Association for Research on Mothering*, 5 (1), 148–156.
20. There are of course other well-known exhibits that attempt to incorporate personal elements of the wearer's perspectives.
21. We are not using "gaze" here only in the more classic scholarly sense of generic theoretical stance but also in a more literal way of one specific person looking at another. We do think and acknowledge that any person's gaze IS filtered and shaped by social, historical, and political influences.
22. See, for example, the critical examination of memory accounts in the first draft/second draft approaches to memory work developed by P. Hampl, "Memory and Imagination," in J. McConkey (Ed.) *The Anatomy of Memory: An Anthology* (New York and Oxford: Oxford University Press, 1996) 201–211. and N. Norquay, "The Other Side of Difference: Memory-work in the Mainstream," *Qualitative Studies in Education*, 6 (3), 1993, 241–251.
23. See Mitchell & Weber, 2000.
24. Jesse, the cowgirl in the movie *Toy Story 2,* provides the entry point to interrogating these cowgirl memories. For an extensive discussion of cowgirl dressing see "Memory Spaces and the Afterlife of Children's Popular Culture" in Claudia Mitchell & Jacqui Reid-Walsh, *Re-*

searching *Children's Popular Culture: Childhood as a Cultural Space* (New York and London: Routledge Taylor & Francis, 2002).
25. bell hooks (1994:45), as cited in Mitchell & Reid-Walsh.
26. Mitchell & Reid-Walsh, 64–65.
27. See Mitchell & Reid-Walsh.
28. Elizabeth Wilson, Keynote address at *Fashion: Making an Appearance*. University of Queensland, Brisbane, Australia, July 2003.
29. See for example, Fiona Carson & Claire Pajaczkowska, Eds., *Feminist Visual Culture* (Edinburgh: Edinburgh University Press, 2001) and Helena Reckett & Peggy Phelan, *Art and Feminism*. (Phaidon Press Limited, 2001).
30. Many of the central themes and images in the work Reckett and Phelan describe—identity, difference, personalizing the political, corporeality—are all themes that have also come to be central to the published narratives of a number of women writing in such areas as education and cultural studies (McWilliam & Taylor, 2001; Steedman, 1989; hooks, 1995; Lesko, 1988; Mitchell & Weber, 1999). In writing about installation, Reckett and Phelan (200) refer to the use of clothing, images from popular culture (Barbie, Marilyn Monroe), childhood artefacts, and household products in such works as Su Richardson's *Burnt Toast* from Feministo (1975–77), Kate Walker's *Death of the Housewife* from Found Objects Assemblage (1974), Annette Messagrer's *Les tortures voluntaires,* 1972, Histoire des robes (1990), Suzanne Lacy and Leslie Laborwitz's performance installation, *In mourning and in rage.* More recent dress installation pieces would include the work of South African artists such as Penny Siopsis on dress-as-memory, or Lianne Lieblin, along with the a gallery installation at Concordia in Montreal called *The Dress Show* where Weber spoke about the "I am a woman now" dress in her gallery talk featured during the exhibition.
31. For a closer look at the "I am a woman dress" as it looked when it was first created in 2000, visit *The Studio* of the Image and Identity Research Collective website: *www.iirc.mcgill.ca*.
32. See also Derry, this volume.
33. Here we are thinking of the work of Norman Denzin on the role of performance within educational research (See N.K. Denzin, "Performance Texts," in W. G. Tierney & Y. S. Lincoln, Eds., *Representation and the Text: Re-framing the Narrative Voice* (Albany, NY: State University of New York Press, 1997, 179–217), as well as the work of Ross Gray on the ways in which performance and the body has been used to disseminate finding on women and breast cancer and men and prostate cancer to audiences of physicians (see R. E. Gray et al. "Making a Mess and Spreading it Around: Articulation of an Approach to Research-Based Theater" In A.P. Bochner & C. Ellis Eds., *Ethnographically Speaking: Autoethnography, Literature, and Aesthetics* (New York: Altamira Press, 2002, 57–75).
34. See also "*Was It Something I Wore?*" and *Curse you Rene Descartes!* this volume.
35. Judith Butler, *Gender Trouble* (New York & London: 1990).
36. "*Was It Something I Wore?*" and "*From Robe to Robe*" have been performed as keynote presentations at the Canadian Association for the Study of Women in Education annual conference held in Toronto, Canada May, 2003, and at the International Federation of Teachers of English conference held in Melbourne, Australia, July, 2003.
37. See Mitchell, this volume. See also Weber, "The Pedagogy of Shoes: Clothing and Self-Study," in K. O'Reilly Scanlon, C. Mitchell and S. Weber, Eds. *Just Who Do We Think We Are? Methodologies for Self-Study in Teacher Education* (New York and London: Routledge Falmer, forthcoming).
38. Weber & Mitchell, 2002a, 2003.
39. Steele, 1989, 7.
40. What we are trying to evoke here is the dialectical nature of meaning construction and identity. Drawing at least partially, on the work of scholars such as Bahktin, Britzman, Foucault,

Merleau Ponty, Griffiths, and Jenkins, we conceive of identity and self, not as fixed and static, but as *ongoing dialectical and embodied processes of interpretation and representation* involving the intersection of personal, social, cultural, political, geographical, physical, material, and psychological aspects of human experience. We construct our selves as we simultaneously are constructed by others.

41. W. J. F. Keenan, "Dress Freedom: The Personal and the Political." In W. J. F. Keenan, Ed., *Dressed to Impress: Looking the Part.* (Oxford and New York: Berg, 2001) 19.
42. Erving Goffman, *The Presentation of Self in Everyday Life* (Garden City, New York: Doubleday, 1959), Tseelon, E. (1995). *The Masque of Femininity: The Presentation of Woman in Everyday Life.* London: Sage Publications.
43. Banim, Green, & Guy (2001, 203-204).
44. Jennifer Craik, *The Face of Fashion. Cultural Studies in Fashion* (London & New York: Routledge, 1994) 4.
45. Lurie (1992).
46. Mitchell and Reid-Walsh, 1998.
47. Mauss (1973, 1985) & Bourdieu (1986).
48. Banim, et al., 2001. As we see in the quote that began this chapter, Warwick and Cavallero use wardrobe moments differently to call our attention to the more historical aspect of identities. (Alexandra Warwick and Dani Cavallaro, *Fashioning the Frame: Boundaries, Dress, and the Body* (Oxford and New York: Berg, 1998) 206.
49. Warwick & Cavallaro, 206.
50. Banim, et al., 1.
51. Buck, 1983.
52. McEwen, *Atonement*, 96-97.
53. McEwen, 97-99.
54. For in depth discussion of various sociocultural aspects of embodiment, see for example, the work of Susan Bordo, Kathy Davis, Jane Arthurs and Jean Grimshaw, Joanne Entwistle, and Gail Weiss referenced at the end of this book.
55. Eileen Green, "Suiting Ourselves" in Guy, Green & Banim, Eds, 2001, 97-116, 110.
56. Green, 110.
57. Kate Gillen (2001) 86.
58. Mitchell & Weber, 1999
59. A. Hansen, "The Day the Heat Went On," in Kleinfled & Yerian, Eds., *Gender Tales: Tensions in the Schools* (New York: St. Martin's Press, 1995).
60. Mitchell, 1998.
61. Charlene Smith, 2000.
62. This is especially true of youth culture. See, for example Laurie Leblanc's *Pretty in Punk: Girls' Gender Resistance in a Boys' Subculture* (New Brunswick, New Jersey, and London: Rutgers University Press, 1999).
63. Deverell, 2001.
64. Ely et al., 1991 See Ely, M.; Anzul, M.; Friedman, T.; Garner, D. & McCormack-Steinmetz, A. (1991). *Doing qualitative research: Circles within circles.*
65. See Max van Manen, *Researching Lived Experience: Human Science for an Action Sensitive Pedagogy.* (London, Ontario: Althouse Press, 1990).

References

Acker, S. *Teachers, Gender and Careers.* New York: Falmer Press, 1989.
Adams, L., and L. Madaras. *Great Expectations.* Boston: Houghton Mifflin Co., 1980.
Albers, S. M. "The Effect of Gender-Typed Clothing on Children's Social Judgments." *Child Study Journal* 28, no. 2 (1998): 137–59.
Alvi, S., H. Hoodfar, and S. McDonough, eds. *The Muslim Veil in North America: Issues and Debates.* Toronto: Women's Press, 2003.
Apter, E. "Splitting Hairs." In *Feminizing the Fetish.* Ithaca: Cornell University Press, 1991.
Arthurs, J., and J. Grimshaw. *Women's Bodies: Discipline and Transgression.* Great Britain: Biddles Ltd., 1999.
Ash, J. "The Aesthetics of Absence: Clothes without People in Paintings." In *Defining Dress: Dress as Object and Meaning,* edited by A. de la Haye and E. Wilson, 128–42. Manchester and New York: Manchester University Press, 1999.
Bailey, K. R. *The Girls Are the Ones with the Pointy Nails.* Ontario: The Althouse Press, 1993.
Bakhtin, N. M. *The Dialogic Imagination.* Translated by C. Emerson and M. Holquist. Austin: Austin University Press, 1986.
Bal, M. *The Molted Screen. Reading Proust Visually.* Stanford, California: Stanford University Press, 1997.
Balzac, H. d. *Une Fille D'eve.* Paris: Garnier-Flammarion, 1965.
Banim, M., E. Green, and A. Guy. "Dis/Continued Selves: Why Do Women Keep Clothes They No Longer Wear." In *Dis/Continued Selves: Why Do Women Keep Clothes They No Longer Wear,* edited by A. Guy, E. Green and M. Banim, 203–20. Oxford: Berg, 2001.
———. "Introduction." In *Through the Wardrobe: Women's Relationships with Their Clothes,* edited by A. Guy, E. Green and M. Banim, 1–20. Oxford: Berg, 2001.
Barnes, R., and J. B. Eicher. *Dress and Gender: Making and Meaning.* New York and Oxford: Berg, 1992.
Barthes, R. *Carmen Lucida.* New York: Farrar, Straus, & Giroux, 1980.
———. *The Fashion System.* New York: Hill and Wang, 1983.
———. *The Pleasure of Text.* London: Cape, 1976.

———. *Roland Barthes by Roland Barthes.* Translated by Richard Howard. New York: Farrar, Straus & Giroux, 1981.
———. *S/Z.* Translated by Richard Miller. New York: Blackwell, 1990.
Baruch, E. H. "Two Interviews with Julia Kristeva." *Partisan Review* 51, no. 2 (1984): 120-32.
Bauer, P., M. Liebl, and L. Stennes. "Pretty Is to Dress as Brave Is to Suitcoat: Gender-Based Property-to-Property Inferences by 4½-Year-Old Children." *Merrill-Palmer Quarterly* 44, no. 3 (1998): 355-77.
Bechdel, A. "Fond Look at the Fab, Funky World of U.S. Feminist Fashion." *Ms.,* July/August 1992, 3.
Beckerman, I. *Love, Loss and What I Wore.* Chapel Hill: Algonquin Books of Chapel Hill, 1995.
Benjamin, W. "The Image of Proust." In *Illuminations: Essays and Reflections,* edited by A. Adrendt, 201-16. New York: Schocken Books, 1968.
Bennett, P. W. "'Who Wore the Pants?'": Dress, Gender and Power, 1850-1914." *History and Social Science Teacher* 20, no. 4 (1990): 221-25.
Benstock, S., and S. Ferriss, eds. *On Fashion.* New Jersey: Rutgers University Press, 1994.
Bentley, M. K. "The Body of Evidence: Dangerous Intersections between Development and Culture in the Lives of Adolescent Girls." In *Growing up Girls: Popular Culture and the Construction of Identity,* edited by S. R. Mazzarella and N. O. Pecora, 209-23. New York: Peter Lang, 1999.
Best, A. *Prom Night: Youth, Schools, and Popular Culture.* New York and London: Routledge, 2000.
Blau, H. "Letting Be Be the Final of Seem. The Future of Illusion." In *Performance in the Postmodern Culture,* Edited by M. Benamou and C. Carmello, 59-77. Madison, WI: Coda, 1977.
Bordo, S. *Unbearable Weight: Feminism, Western Culture and the Body.* Berkeley: University of California Press, 1993.
Botsford, F. M. *Solitaire: The Intimate Lives of Single Women.* Toronto: MacFarlane, Walter and Ross, 2001.
Bourdieu, P. "The Biographical Illusion." *Actes de la Recherche en Science Sociales* 62, no. 3 (1986): 69-72.
Braziel, J. E., and K. LeBesco, eds. *Bodies out of Bounds: Fatness and Trangression.* Berkeley, Los Angeles, and London: University of California Press, 2001.
Breward, C. *The Culture of Fashion.* Manchester and New York: Manchester University Press, 1995.
Britzman, D. P. "The Terrible Problem of Knowing Thyself: Toward a Poststructural Account of Teacher Identity." *Journal of Curriculum Theorizing* 9, no. 3 (1992): 23-46.
Brumberg, J. J. *The Body Project: An Intimate History of American Girls.* New York: Random House, 1997.
Brunner, D. D. "Silent Bodies: Miming Those Killing Norms of Gender." *Journal of Curriculum Theorizing* 12, no. 1 (1996): 9-15.
Brunsma, D. L. "School Uniforms: A Critical Review of the Literature. From Inquiry to Practice." 18. Bloomington: Phi Delta Kappa, 2002.
Brunsma, D. L., and K. A. Rockquemore. "The Effects of Student Uniforms on Attendance, Behavior Problems, Substance Use, and Academic Achievement." *Journal of Educational Research* 92, no. 1 (1998): 53-62.
Buchler, J. *Nature and Judgment.* New York: Columbia University, 1955.
Buck, A. "Clothes in Fact and Fiction." *Costume* 17 (1983): 89.
Bullock, K. *Rethinking Muslim Women and the Veil.* Herdon: International Institute of Islamic Thought, 2002.
Butler, J. *Bodies That Matter: On the Discursive Limits of "Sex."* New York: Routledge, 1993.

———. *Gender Trouble: Feminism and the Subversion of Identity*. New York and London: Routledge, 1990.
Carson, F., and C. Pajaczkowska, eds. *Feminist Visual Culture*. Edinburgh: Edinburgh University Press, 2001.
Caruso, P. "Individuality vs. Conformity: The Issue Behind School Uniforms." *NASSP Bulletin* 80, no. 581 (1996): 83–88.
Cavallaro, D., and A. Warick. "Introduction: The Body in Philosophy and Theories of Representation." In *Fashioning the Frame: Boundaries, Dress and Body*, edited by D. Cavallaro and A. Warick, 1–22. Oxford: Berg, 1998.
Chapkis, W. *Beauty Secrets: Women and the Politics of Appearance*. Boston: South End Press, 1986.
Chodorrow, N. *The Reproduction of Mothering. Psychoanalysis and the Sociology of Gender*. Berkeley: University of California Press, 1978.
Church, K., and L. Church. "Needle and Pins: Dialogue on a Mother/Daughter Journey." *Journal of the Association for Research on Mothering* 5, no. 1 (2003): 148–56.
Clifford, J. "On Ethnographic Allegory." In *Writing and Culture: The Poetics and Politics of Ethnography*, edited by J. Clifford and G. Marcus. Berkeley: University of California Press, 1986.
Cohn, C. C., and L. Siegel. "Should Students Wear Uniforms." *Learning* 25, no. 2 (1996): 38–39.
Cooke, K. *Real Gorgeous: The Truth About Body and Beauty*. New York: London, 1996.
Craik, J. *The Face of Fashion: Cultural Studies in Fashion*. London and New York: Routledge, 1994.
———. "'I Must Put My Face on': Making up the Body and Making out the Feminine." *Cultural Studies* 3 (1989): 1–24.
Crane, D. *Fashion and Its Social Agenda: Class, Gender and Identity in Clothing*. Chicago and London: The University of Chicago Press, 2000.
Culler, J. *Roland Barthes*. New York: Oxford University Press, 1983.
Davis, F. *Fashion, Culture and Identity*. Chicago: University of Chicago Press, 1992.
Davis, K., ed. *Embodied Practices: Feminist Perspectives on the Body*. London: Sage, 1997.
Davis-Floyd, R. *Birth as an American Rite of Passage*. Los Angeles: University of California Press, 1992.
de la Haye, A. *The Cutting Edge: 50 Years of British Fashion, 1947–1997*. Woodstock, NY: Overlook Press, 1997.
de la Haye, A., and E. Wilson. "Introduction." In *Defining Dress: Dress as Object and Meaning*, edited by A. de la Haye and E. Wilson, 1–9. Manchester and New York: Manchester University Press, 1999.
———, eds. *Defining Dress: Dress as Object and Meaning*. Manchester and New York: Manchester University Press, 1999.
de Lauretis, T. A. *Technologies of Gender: Essays on Theory Film and Fiction*. Bloomington and Indianapolis: Indiana University Press, 1987.
DeMitchell, T. A. "Pants and Hats: Dress Codes and Expressive Conduct as Speech." *International Journal of Education reform* 8, no. 4 (1999): 4–13.
DeMitchell, T. A., R. Fossey, and C. Cobb. "Dress Codes in Public Schools: Principals, Policies and Precepts." *Journal of Law and Education* 29, no. 1 (2000): 31–49.
Denzin, N. "Performance Texts." In *Representation and the Text: Re-Framing the Narrative Voice*, edited by W. G. Tierney and Y. S. Lincoln, 179–217. Albany, NY: State University of New York Press, 1997.
Dickinson, P. *Here Is Queer: Nationalisms, Sexualities and the Literatures of Canada*. Toronto: University of Toronto Press, 1999.
Didion, P. *On Keeping a Notebook: Slouching toward Bethlehem*. New York: Dell, 1961.
Dinnerstein, D. *The Mermaid and the Minotaur: Sexual Arrangements and Human Malaise*. New York: Harper, 1976.

Dunseath, K., ed. *A Second Skin: Women Write About Their Clothes*. London: Women's Press, 1998.
Dyck, I. "Further Notes on Feminist Research: Embodied Knowledge in Place." In *Further Notes on Feminist Research: Embodied Knowledge in Place*, edited by P. Moss. Oxford: Blackwell, 2002.
Earle, W. A. *Autobiographical Consciousness*. Chicago: Quadrangle, 1972.
Eicher, J. B., ed. *Dress and Ethnicity*. Oxford and Washington: Berg, 1995.
Eicher, J. B., and M. E. Roach-Higgins. "Definition and Classification of Dress: Implications for Analysis of Gender Roles." In *Dress and Gender: Making and Meaning*, edited by R. Barnes and J. B. Eicher, 1–28. New York and Oxford: Berg, 1992.
Ely, N., M. Anzul, T. Friedman, D. Garner, and A. McCormack-Steinmetz. *Doing Qualitative Research: Circles within Circles*. London and Philadelphia: Falmer Press, 1991.
Entwistle, J. "The Dressed Body." In *Real Bodies: A Sociological Introduction*, edited by M. B. Evans and E. Lee, 133–50. New York: Palgrave, 2002.
Entwistle, J., and E. Wilson, eds. *Body and Dressing*. Oxford and New York: Berg, 2001.
Evans, M. B., and E. Lee, eds. *Real Bodies: A Sociological Introduction*. New York: Palgrave, 2002.
Fairfax, C. *A Brief Introduction to English Academic Costume* [cited March 6 2003]. Available from http://home.uchicago.edu/~atterlep/costuming/academic%20clothing.htm.
Flannery, M. C. "Dressing in Style? An Essay on the Lab Coat." *American Biology Teacher* 61, no. 5 (1999): 380–83.
Fontanel, B. *Support and Seduction: A History of Corsets and Bras*. New York: Henry N. Abrams, 1997.
Foucault, M. *The Care of the Self: The History of Sexuality, Vol III*. Translated by Robert Hurley. New York: Pantheon, 1986.
———. *The History of Sexuality, Vol I: An Introduction*. Translated by Robert Hurley. New York: Pantheon, 1978.
———. *Power/Knowledge: Selected Interviews and Other Writings 1972–1977*. Edited by C. Gordon. London: Harvester, 1980.
Fowler, M. *The Way She Looks Tonight: Five Women of Style*. Toronto: Random House, 1996.
Franklin, A. "Black Women and Self-Presentation: Appearing in (Dis)Guise." In *Through the Wardrobe: Woman's Relationships with Their Clothes*, edited by A. Guy, E. Green and M. Banim, 137–50. Oxford: Berg, 2001.
Franklin, E., et al. "Dress: Images of America. Elementary Version." ERIC, 1980.
Fussell, P. *Uniforms: Why We Are What We Wear*. New York: Houghton-Mifflin, 2002.
Gallop, J. *The Daughter's Seduction: Feminism and Psychoanalysis*. Ithaca: Cornell University Press, 1982.
Gilbert, P., and S. Taylor. *Fashioning the Feminine: Girls' Popular Culture and Schooling*. Sydney: Allen & Unwin, 1991.
Gillen, K. "Choosing an Image: Exploring Women's Images through the Personal Shopper." In *Through the Wardrobe: Women's Relationships with Their Clothes*, edited by A. Guy, E. Green and M. Banim, 71–96. Oxford: Berg, 2001.
Gilligan, C. *In a Different Voice: Psychological Theory and Women's Development*. Cambridge: Harvard University Press, 1982.
Goffman, E. *The Presentation of Self in Everyday Life*. Garden City, NY: Doubleday, 1959.
Goodrum, A. "Land of Hip and Glory: Fashioning the 'Classic' National Body." In *Dressed to Impress: Looking the Part*, edited by W. J. F. Keenan, 85–104. Oxford and New York: Berg, 2001.
Gray, R. E., V. Ivonoffski, and C. Sinding. "Making a Mess and Spreading It Around: Articulating an Approach to Research-Based Theater." In *Ethnographically Speaking: Autoethnography, Literature, and Aesthetics*, edited by A. P. Bochner and C. Ellis, 57–75. Walnut Creek: Altamira Press, 2002.

Green, E. "Suiting Ourselves: Women Professors Using Clothes to Signal Authority, Belonging and Personal Style." In *Through the Wardrobe: Women's Relationships with Their Clothes*, edited by A. Guy, E. Green and M. Banim, 97–116. Oxford: Berg, 2001.
Gregson, N., and L. Crewe. *Second-Hand Cultures*. Oxford and New York: Berg, 2003.
Griffiths, M. *Feminisms and the Self: The Web of Identity*. New York: Routledge, 1995.
Grumet, M. *Bitter Milk: Women and Teaching*. Amherst: University of Massachusetts Press, 1988.
———. "Scholae Personae: Masks for Meaning." In *Pedagogy: The Question of Impersonation*, edited by J. Gallop. Bloomington, IN: Indiana University Press, 1995.
Grumet, M., and W. F. Pinar. *Toward a Poor Curriculum*. Dubuque, IA: Kendall/Hunt, 1976.
Guindi, Fadwa El. "Veiling Resistance." *Fashion Theory*. Volume 3, Issue 1 (March 1999) 51–80.
Gumpert, L. *Christian Boltanski*. Paris: Flammarion, 1994.
———. "The Life and Death of Christian Boltanski." In *Lessons of Darkness*, edited by L. Gumpert and M. J. Jacob, 59. Chicago: Ausstellungskatalog, 1988.
Guy, A., E. Green, and M. Banim, eds. *Through the Wardrobe: Women's Relationships with Their Clothes*. Oxford and New York: Berg, 2001.
Hampl, P. "Memory and Imagination." In *The Anatomy of Memory: An Anthology*, edited by J. McConkey, 201–11. New York and Oxford: Oxford University Press, 1994.
Hansen, A. "The Day the Heat Went On." In *Gender Tales: Tensions in the Schools*, edited by J. S. Kleinfield and S. Yerian, 131–37. New York: St. Martin's Press, 1994.
Hargreaves-Mawdsley, W. N. *A History of Academic Dress in Europe until the End of the Eighteenth Century*. Oxford: Clarendon Press, 1963.
Heidegger, M. "Origin of the Work of Art." In *Philosophies of Art and Beauty: Selected Readings in Aesthetics from Plato to Heidegger*, edited by A. Hofstadter and R. Kuhns, 647–708. Chicago: University of Chicago Press, 1976.
Hirsh, M. "Masking the Subject: Practicing Theory." In *The Point of Theory*, edited by M. Bal and I. E. Boer. New York: Continuum, 1994.
Hoffler-Riddick, P. Y., and K. J. Lassiter. "No More 'Sag Baggin': School Uniforms Bring the Focus Back to Instruction." *Schools in the Middle* 5, no. 4 (1996): 27–28.
Holiday, R., and J. Hassard, eds. *Contested Bodies*. London and New York: Routledge, 2001.
Hollander, A. *Seeing through Clothes*. New York: Viking Press, 1978.
hooks, b. *Art on My Mind: Visual Politics*. New York: New Press, 1995.
Howard, R. "Remembering Roland Barthes." In *Signs in Culture: Roland Barthes Today*, edited by S. Ungar and B. R. McGraw. Iowa City: University of Iowa Press, 1989.
Howey, N. *Dress Codes: Of Three Girlhoods—My Mother's, My Father's, and Mine*. New York: Picador, 2002.
Ingraham, C. *White Weddings: Romancing Heterosexuality in Popular Culture*. New York: Routledge, 1999.
Isaacson, L. "Student Dress Policies." 4. Eugene: University of Oregon, 1998.
Jenkins, R. *Social Identity*. London: Routledge, 1996.
Joesph, N. *Uniforms and Nonuniforms: Communication through Clothing*. New York: Greenwood Press, 1986.
Joselit, J. W. *A Perfect Fit: Clothes, Character and the Promise of America*. New York: Henry Holt and Company, 2001.
Justice-Malloy, R. "Little Girls Bound: Costume and Coming of Age in the *Sears Catalogue* 1906–1927." In *Delinquents & Debutantes: Twentieth Century American Girls Cultures*, edited by S. A. Inness, 109–33. New York and London: New York University Press, 1998.
Kaiser, S., J. Chandler, and T. Hammidi. "Minding Appearance in Female Academic Culture." In *Through the Wardrobe: Women's Relationship with Their Clothes*, edited by A. Guy, E. Green and M. Banim, 117–36. Oxford: Berg, 2001.

Kandioyti, D. "Bargaining with Patriarchy." In *The Women, Gender and Development Reader*, edited by V. Nialini and L. Duggan. Halifax: Fernwood Publishing company, 1997.
Keenan, W. J. F. "Dress Freedom: The Personal and Political." In *Dressed to Impress Looking the Part*, edited by W. J. F. Keenan, 182–83. Oxford and New York: Berg, 2001.
———. "Introduction: 'Sartor Resartus' Restored." In *Dressed to Impress: Looking the Part*, edited by W. J. F. Keenan, 1–49. Oxford and New York: Berg, 2001.
———, ed. *Dressed to Impress: Looking the Part*. Oxford and New York: Berg, 2001.
Kidwell, C. B., and V. Steele. *Men and Women: Dressing the Part*. Washington: Smithsonian Institution Press, 1989.
King, K. A. *Should School Uniforms Be Mandated in Elementary Schools?* New Century School, 1998 [cited March 7 2003]. Available from http://www.danenet.wicip.org/ncs/forumuniformseval.htm.
Kommer, D. "Beyond Fashion Patrol: School Uniforms in the Middle Grades." *Middle School Journal* 30, no. 5 (1999): 23–26.
Kristeva, J. *The Power of Horror: An Essay on Abjection*. Translated by L. S. Roudiez. New York: Columbia University Press, 1992.
———. *Tales of Love*. Translated by L. S. Roudiez. New York: Columbia University Press, 1987.
Kuhn, A. *Family Secrets: Acts of Memory and Imagination*. London and New York: Verso, 1995.
Kuhn, M. J. "Student Dress Codes in Public Schools: Multiple Perspectives in the Courts and Schools on the Same Issue." *Journal of Law and Education* 25, no. 1 (1996): 83–106.
Kundera, M. "After Word: A Talk with the Author by Philip Roth." In *The Book of Laughter and Forgetting*, 234–35. New York: Viking Penguin, 1981.
Lane, K. E., S. L. Schwartz, M. D. Richardson, and D. W. VanBerum. "You Aren't What You Wear." *American School Board Journal* 181, no. 3 (1994): 64–65.
Lawler, S. *Mothering the Self: Mothers, Daughters, Subjects*. New York and London: Routledge, 2000.
Leblanc, L. *Pretty in Punk: Girls' Gender Resistance in a Boys' Subculture*. New Brunswick, NJ: Rutgers University Press, 1999.
Lesko, N. "The Curriculum of the Body: Lessons from a Catholic High School." In *Becoming Feminine: The Politics of Popular Culture*, edited by L. G. Roman, L. K. Christian-Smith and E. Ellsworth, 123–42. London: Falmer Press, 1988.
Lewis, R., and K. Rolley. "Ad(Dressing) the Dyke: Lesbian Looks and Lesbians Looking." In *Outlooks: Lesbian and Gay Sexualities and Visual Cultures*, edited by P. Horne and R. Lewis, 178–90. London and New York: Routledge, 1996.
Linneburgh, E. "Kanga: Popular Cloths and Messages." In *African Popular Culture*, edited by K. Barber, 138–41. Bloomington & Indianapolis: Indiana University Press, 1997.
Lumsden, L. "Uniforms and Dress Code Policies." 4. ERIC (ED454568): University of Oregon, 2001.
Lumsden, L., and G. Miller. "Dress Codes and Uniforms." *Research Roundup* 18, no. 4 (2002): 1–4.
Lunce, S. E. *Academic Costumes and Regalia: A Brief History and Chronology* 1996 [cited March 7 2003]. Available from http://www.tamiu.edu/~slunce/regalia.htm.
Lurie, A. *The Language of Clothes*. London: Bloomsbury, 1992.
Mak, M., and C. A. Mitchell. "Unwanted Images: Gender-Based Violence in the New South Africa." (7 minutes) edited by M. Mak and C. A. Mitchell: Canada South Africa Education Managment Programme, 2000.
Malossi. *The Style Engine: Spectacle, Identity, Design, and Business: How the Fashion Industry Uses Style to Create Wealth*. New York: The Monaceli Press, 1998.
Mauss, M. "A Category of the Human Mind: The Notion of the Person, the Notion of Self." In *The Category of Person*, edited by M. Corrithers, S. Collins and S. Lukas, 1–24. Cambridge: Cambridge University Press, 1985.

———. "Techniques of the Body." *Economy and Society* 2, no. 1 (1973): 70–87.
Mavor, C. *Becoming: The Photographs of Clementina Viscountess Hawarden*. Durham and London: Duke University Press, 1999.
———. "Collecting Loss." In *Becoming: The Photographs of Clementina Viscountess Hawarden*, 113–37. Durham and London: Duke University Press, 1999.
Mazzarella, S. R. "The 'Super Bowl of All Dates'. Teenage Girls' Magazines and Co-Modification of the Perfect Prom." In *Growing up Girls: Popular Culture and the Construction of Identity*, edited by S. R. Mazzarella and N. O. Pecora, 97–112. New York: Peter Lang, 1999.
McRobbie, A. "Second-Hand Dresses and the Role of the Ragmarket." In *Zoot Suits and Second-Hand Dresses: An Anthology of Fashion and Music*, edited by A. McRobbie, 23–40. London: Macmillan, 1989.
———, ed. *Zoot Suits and Second Hand Dresses: An Anthology of Fashion and Music*. Houndsmill: Macmillan, 1989.
McWilliam, E., and P. G. Taylor, eds. *Pedagogy, Technology and the Body*. New York: Peter Lang, 2001.
Mellencamp, P. "The Unfashionable Male Subject." In *Gender: Literacy and Cinematic Representation*, edited by J. Ruppert, 17–24. Gainesville: University Press of Florida, 1989.
Merleau-Ponty, M. *Phenomenology of Perception*. London: Routledge & Kegan-Paul, 1962.
Metz, C. "Photography and Fetish." *October* 34 (1985).
Miles, A., and G. Finn, eds. *Feminism in Canada: From Pressure to Politics*. Montreal: Black Rose Books, 1982.
Minot, L. "Girl Clothes in a Box." *Bad Subjects: Political Education for Everyday Life*, no. 10. Available Online: http://eserver.orf/bs/10/Minot.html. (1993).
Mitchell, C. A. "Oh No, We Want to Go Farther Than That! Women and Education Management in Zambia." Lusaka: Ministry of Education, UNICEF, 1998.
Mitchell, C. A., and J. Reid-Walsh. "Mail-Order Memory Work: Towards a Methodology for Uncovering the Experiences of Covering Over." *Review of Education/Pedagogy/Cultural Studies* 20, no. 1 (1998): 57–75.
———. "Memory Spaces and the Afterlife of Children's Popular Culture." In *Researching Children's Popular Culture: Childhood as a Cultural Space*, 47–78. New York and London: Routledge Taylor and Francis, 2002.
Mitchell, C. A., J. Reid-Walsh, and J. Larkin. "Visualizing the Politics of Innocence in the Age of AIDS." *Sex Education* (In Press).
Mitchell, C. A., and S. J. Weber. *Reinventing Ourselves as Teachers: Beyond Nostalgia*. London and Philadelphia: Falmer Press, 1999.
———. "Undressing and Redressing the Teacher's Body." In *Reinventing Ourselves as Teachers: Beyond Nostalgia*. London: Falmer Press, 1999.
Mlamleli, O. et al. *Opening Our Eyes: Addressing Gender-Based Violence in South African Schools—a Module for Educators*. Pretoria, South Africa: National Department of Education, 2001.
Morris, T. L., J. Gorham, S. H. Cohen, and D. Huffman. "Fashion in the Classroom." *Communication Education* 45, no. 2 (1996): 135–49.
Munt, S. R. "The Butch Body." In *Contested Bodies*, edited by R. Holiday and J. Hassard. London and New York: Routledge, 2001.
Murphy, C. "Imaternity Creates a New Identity Online." *Information week* 2000.
Murray, R. K. "The Impact of School Uniforms on School Climate." *NASSP Bulletin* 81, no. 592 (1997): 106–12.
Naples, N., and M. Desai. *Women's Activism and Globalization: Linking Local Struggles and Transnational Politics*. New York and London: Routledge, 2002.
Nelson, A. "The Pink Dragon Is Female: Halloween Costumes as Gender Markers." *Psychology of Women Quarterly* 24 (2000): 127–44.

Norquay, N. "The Other Side of Difference: Memory-Work in the Mainstream." *Qualitative Studies in Education* 6, no. 3 (1993): 241–51.
Oliver, K. *Reading Kristeva: Unraveling the Double-Bind*. Bloomington: Indiana University Press, 1993.
Olney, J. *Metaphors of Self: The Meaning of Autobiography*. Princeton: Princeton University Press, 1972.
Orenstein, P. *School Girls: Young Women, Self-Esteem and the Confidence Gap*. New York: Doubleday, 1994.
Ovenden, G. *Clementina, Lady Hawarden*. London: Academy Editions, 1984.
Padgett, J. B. "Teacher's Perceptions of the Effect Uniforms or Strict Dress Codes Have on Elementary School Children." ERIC (ED347141), 1998.
Penelope, J. *Speaking Freely: Understanding the Lies of the Fathers' "Tongues."* Toronto: Pergamon Press, 1990.
Peters, J. F. "Youth Clothes-Shopping Behavior: An Analysis by Gender." *Adolescence* 24, no. 95 (1989): 575–80.
Phillips, P. A., and L. R. Smith. "The Effects of Teacher Dress on Student Perceptions." ERIC (ED347151), 1992.
Price, R. "For the Family." In *Immediate Family*, edited by S. Mann. New York: Aperture, 1992.
Proust, M. *Swann's Way Vol I, in Search of Lost Time*. Translated by C. K. S. Moncrieff and T. Kilmartin. New York: Random House, 1992.
Reckett, H., and P. Phelan. *Art and Feminism*. London and New York: Phaidon Press Limited, 2001.
Reilly, L. B. "Gender Specific Aspects of Children's Clothing and Teacher Student Interaction." ERIC (ED457086), 2001.
Riggins, S. *The Socialness of Things: Essays on the Socio-Semiotics of Objects*. New York: Mouton de Gruyter, 1994.
Roach, K. D. "Effects of Graduate Teaching Assistant Attire on Student Learning, Misbehaviors, and Ratings of Instructions." *Communication Quarterly* 45, no. 3 (1997): 125–41.
Rose, L. "Freud and Fetishism: Previously Unpublished Minutes of the Vienna Psychoanalytic Society." *Psychoanalytic Quarterly* 57, no. 2 (1988): 147–65.
Rossetti, C. "Goblin Market." In *The Complete Poems of Christina Rossetti Vol I*, edited by Crump, 191–216. Baton Rouge: Louisiana State University Press, 1979.
Rubenstein, R. P. *Dress Codes: Meanings and Messages in American Culture*. Boulder: West View Press, 1995.
Said, E. *Orientalism*. New York: Vintage, 1979.
Scheuring, S. "Heavy Duty Denim: 'Quality Never Dates.'" In *Zoot Suits and Second-Hand Dresses: An Anthology of Fashion and Music,* edited by A. McRobbie, 225–36. London: Macmillan, 1989.
Schneider, A. "Frumpy or Chic? Tweed or Kente? Sometimes Clothes Make the Professor: Academic Wardrobe Selection Can Involve Ideology, Discipline and Job-Hunting Strategy." *The Chronicle of Higher Education* 23 (1998): 17–19.
Secor, A. J. "The Veil and Urban Space in Istanbul: Women's Dress Mobility and Islamic Knowledge." *Gender, Place, and Culture* 9, no. 1 (2002): 5–22.
Seng, Y. J., and B. Wass. "Traditional Palestinian Wedding Dress as a Symbol of Nationalism." In *Dress and Ethnicity: Changes across Space and Time*, edited by J. B. Eicher, 227–54. Oxford: Berg, 1995.
Shadley, G. "School Uniforms, Eros, and Mixed Messages." Paper presented at the The Annual Congress of the Canadian Association for the Study of Women in Education, Halifax 2003.
Shattuck, R. "Lost and Found: The Structure of Proust's Novel." In *The Cambridge Companion to Proust,* edited by R. Bales, 74–84. Cambridge, England: Cambridge University Press, 2001.

Shaw, J. W. *Academical Dress of British and Irish Universities.* Chichester, UK: Philimore, 1995.
Shilling, C. *The Body and Social Theory.* London: Sage, 1993.
Smith, C. *Proud of Me.* London: Penguin, 2000.
Smith, M. K. et al. "Image and Identity: Clothing and Adolescence in the 1990's." ERIC (ERD389663), 1990.
Sontag, S. *On Photography.* New York: Farrar, Straus, & Giroux, 1973.
Spector, D. "The Woman Who Married." In *At Our Core: Women Writing about Power,* edited by S. Halderman Mertz, 124-25. Watsonville, CA: Papier-Mache Press, 1998.
Speer, T. L. "Fashion That Works . . . Or Not." *Techniques: Making Education and Career Connections* 73, no. 8 (1998): 39-41.
Spence, J. "Flying on One Wing." In *Through the Wardrobe: Women's Relationships with Their Clothes,* edited by A. Guy, E. Green and M. Banim, 173-88. Oxford and New York: Berg, 2001.
Stallybrass, P. "Worn Worlds: Clothing, Mourning, and the Life of Things." In *Cultural Memory and the Construction of Identity,* edited by D. Ben-Amos and L. Weissberg, 35-50. Detroit: Wayne State University Press, 1999.
Steedman, C. *Landscape for a Good Woman: A Story of Two Lives.* New Brunswick, NJ: Rutgers University Press, 1987.
———. "Prisonhouses." In *Teachers: The Culture and Politics of Work,* edited by M. Lawn and G. Grace, 117-29. Philadelphia: Falmer Press, 1989.
Steele, V. *The Corset: A Cultural History.* New Haven and London: Yale University Press, 2001.
———. "Dressing for Work." In *Men and Women: Dressing the Part,* edited by C. B. Kidwell and V. Steele, 64-91. Washington, D.C.: Smithsonian Institute, 1989.
———. *Shoes: A Lexicon of Style.* New York: Rizzoli, 1999.
Steinhauer, J. "The Maternity Blues: What to Wear." *New York Times,* June 29 1997, I 34.
Stewart, M. "A Letter from Martha." *Martha Stewart Weddings* 2002, 50.
Stewart, S. *On Longing: Narratives of the Miniature, the Gigantic, the Souvenir Collection.* Durham, NC: Duke University Press, 1993.
Swain, J. "The Right Stuff: Fashioning an Identity through Clothing in a Junior School." *Gender and Education* 14, no. 1 (2002): 53-69.
Tanenbaum, L. *Slut: Growing up Female with a Bad Reputation.* New York: Perennial, 2000.
Tannen, D. *Gender and Conversational Interaction.* New York: Oxford University Press, 1993.
Taylor, L. *The Study of Dress History.* Manchester and New York: Manchester University Press, 2002.
Tseelon, E. *The Masque of Femininity: The Presentation of Woman in Everyday Life.* London: Sage Publications, 1995.
———. "Ontological, Epistemological and, Methodological Clarifications in Fashion Research: From Critique to Empirical Suggestions." In *Through the Wardrobe: Women's Relationships with Their Clothes,* edited by A. Guy, E. Green and M. Banim, 237-56. Oxford and New York: Berg, 2001.
Turner, V. *The Forest of Symbols: Aspects of Ndembu Ritual.* Ithaca, NY: Cornell University Press, 1967.
Tyrnauer, M. "Empire by Martha." *Vanity Fair* 2001, 364-402.
Underhill, P. *Why We Buy: The Science of Shopping.* New York: Simon and Schuster, 1999.
Unknown. "True Love Returns: American Rediscovers Its Heartland." *The Economist,* July 27, 2002 2002, 31.
Uys, J. "The Gods Must Be Crazy." edited by J. Uys. Botswana: Fox, 1984.
van Manen, M. *Researching Lived Experience: Human Science for an Action Sensitive Pedagogy.* London, Ontario: The Althouse Press, 1990.
Wang, and Meng. *Numbers in the Eyes of the Chinese.* Beijing: Tuanjie Publications, 2000.

Warwick, A., and D. Cavallaro. *Fashioning the Frame: Boundaries, Dress, and the Body*. Oxford and New York: Berg, 1998.

Weber, S. J. "The Narrative Anecdote in Teacher Education." *Journal of Education For Teaching* 19, no. 1 (1993): 71–82.

———. "The Pedagogy of Shoes: Clothing and Self-Study." In *Just Who Do We Think We Are: Methodologies for Self-Study,* edited by K. O'Reilly-Scanlon, C. A. Mitchell and S. J. Weber. London and New York: Routledge-Falmer, Forthcoming.

Weber, S. J. & S. Cloutier, *Prom dress #1: I am a women now* (material latex and fabric). Featured during S. J. Weber, "Dresses: The Dance of Identity." Lecture at The Dress Show, Leonard & Bina Ellen Art Gallery, Concordia University, Montreal, Quebec. 2003.

Weber, S. J., and C. A. Mitchell. "Clothes Make the Teacher? Adornment and Identity." In *"That's Funny You Don't Look Like a Teacher." Interrogating Images and Identity in Popular Culture,* 54–71. London: Falmer Press, 1995.

———. *'That's Funny You Don't Look Like a Teacher'. Interrogating, Images and Identity in Popular Culture*. London: Falmer Press, 1995.

———. *Dress fitting*. Documentary digital video 25 min. digital video. Directed by S. J. Weber, based on research conducted by S. J. Weber and C. A. Mitchell. An Image and Identity Research Collective Production. Concordia University, Montreal. 2001.

———. "Using Visual Artistic Modes of Representation for Self-Study." In *International Handbook of Self-Study of Teaching and Teacher Education Practices,* edited by J. Loughran, M. Hamilton, V. LaBoskey and T. Russell. Dordrect: Kluwer Academic Publishers, 2004.

Weber, S. J., and C. A. Mitchell. "Bodies of Knowledge, Knowledge of Bodies: A Performance." Paper presented at the 4th Canadian Association for Studies on Women in Education Summer Institute, Toronto, Ontario 2002.

———. "Tunic Wars: Act 2 of Bodies of Knowledge, Knowledge of Bodies: A Performance." Paper presented at the 4th Canadian Association for Studies on Women in Education Summer Institute, Toronto, Ontario 2002.

Weiss, G., and H. F. Haber, eds. *Perspectives on Embodiment: The Intersections of Nature and Culture*. New York and London: Routledge, 1999.

Wentzel, P. *Pumpkin Maternity Online* 2001 [cited March 29 2001]. Available from www.pumpkinmaternity.com.

West, C., K., D. K. Tidwell, A. K. Bomba, and P. A. Elmore. "Attitudes of Parents About School Uniforms." *Journal of Family and Consumer Sciences: From Research to Practice* 91, no. 2 (1999): 92–96.

White, E. *Marcel Proust*. New York and London: Viking Penguin, 1999.

Wilson, E. "Keynote Address." Fashion: Making an Appearance, University of Queensland, Brisbane, Australia 2003.

Workman, J. E., and K. K. P. Johnson. "Effects of Conformity and Nonconformity to Gender-Role Expectations for Dress: Teachers Versus Students." *Adolescence* 29, no. 113 (1994).

Wright, L. "The Suit: A Common Bond or Defeated Purpose?" In *The Gendered Object,* edited by P. Kirkham, 153–61. Manchester and New York: The Manchester University Press, 1996.

Yee, A. *"China Chic": From Dragon Robes to Mao Suits* 1999 [cited June 22 2002]. Available from www.nytimes.com.

Zirkel, P. A. "A Uniform Policy." *Phi Delta Kappan* 79, no. 7 (1998): 550–51.

Zuhur, S. *Revealing, Reveiling: Islamist Gender Ideology in Contemporary Egypt*. New York: State University of New York Press, 1992.

Contributors

Sandra Weber is Professor of Education and a Fellow at the Simone de Beauvoir Institute at Concordia University where she teaches courses on gender, language, curriculum, image-based research methods, and the popular culture of technology. Co-founder of the *Image and Identity Research Collective* (www.iirc.mcgill.ca), and the author of more than fifty articles and book chapters, Weber is currently directing one funded research project on body, dress, and identity and another on Digital Girls.

Claudia Mitchell is a Professor in the School of Education at the University of Natal. Her research interests include youth and AIDS prevention, gender and development, gay and lesbian youth literature, South Africa young adult literature, teachers' professional identity, girlhood, and popular culture. Methodologically, she is particularly interested in arts-based/image-based approaches to youth participation. Her most recent book, *Researching Children's Popular Culture: The Cultural Spaces of Childhood* (with Jacqueline Reid-Walsh) was published by Routledge in 2002.

Together, **Weber and Mitchell** have co-authored several books (*That's Funny, You Don't Look Like a Teacher: Interrogating Images of Identity in Popular Culture* (London: Falmer Press, 1995), and *Reinventing Ourselves as Teachers: Beyond Nostalgia* (London: Falmer Press, 1999); and co-produced two documentaries on dress/girlhood/youth culture (*Canadian Pie*, 2002 [with Monica Mak] and *Dress Fitting*, 2000). They are currently editing a book (in collaboration with Kathleen O'Reilly Scanlon) called *Just Who Do We Think We Are? Methodologies for Self-Study in Education*, to be published in 2004 by Falmer-Routledge.

Ilana Abramovitch is the Manager of Curriculum in New York's Museum of Jewish Heritage—A Living Memorial to the Holocaust, and has served as consultant for numerous Jewish Art festivals. She is the co-editor (with Seán Galvin) of *The Jews of Brooklyn* (2001, Brandeis University Press).

Roksana Bahramitash a full time faculty member at Iran's women-only university in 1986, earned her Ph.D. from McGill University in Montreal. She has worked on Islamisation and women's economic power in Indonesia for CIDA and the International Labour Organization in Geneva. Her first post-doctoral fellowship from University of Simon Fraser, on globalization, was followed by a second from SSHRC on the impact of political Islam on women's economic role in Iran, Egypt and Turkey. Her work can be found in the *International Journal of Politics, Culture, and Society* and the *Brown Journal of World Affairs*. Winner of the Ross Award, she has published over twenty articles on her research to date.

Kathryn Church is Research Associate for the RBC Institute for Disability Studies Research and Education, and Adjunct Professor for the School of Disability Studies, both at Ryerson University. Her work explores suppressed or invisible histories, innovative research methods and alternative forms of writing/representation. From 1997 to 2001, she was curator of an award-winning museum exhibit entitled "Fabrications: Stitching Ourselves Together."

Ardra L. Cole is Professor and Co-director of the Centre for Arts-informed Research at the University of Toronto. She can often be found rummaging in used and vintage clothing stores.

Xiao Lan Curdt-Christiansen is a Ph.D. candidate in the Department of Second Language Education at McGill University, Montreal. She was born in China and grew up in Beijing. She has lived in Denmark, but has resided in Montreal for the last seven years with her family. Her research interests are literacy practices in multilingual contexts, language and socialization, and language and cultural identity. Her dissertation topic is "Triliteracy practices among Chinese children in Quebec." She is currently engaged in a research project concerning the language acquisition, literacy practices and identity construction of immigrant children in heritage language schools.

Catherine Derry is a doctoral student in Education at McGill University. Her research interests include memory work, self-study, arts-based research, "fitting in," and gender studies. Catherine is currently working on her first book, co-authored with Sandra Weber, *Afraid to Go to School: Women Remember Childhood Exclusion and Bullying*.

Madeleine R. Grumet is a Professor of Education and Communication Studies at the University of North Carolina at Chapel Hill. Her scholarship addresses arts and humanities education, feminist theory, and performance theory, topics addressed in her book, *Bitter Milk: Women and Teaching,* and in numerous articles and book chapters. Dr. Grumet has taught at Hobart and William Smith Colleges, and has served as Dean of the School of Education at Brooklyn College, City University on New York, and at the School of Education at UNC.

Charlotte Hussey has a B.A. from Wheaton College in Massachusetts, an M.A. from Concordia University in Montreal, an M.F.A. from Warren Wilson College in North Carolina and a Ph.D. from McGill University in Montreal. Having immigrated to Canada in 1974, she now teaches Creative Writing and Composition at McGill University. She is also the author of *Rue Sainte Famille* (1990, Véhicule Press).

J. Gary Knowles is Professor of Adult Education and Co-director of the Centre for Arts-informed Research at The Ontario Institute for Studies in Education of The University of Toronto. He teaches courses on environmental education and teacher development, qualitative inquiry from life history, arts-informed and reflexive perspectives. Besides teaching he encourages thesis writers to move outside "the conventional" and write manuscripts that convey passion, humility, and ambiguity yet communicate on multiple levels and with audiences beyond the academy. Gary is also an exhibiting visual artist who mainly works with water media on paper and canvas. Recent book publications include: with Lorri Neilsen and Ardra L. Cole, *The Art of Writing Inquiry,* with Ardra L. Cole, *Lives in Context: The Art of Life History Research* and *Researching Teaching: Exploring Practice through Reflexive Inquiry.*

Annette Kuhn is a Professor of Film Studies, Director of Research, Director of the MA program in Visual Culture, and the Departmental Disability Officer at the Institute for Cultural Research of Lancaster University, UK. Her research interests include film studies, visual culture, film history, cultural history, cultural memory, and science-fiction cinema. Her publications include *Family Secrets: Acts of Memory and Imagination* (1995 & 2002, Verso), *An Everyday Magic: Cinema and Cultural Memory* (2002. I.B. Tauris), *Women's Pictures: Feminism and Cinema,* 2nd Ed. (1994, Verso), *Cinema, Censorship and Sexuality* (1988, Routledge), *The Power of the Image: Essays on Representation and Sexuality* (1985, Routledge and Kegan Paul), and *Women's Pictures: Feminism and Cinema* (1982, Routledge and Kegan Paul), to name a few.

Born and raised in Ottawa, sculptor **Lyse Lemieux** has lived and worked in Vancouver for over twenty-five years. Her exploration of the tunic has led her to work with glass, neoprene, beeswax, and more recently rubber latex—ephemeral and vulnerable materials that speak to the presence and the absence of the body. After working for years as a producer and journalist in radio and television, Lemieux maintains an interest in works that are multidisciplinary. She is presently working on a collaborative music and dance installation titled *SKINS: À Fleur de peau* with choreographer Barbara Bourget and composer performer Marguerite Witvoet. As a young girl, Lemieux went to a Catholic school where female students wore the required *navy blue tunic*. In her most recent works Lemieux explores the role of the tunic as both witness and victim of Transformation.

Kathleen O'Reilly-Scanlon received her Ph.D. from McGill University. She is currently assistant professor at the University of Regina where she teaches undergraduate and graduate courses in language arts, literacy and curriculum. Her research interests include memory work, self-study, critical pedagogy, and Indigenous education.

Carol Mavor is associate Professor of Art at the University of North Carolina at Chapel Hill. She is the author of *Pleasures Taken: Performances of Sexuality and Loss in Victorian Photographs* (1995, Duke University Press), and *Becoming: The Photographs of Clementina, Viscountess Hawarden* (1999, Duke University Press).

Jennifer Musial is a graduate student at Bowling Green State University, and is currently finishing a graduate certificate in Women's Studies. She recently completed her Master's thesis entitled "Transgressive Embodiment: Containing the Pregnant Body in Popular Culture" through the Popular Culture department at BGSU. Her work can also be found in the Association for Research on Mothering, special journal issue: *Mothering, Popular Culture and the Arts* (2003). She is co-editing a book about plastic surgery due to be published in 2004/2005 and is a regular editor for the cultural studies e-journal, *Reconstruction*. Her latest project is to develop feminist media pedagogy for younger students, so she is currently putting together a curriculum model to incorporate critical media literacy into the elementary school classroom.

Lorri Neilsen (who writes poetry with Glenn after her name, in honor of her grandmother) teaches qualitative inquiry and writing at Mount Saint Vincent University in Halifax, Nova Scotia. Her most recent book is *All the Perfect Disguises* (2003), a collection of poetry that won the Poet's Corner Award. Other publications include *Knowing her Place: Research Literacies and Feminist Occasions* (winner of NCTE's Meade Award), *A Stone in My Shoe, Literacy and Living,* and (with co-editors A. Cole, J.G. Knowles and T. Luciani) *The Art of Writing Inquiry* and *Pro-*

voked by Art: Theorizing Arts-Informed Inquiry. She lives in Hubbards, Nova Scotia and is currently working on a collection of essays and another poetry manuscript.

Liz Ralfe lives in Durban, South Africa. She is married with three daughters. She is a lecturer in Language Education in the Faculty of Education, University of Natal. Her research interests include multi-cultural and multi-lingual education. In her spare time she enjoys theater, cinema, music and sewing.

Joan Reider lives in Montreal with her husband. The mother of six and the grandmother of nine, she is devoted to her family. Although she started writing poetry and plays for fun at the age of 14, she only acknowledged her love of words in recent years. She wrote a collection of poems for her 70th birthday, and now enjoys writing essays and commentaries about everyday life.

Born and raised in New York, **Kathy Sands** has lived in Canada for over thirty years. A photographer since the age of thirteen, she has taught photography in Montreal and Toronto, and has exhibited in Connecticut, New York and Florida. After an auto accident left her seriously injured eleven years ago, Sands turned to writing, and recently completed her Doctorate in Adult Education at OISE. Her dissertation used multiple genres (poetry, prose and visual imagery) to explore her own creative journey at midlife.

Celeste N. Snowber is a dancer, educator, and writer and Assistant Professor in the Faculty of Education at Simon Fraser University in Burnaby, British Columbia, Canada. She works in the area of dance education, arts-based educational research, and teacher education. She is the author of *Embodied Prayer* and *In the Womb of God* and has published articles and poetry in the *Journal of Curriculum Theorizing, Educational Insights, English Quarterly, Teacher Education Quarterly,* and *Qualitative Inquiry*. Celeste continues to perform themes of embodiment through modern dance, improvisation, and poetry and is presently finishing a manuscript, entitled, *Ocean Lover,* which explores the natural landscape as a metaphor for spiritual formation. She lives with her three lively boys, aged 11, 11, and 15 in Port Moody, British Columbia.

Candis Steenbergen is a Ph.D. Candidate in Humanities: Interdisciplinary Studies in Society and Culture at Concordia University, where she is also a lecturer in Women's Studies and Education. Interested in spaces where feminisms lurk, her research examines the interplay between and influences of feminisms, sexuality, and popular culture on the complicated and often paradoxical politics of women of her "generation." She enjoys digging up and playing with feminist identities, the fissures of theory and practice, and feminist politics. She was guest editor for

Canadian Woman Studies' special issue on young feminisms (Winter/Spring 2001), and her work appears in *Turbo Chicks: Talking Young Feminisms* (2001, Sumach Press).

Jo Visser is a part-time lecturer at McGill University and a high school teacher. Her research explores issues of women's identity, self expression, and the dichotomy between the domestic and public realms, through visual arts, the creation of a "living research wall," writing, teaching, cooking, and, on occasion, obsessively rearranging the furniture.

Name Index

Alvi, Sajida, 205, 273
Amis, Martin, 235
Apter, Emily, 15–16, 35–36, 273
Arthurs, Jane and Jean. Grimshaw, 272–273

Bakhtin, N. Mikhail, 273
Balzac, Honoré de, 29, 37, 190, 273
Banim, Maura, Eileen Green & Ali Guy, 8, 9, 81, 261–263
Barnes, R., and J. B. Eicher, 273, 276
Barthes, Roland, 8, 18–21, 28–37, 255, 274
Barthes, Henriette, 18
Bechdel, Alison, 274
Benjamin, Walter, 34
Best, Amy, 51, 54–55, 274
Blau, Herbert, 93
Boltanski, Christian, 15, 239
Bordo, Susan, 272, 274
Bourdieu, Pierre, 190, 262, 272, 274
Breward, Christopher, 9, 274
Britzman, Deborah P., 271, 274
Buchler, Justus, 270, 274
Butler, Judith, 260, 271, 274

Carlyle, Thomas, 251
Cavallaro, Dani, and Alexandra Warwick, 272, 275, 282
Chapkis, Wendy, 8, 275

Chodorrow, Nancy, 275
Clifford, James, 17, 36
Cooke, Kaz, 275
Craik, Jennifer, 261, 272, 275
Crane, Diane, 9, 65, 275

Davis-Floyd R., 275, 273
Davis Fred, 252, 269, 275
Davis, Kathy, 272, 275
de la Haye, Amy, 9, 275
de Lauretis, Teresa., 73, 81, 104, 275
Denzin, Norman, 271, 275
Dickinson, Peter , 81, 275
Didion, Joan, 89, 92, 98
Dinnerstein, Dorothy, 98, 275
Douglas, Mary, 131
Dunseath, Kirsty, 275

Eicher, Joanne. B., 9, 186, 269, 276
Entwistle, Joanne, 8, 269, 276
Evans, Mary B. and Ellie Lee, 276

Finn, Geraldine, 76, 81
Fontanel, B, 276
Foucault, Michel, 73, 271, 276
France, Anatole, 251
Franklin, Anita, 276
Freud, Sigmund, 15, 35, 91

Fussell, Paul, 270, 276
Geertz, Clifford, 8
Gallop, Jane, 98, 276
Gillen, Kate, 97-98, 266, 276
Gilligan, Carol, 98, 276
Goffman, Erving, 78, 81, 261, 276
Goodrum, A., 270, 276
Green (see Banim, Green & Guy)
Gregson, Nicky, and Louise Crewe, 277
Griffiths, Morwenna, 272, 277
Grosz, Elizabeth, 131
Grumet, Madeleine, 7, 98, 104, 252, 277
Guindi, Fadwa El., 205, 277
Gumpert, Lynn, 29, 36-37, 277
Guy (see Banim, Green & Guy)

Hampl, Patricia, 270, 277
Heidegger, Martin, 254, 270
Holiday, Ruth, and John Hassard, 277
Hollander, Anne, 9, 277
Hoodfar, Homa., 205, 273
hooks, bell, 256-257, 271, 277
Howey, Noelle, 277

Ingraham, Chris, 174, 277

Joselit, Jenna Weissman, 277

Kaiser, S., J. Chandler, and T. Hammidi, 81, 190, 277
Keenan, William J. F., 82, 269, 272
Kristeva, Julia, 92, 97-98, 127, 131, 136, 274
Kuhn, Annette, 7, 111, 125, 278
Kundera, Milan, 24, 37, 278

Lamont, Elizabeth, 257
Leblanc, Lauraine, 54, 272, 278
Lesko, Nancy, 271, 278
Lewis, Reina, and Katrina Rolley, 278
Lurie, Alison, 261, 272, 278

Malossi, Giannino, 278
Mary Kay, 224
Mauss, Marcel, 262, 272, 278
Mavor, Carol, 7, 15
Mazzarella, Sharon R., 54-55
McRobbie, Angela, 279, 280
McWilliam, Elizabeth, 271

Mellencamp, P., 279
Merleau-Ponty, Maurice, 279
Metz, Christian, 36
Miles, Angela, 81
Mitchell, Claudia, 7, 8, 53-55, 63, 65, 83, 88, 256, 269-272, 275, 278, 279, 282
Morris, Tracy, L., Joan Gorham, Stanley H. Cohen, and Drew Huffman, 279
Munt, Sally R., 279

Nair, Mira, 179
Naples, Nancy A., and Manisha Desai, 232, 279
Nelson, Adie, 279
Norquay, Naomi, 270, 280

Oakley, Ann, 163
Oakley, Annie, 41, 163
Oliver, Kelly, 98
Olney, James, 91, 109
Orenstein, Peggy, 55
Ovenden, Graham, 36

Penelope, Julia, 88
Peters, John F., 280
Plato, 97, 219
Price, Reynolds, 28
Proust, Marcel, 32-37

Reid-Walsh, Jacqueline, 257
Reckett, H., and P. Phelan, 271, 280
Riggins, Stephen H., 270, 280
Roach, K. D., 280
Rossetti, Christina, 23, 36
Rubenstein, Ruth P., 280

Said, Edward, 280
Salvation Army, 230,
Sartre, John-Paul, 96
Scheuring, S., 280
Schneider, Alison, 81
Secor, Anna J., 280
Seng, Y. J., and B. Wass. , 280
Shadley, Gillian, 65
Shah, Reza, 193
Shilling, Chris, 281
Smith, Charlene, 267, 272, 278, 280, 281
Sontag, Susan, 19, 26, 37

Spears, Britney, 65
Spector, Donna, 281
Speer, Tibbett L., 281
Spence, Jo, 281
Stallybrass, Peter, 36
Steedman, Carolyn, 271, 281
Steele, Valerie, 9, 154, 190, 253, 254, 261, 270, 271, 278, 281
Steinem, Gloria, 178
Stewart, Martha, 173
Swain, Jon, 281

Tanenbaum, Leora, 54
Tannen, Deborah, 88
Taylor, Lou, 4, 8, 255, 269–271, 276, 279, 281
Tseëlon, Efrat, 7, 9, 261, 272, 281

Twiggy, 197
Turner, Victor, 136

Underhill, Paco, 281

van Manen, Max, 8, 163

Wang, Guangmei, 187, 188
Warwick, Alexandra, and Dani Cavallar, 272, 282
Weber, Sandra, 1, 53, 54, 57, 61, 76, 88, 99, 258, 259, 269–272, 279, 282
Weiss, Gail, and H. F. Haber, 272, 281
Wilson, Elizabeth, 9

Zuhur, Sherifa, 205, 282

Subject Index

Academy, academic wear, 5, 73–82, 83–88, 89–98, 99–104, 105–107, 185, 190, 260, 266, 276
accessories, 20, 138, 178, 230, 260, 262; bags (shopping and bookbags); 16, 35, 42, 43, 142; beads, 15, 16, 33, 35, 167, 213, 264; belts, 62, 74, 244, 247; Birkenstocks 224; boa, 53; bonnet, 139, 213; boots, 11, 53, 54, 77 (cowboy), 80, 105, 144, 244, 257; bows, 58, 128, 131, 138, 141, 165, 173, 178; buttons, 17, 33, 40, 79, 83, 184, 185, 264; date as accessory, 49–50; caps (sailor and academic), 17, 102; clogs, 90, 105; corsage, 48, 49, 50, 143, 258; dickey, 208; earrings, 142, 143, 144; glasses, 63, 84, 85, 86, 195, 202, 208, 232; glass slippers , 58; gloves, 20, 138, 139, 163, 178, 195, 202, 208; handbags (purses, pocketbooks), 20, 94, 138–139, 209, 235; hats, 12, 20, 21, 33, 138, 173, 178, 188, 195 202, 208, 262; high heels, 48, 105, 11, 105, 135, 163, 262, 264, 265; jewelry, 64, 140, 142, 147; kappie, 213; lockets, 24; necklace, 50, 143, 264; pearls, 12, 15, 23, 40, 133, 264; pumps (*see* high heels); purse (*see* handbags); ribbons, 12, 16, 23, 33, 35, 139, 141; rings, 130, 132, 204; sandals, 102, 105; scarf, scarves, 75, 77, 133, 191–200–205, 207–209; shoes (*see also* "high heels"), 11, 48, 57–58, 61, 64, 76, 91, 105, 138, 139, 163, 178, 224, 233, 237–240, 245,

accessories *(continued)*
  260, 264, 265; slippers (*see also* glass slipper) 239; socks, 29, 61, 63, 64, 90, 103, 106, 138, 142, 144 watches, 75, 77, 244
adolescence/adolescents, 45–56, 63–64, 157, 197, 208, 258
advertising and marketing, 65, 106, 130, 135, 150, 224, 255 *see also* magazines, catalogues
agency, 86, 131; *see also* empowerment
aging, 6, 102, 147, 195
AIDS *see* HIV/AIDS,
appearance, 115, 117–121, 128, 132, 133, 138–141, 147, 252, 254, 261
audience, 84, 86, 174, 260–261, 285 *see also* gaze, performance, "the wearer's view"
autobiography, 4, 6, 92, 256. 269 ; *see also* "dress story"
autobiographic inquiry, 6, 91, 269

beauty/beautiful, 3, 22, 24, 32, 34, 46, 47, 48, 50, 51, 53, 102, 113, 114, 120, 130, 151, 173, 175, 187, 188, 194, 195, 213, 223, 225
beauty myth, 47, 130, 131, 135, 154
birth, 5, 17, 113, 115, 127, 194, 237, 245
birth-to-death, 5, 29
body, 4, 5, 6, 16, 19, 20, 21, 24, 26, 29, 35, 47, 64, 75, 79, 80, 81, 90, 97, 113, 128, 130, 178, 193, 208, 220, 223, 224, 225–228, 230, 236,

body, *(continued)*
  237, 239, 242, 247, 256, 260, 261, 262, 266, 267; sexualized, 87; *see also* dress-body
body image, 4, 6, 47, 75
body size, 6, 47, 48, 54, 75, 152, 241; fat, 47, 125
brand, 79, 184; Buster Brown, 61; Chanel, 254; Oxford, 61, 64
bric-a-brac, 16, 20
Burda, 198

catalogues, 63, 127–136, 243, 244, 245, 260, 263
ceremony, 39, 45, 102, 188, 244, 255
childhood, 6, 21, 25, 26, 28, 29, 30, 46, 48, 50, 114, 115, 117, 121, 138, 146, 174, 179, 188, 193, 194, 208, 253, 256, 257, 258, 267
children, 30, 61, 63, 64, 65, 89, 93, 96, 97, 115, 117, 118, 119, 131, 174, 188, 257, 266
class, 16, 23, 62, 63, 65, 79, 81, 91, 117, 118, 123, 128, 133, 135, 174, 186, 194, 195, 196, 197, 199, 201, 204, 213, 230, 262, 266
closet, closets, 4, 21, 23, 29, 30, 41, 73, 75, 76, 79, 80, 81, 99, 141, 142, 144, 172, 173, 235, 239, 262
clothes, 4–8, 11–12, 24, 29, 75–81, 104, 118–120, 133, 142, 145, 184, 186, 187, 189, 217, 225, 230, 251, 253–258, 261–264, 262; academic gown, 99–104, 260; baby dress, 16, 31; baby doll dress, 131; bathing suit, 139; bathrobe, 6; black dress, 50, 53, 54, 224, 229–238; blouses, 21, 41, 61–65, 83, 105, 138, 139, 149, 257; bridesmaid's dress, 164; burial dress, 239–245, 268; business suit, 74, 253, 254; business attire, 130, 131; casual, 74, 86, 105, 140, 197, 263, 268; catsuit, 74; Chinese dress, 183–190; civvies, 268; cloak, 33, 35; coats, 11, 16, 21, 33, 41, 42, 62, 75, 103, 199, 208, 243, 276; Communion dress, 39–43; cowboy suit, 244; cowgirl suit, 256, 257; doll clothes, 224; dresses, 11, 29, 239; Easter dress, 31, 35; fancy dress, 22–24, 47, 121, 123, 124; fur coats, 243; gowns, 99–104, 165–167, 173–177, 186, 241, 243, 254, 255, 258; hand-me-downs, 62, 91, 262; hip huggers, 91; hoodies, 79, 80; hospital gown, 268; housedress, 90; isishweshwe, 211–218; jackets, 6, ⎯, 86, 87, 91, 103, 105, 138, 184, 185, 243;

clothes *(continued)*
  254, 255, 267; jeans, 12, 65, 74, 75, 77, 90, 103, 106, 107, 130, 144, 158, 175, 257; kilts, 62, 65, 138, 139; Mao suits, 187, 282; Maternity, 127–136, 281, 282; military uniforms, 187, 188; miniskirt, 197, 198; nightdress, 31, old, 15, 16, 22, 24, 30, 33, 35, 47, 62, 106, 144, 200, 252, 264; outfit, 3, 41, 49, 50, 53, 61, 77, 86, 107, 117, 139, 184, 185, 192, 208, 209, 213, 217, 239, 240, 252–254, 257, 263–265; pants (*see also* trousers), 17, 74, 95, 101, 103, 105, 106, 135, 153, 189, 240, 243, 265, 274, 275; pant suit, , 240; party dress, 40; petticoat, 23, 35, 264; power suit, 77, 185; princess dress, 245; prom dress, 45–55, 239–244, 258–260, 282; Red River Winter Coat, 208; robe, 89–99, 101, 103, 104, 157, 177, 271; school uniforms, 61–65, 67–71, 266–268, 274, 275, 277–280, 282; second hand, 62, 74, 106, 194, 230, 254, 277, 279, 280; shirts, 29, 49, 50, 75, 77, 91, 105, 243, 244; shorts, 11, 31, 106, 223; skirts, 24, 26, 31, 35, 41, 62, 63, 74, 75, 77, 80, 84, 87, 105, 107, 139, 146, 149, 177, 178, 184, 185, 190, 195, 212, 214–217, 220, 230, 231, 233, 236, 240, 241, 254, 257, 262, 265, 267; suits, 39, 49, 74, 77, 85–87, 105, 147, 149, 153, 184–186, 189, 190, 208, 230, 244, 252–254, 260, 282; sweaters, 12, 24, 29, 32, 42, 64, 75, 77, 79, 80, 86, 106, 135, 144, 240; tank tops, 105–107, trousers (*see also* pants) 29, 62, 188, 192, 197, 199, 254, 265; t-shirts, 75, 79, 80, 106, 130, 133, 144, 268; track suit, 142; tunics. 61–65, 67–71, 106, 267, 282; turtleneck, 85, 86, 106, 260; underskirt, 23; uniform (*see also* school uniforms and military uniforms) 17, 103, 200, 254, 270, 277; wedding dress, 6, 165–180, 240, 243, 244, 255, 268–270, 280; winter coats, 21, 41, 62, 75, 208; work clothes, 62, 230; zoot suit, 279, 280; *see also* academic wear, dress
clothing, 4–5, 7, 15, 20, 21, 33, 46, 65, 77, 85, 87, 90, 91, 119, 120, 128, 130–136, 140–142, 146, 151, 186, 187, 212, 214, 215, 252–254, 256–258, 260–263, 266–269; as art, 26, 67–71, 172, 255, 257–258; as memory prompt, 121, 256, 257; as site of struggle, 118
color, 17, 35, 46, 48, 49, 80, 130, 139, 145, 184,

Subject Index • 295

color *(continued)*
185, 209, 215, 240–242, 247; black, 12, 45, 46, 49, 50, 53, 54, 57, 74, 77, 80, 85, 86, 89, 101, 103, 105, 106, 135, 138, 141, 184, 185, 190, 192, 199, 201, 202, 204, 224, 229, 230, 231, 235–237, 245, 260, 263, 264; green, 11, 26, 62, 89–98, 139, 163, 172, 187, 241, 264; pink, 45, 48, 50, 51, 53, 130, 148–151, 186, 208, 264; red, 41, 57–58, 80, 101, 186, 189, 190, 208, 247; white, 11, 12, 16, 17, 29, 31, 35, 40, 41, 61, 63, 79, 130, 138, 139, 141, 142, 149, 167–169, 172–174, 178, 179, 184, 185, 188, 190, 208, 213, 216, 223, 237, 238, 240, 245, 257

commodification, 4, 127–135, 196, 266

consumerism, 127–135, 176, 200, 202 *see also* commodification, shopping

context, 4–6, 78, 112, 113, 119, 124, 192, 254, 255, 261, 267, 268

contradiction, 5, 80, 91, 93, 119, 120, 124, 163

control, 49, 64, 73, 81, 145, 252

corsets, *see* undergarments

Cosmopolitan, 199

costume, 28, 33, 41, 48, 120, 121, 123, 124, 153, 174, 177, 212, 213 *see also* clothes, dress

cross-dressing, 192, 195

Crouching Tiger, Hidden Dragon, 188

culture, 4, 118, 127, 130, 133, 187, 193, 212, 213, 216, 217, 254, 255, 266; subculture, 255, 268

dance/dancing, 24, 31 49, 58, 140, 194, 197, 201, 208, 241, 243

daughter, *see* "mother-daughter" relationship

death, 16, 21, 24, 29, 95–97, 144, 237, 239–245, 242, 247 *see also* burial dress, loss, mourning

designs/designing, 50, 91, 128–133, 172–177, 184–185, 214–215, 255, 258 *see also* dressmaking and fashion

designer/designers, 65, 133, 173, 209, 214 *see also* dressmakers

desire , 67–70, 97, 107, 112–124, 179, 188,197, 199, 258, 262, 267

dialectics, 93, 261, 271, 272

dress; and fit 47, 79, 174, 177, 178, 186, 192, 230, 243, 262; as communication 45, 78, 186, 189, 212, 254; as disappointment 53; as embodiment 6, 255, 260, 261–262; as empowering 43, 186; and humiliation/ shame 42, 263; and literature 7, 263–264; as

dress *(continued)*
method of inquiry 5, 253; as performance/presentation of self 78, 80–101, 251–252, 260–263; as phenomenon 251–271; as pleasure 118, 208, 257, 260; as resistance/defiance/protest 42–43, 54, 64, 80, 99, 101, 124, 166, 172–173, 199, 200–202, 225, 265, 267; as restriction 46–50, 61–65, 147–154, 236; and rituals 39, 179, 258; as sexual display 87, 167, 177, 258, 266, 267; as sign 204, 254; as social marker *(see also* class, dress codes) 5, 51, 186, 189, 254, 255, 263, 266; as symbol/metaphor 5, 32, 51, 62, 64, 77, 103, 173, 185, 186, 187, 188, 189, 192, 199, 200, 204, 212, 254, 258, 260; as transformative 53, 286,238, 265; *see also* clothes, dress styles, designing, dressing, dress codes, dress meanings, dress stories

dress-body, xiv, 7, 8, 77, 90, 261, 268; *see also* dress as embodiment

dress codes, 102, 103, 186, 194, 200, 236, 240, 261; *see also* dress meanings

dressed; over-dressed 240; well-dressed 185–186, 199, 252, 253; inappropriately dressed 42, 158, 265; appropriately dressed 74, 90, 132, 139; *see also* dressing

dresses-in-use, 6

dressing, 138, 261, 262; deciding what to wear 23, 80, 91, 101, 252, 262–263; as personal choice 80, 258, 261; as political decision 80, 191–205, 254, 265–269; for comfort/convenience 74, 75, 107, 142, 144, 177, 178, 209, 265; power dressing 131, 185–87; dressing the part 81, 186, 256; to fit in 46, 55, 261; undressing, undressed 90, 138, 194, 195, 238, 225–228 243, 244; dressing up (fancy/elegant) 115, 118–124, 138, 164, 188, 240, 257; *see also* dress and dressed

dressmaking/dressmaker, 117, 118, 135, 172, 174, 177, 184, 196, 197, 216, 255; *see also* seamstress, design

dress meanings, 4, 6, 7, 77, 80, 103, 167, 169, 189, 192, 203, 215, 253–256, 261, 265, 266; connotative, 78, 255; denotative, 78, 255; *see also* dress as symbol

dress moments, *see* wardrobe moments

dress stories, 3–6, 6–7, 8, 17, 251, 254, 256, 260, 265, 266, 267, 268

Dress Studies, 6, 268–269

education, 62, 79, 89, 91, 93, 94, 97, 108; autobiographical accounts 89; narrative of educational experience 91–92, 96; educational experience 89–93, 96; *see also* schooling, teaching
embodiment. 4, 7, 87, 127, 128, 130, 132, 260, 261, 262; dress and embodiment 5; clothing as a mode of 8, 261
embodied, embodied experience 7, 128, 151; embodied identity 262; embodied appearance 87, 266; embroidery, 15 186, 188; empowerment, 186, 267
experience, meaning of 4; social experience 6, 128; experience of clothes/dress 6, 7, 262, 265, 269; everyday experience 7, 8, 263; experiences of/with the mother 18,19; shopping experience 47, 128; experience of pregnancy 93, 128, 132; living experience 186, 187, 196; experience of discrimination 202
ethnography, 269

fabric, 15, 20, 32, 34, 75, 91, 119, 150, 151, 163, 169, 173, 174, 177, 178, 184, 197, 208, 212, 214, 215, 216, 240, 241, 258, 266, 268; cotton, 16–18, 26, 29, 31, 35, 62, 105–107, 133, 196, 199, 214, 216, 226; denim, 77, 80, 85, 106, 257, 280; fur 15, 33, 138, 243; lace, 106, 107, 163, 174, 177, 178, 229, 241; polyester, 142, 240, 245; satin, 12, 16, 35, 46, 48, 89, 163, 169, 184; silk, 16, 21, 23, 35, 91, 149, 173, 175, 178, 184–190, 230, 243, 264; synthetic 90, 142, 147, 174; tartan 63, 115, 138, 139; fashion, 90, 101, 103, 128, 131, 134, 135, 140, 141, 142, 146, 148, 184, 185, 187, 188, 189, 197, 198, 199, 200, 219, 247, 255, 265; faux pas, 77
fashionable, 154, 187, 188, 197, 198, 199
fashion magazines, , 47, 48, 135, 140, 196, 198, 199, 220, 245, 251
father, 17, 18, 21, 24, 26, 28, 29, 30, 35, 43, 45, 50, 62, 94, 113–115, 117, 123, 140, 197, 198, 257, 260
feminine, 16, 46, 49, 80, 119, 185, 187, 254
femininity, 79, 120, 124, 130, 131, 133, 135, 186
feminisms, 75, 76, 81, 89, 199
feminist, feminists, 74, 75, 79, 80, 84, 89, 103, 151, 178, 200, 256, 258, 265, 268, 269
fetish, fetishism, 15, 16, 20, 24, 26

garments, *see* clothes
gaze, 18, 77, 79, 97, 119, 125, 191, 256, 262, 263, 264, 265; camera's, 18; imagined, 262; viewer's, 255; wearer's, 5, 255, 265, 268; *see also* audience, performance, "the wearer's view"
gender, gender identity, 49, 73, 77–80, 93, 118–120, 128, 192, 230
girlie/girly, 45, 79, 107, 131
graduation/convocation, 64, 99, 101–103, 139, 241
grandmother, 16, 17, 18, 21, 29, 34, 35, 48, 140, 193, 195, 196
"grrrl gear", 75
The Gods Must Be Crazy, 255

hats, *see* accessories
hair, 12, 16, 17, 23, 28, 47, 48–50, 63, 76, 79, 84, 90, 102, 106, 123, 138, 139, 142, 143, 194–198, 208, 223, 244
haute couture, *see* designer, dressmaking, style
health, 154, 268
hems, hemlines, 26, 31, 35, 62, 77, 184, 186, 264
heteronormativity, 130, 132, 174, 258, 267, 268
hijab, 191–204
hippie, 223
HIV/AIDS, 8, 258, 267, 268, 279
Hollywood, 169, 199, 200, 208
Holocaust, 232–234, 284

identity, 4–8, 46, 49, 75, 76, 78, 96, 119, 124, 128, 131, 133, 144, 164, 178, 179, 183–190, 192, 197–199, 202, 211–217, 227, 235, 251–255, 258, 261, 265, 271; dialectics of, 261; cultural identity, 189, 253, 254; professional identity, 6, 251, 252; *see also* self
Image and Identity Research Collective (IIRC), 5, 8, 54, 271
images, 6, 21, 24, 26, 28, 30, 77–79, 112, 128, 130, 135, 153, 154, 196, 253, 261, 265
infantilization, 128, 130–132, 135
In the Mood for Love, 188

Subject Index • 297

interviewing/qualitative research methods, 4, 5, 46, 50, 252, 261

lace, see fabrics
loss, 15–35, 96, 97, 113, 114, 159, 256; *see also* death and mourning
love, 18, 21, 28, 93, 96, 113–115, 118, 120, 178, 258

make-up, 50, 64, 84, 152, 196, 198, 220, 223; lipstick, 17, 102, 143, 198, 223, 224, 264
Marks and Spencer's, 212
marriage, 17, 140, 145, 148, 153, 167–169, 171–179
masquerade, 120, 123, 124, 254
material, *see* fabric
material culture, 4, 5, 8, 258, 269, 270
media, 4, 46, 79, 127, 174, 200, 263
memory, memories, 4, 5, 16, 18, 24–26, 30, 33, 35, 51, 85, 95, 112, 114, 121, 147, 174, 188, 193, 196, 208, 253, 256, 257
memory work, 5, 253, 256, 269
metaphor, 18, 19, 32, 34, 91; *see also* dress as symbol
mind/body duality, 92, 102, 103, 104
mirror, 11, 12, 23, 35, 41, 102, 143, 175, 196, 197, 219, 223, 237, 261, 263, 264, 265
Monsoon Wedding, 179
mother-daughter relationships, 16, 22–26, 31, 35, 50–54, 115–124, 217, 239–245, 243, 255, 258
mourning, 20, 29, 215, 244 *see also* death and loss
multiple meanings, 81, 193, 255

narrative, 4–8, 17, 91–94, 96, 253, 254, 256, 260, 262, 267–269, 271, 278
New Year's Eve, 53, 241
"not just any dress", 5, 35
nudity, 101, 112

Other, 192, 266, 268

paradox, 75, 120
pedagogy, 75, 80, 86, 90, 91, 252, 253; , and curriculum theory, 89
performance, 76, 78, 80, 81, 85, 86, 90, 93, 119, 123, 124, 260, 263; *see also* audience, gaze, "the wearer's view"

photographs, photography, 4, 5, 7, 15–35, 50, 51, 53, 62, 85, 86, 99, 101, 111–125, 141, 143, 152–154, 220, 253–256; album, 16, 17, 18, 21, 24, 30, 35, 51, 53; scrapbooks, 16
poetic inquiry, 5, 269
politics, 74, 77, 79, 81, 85, 141, 188, 193, 194, 198, 199, 204, 266, 267
popular culture, 46–49, 65, 75, 79, 84, 127, 135, 174, 184, 188, 223, 251, 256–258, 262
portraits, *see* photographs
pregnancy, pregnant, 127–136, 258, 267
presentation of self, *see* self, dress as performance/presentation
professor, *see* teacher
prom, 45–54, 78, 239–245, 258, 259

qi pao, 188

race, 78, 130, 174, 196, 212, 213, 216
referent, 18–19, 29
relics, 15, 20, 103
religion, 26, 39, 40, 62, 70, 71, 130, 148, 192, 195, 200–202, 204, 213, 232, 254, 265
representation, 88, 91, 117, 128–135, 173, 186, 189, 193, 197, 202, 251, 258, 260, 261, 269; *see also* dress as symbol
research, research methods, 4–8, 81, 93, 163, 165, 251–256, 260, 269–270
revolution, 106, 187, 198–200, *see also* dress as resistance
rituals/rites of passage, 5, 39, 46, 128, 139, 148, 179, 193, 232, 240, 244, 258, 267 *see also* weddings, communions, proms

school/schooling, 16, 26, 40–42, 45, 54, 62–65, 71, 83, 84, 139; *see also* education
seamstress, 32, 33, 35, 172, 177; *see also* dress design/dressmaker
self, 21, 25, 28, 46, 49, 54, 73, 80, 91, 115, 132, 164, 192, 216, 219, 256, 262, 263; presentation of self/self image, 6, 46, 80–81, 91, 106, 135, 252, 261–262
self-study, 8, 88, 269
Seventeen, 48, 245
sewing 32, 33, 177, 197, 214–216; as metaphor 31–35; *see also* dressmaking
sex, sexuality, 15, 23, 46, 63, 78, 84, 96, 130, 132, 168, 258, 267; safe sex, 258; sex-based

sex, sexuality *(continued)*
  abuse/harassment/violence 83, 168, 195–196, 267–268; heteronormativity, 130, 174, 267, 268; sex-based segregation, 203; sex-roles (see gender); sexualize, 132 , 266
shoes, *see* accessories
shopping, 45–54, 91, 128, 132, 133, 175–177, 214, 230, 262
social class, *see* class
social justice, 198, 200, 204
social mores/norms, 46, 54, 78, 119, 124, 139, 140–141
social expectations/obligations, 4, 54, 185
social role, 128, 195 *see also* gender
social status, 49, 65, 103, 123, 133, 128, 151, 186
social structures/systems, 4, 187, 204, 263
stains/stained, 3, 70, 74, 78, 79, 81, 90, 96, 103, 113, 142
stereotypes, 78, 79, 80, 103
stores, *see* shopping
students, 74, 78–80, 92–97, 102, 104
student-teachers, 74, 83–87
style/stylish, 49, 57, 61, 63, 74–76, 79, 128, 131, 133, 149, 152, 196, 208, 212, 230, 240
symbol, *see* representation *and also* dress as symbol

tailor *see* dress design/dressmaking
taste (in clothes) 33, 46, 49, 140, 198, 257, 258
teachers, 39, 74, 75, 76, 77, 84–86, 94, 103–104, 139, 251–253, 260, 267; *see also* education, school,
teenagers, *see* adolescence/adolescents
thrift shop, 74, 230, 254 *see also* clothes, shopping

undergarments/underwear, 61, 95, 101,106–107, 146, 149, 150,152, 229, 239, 264; bloomers, 61, 63, 65,146; bra, 12, 106, 107, 178, 243, 239; corset, 6, 23, 145–154, 178; lingerie, 22, 79, 91, 141, 208, 229; negligee, 97; pantyhose, 239; panties, 107, 146, 178, 239; slip, 29, 149, 229, 231, 236, 239, 243; stockings (*see also* accessories), 195, 243, 244; underpants, 61, 115, 243, 244; undershirt, 149; underskirt, 24

veil, 191–204, 208; *see also* hijab and wedding
voice, 32, 76, 83, 86, 91, 114, 143, 158, 232, 234, 236, 244
Vogue, 106,199

Wall Street Journal, 235
wardrobe, 74, 75, 80, 91, 139, 208, 209, 263
"wardrobe moment" 74, 85, 144, 147, 262, 263; *see also* dressing
wearing/worn, see clothes, dress, dressing
wearer's view, 5, 79, 254–255, 262–265, 268; *see also* gaze, wardrobe moment
weddings, 50, 140, 164, 165, 168, 172–180, 244; bouquets, 173; date, 185; dresses (*see* clothes); photographs, 21, 255; rings, 130, 132; veil, 16, 173; *see also* rituals/rites of passage
work/working/workplace, 3, 30, 33, 45, 62, 106, 117–120, 141, 142, 147–49, 194, 201, 212, 213, 230–233, 241, 252, 266; *see also* teaching